320.971 Kinsella, Warren.,
KIN Kicking ass in Canadian politics /

WEST NIPISSING PUBLIC LIBRARY
WNP026594

KICKING ASS
IN CANADIAN
POLITICS

KICKING ASS

IN CANADIAN POLITICS

WARREN KINSELLA

COPYRIGHT © 2001 BY WARREN KINSELLA

All rights reserved under International and Pan-American Copyright Conventions. No part of this book may be reproduced in any form or by any electronic or mechanical means, including information storage and retrieval systems, without permission in writing from the publisher, except by a reviewer, who may quote brief passages in a review. Published in 2001 by Random House Canada, a division of Random House of Canada Limited.

Random House Canada and colophon are trademarks.

National Library of Canada Cataloguing in Publication Data

Kinsella, Warren, 1960–
Kicking ass in Canadian politics

ISBN 0-679-31085-1

1. Canada—Politics and government—1984– . I. Title.

FC635.K55 2001   320.971   C2001-900845-7
F1034.2.K56 2001

www.randomhouse.ca

Text design: Daniel Cullen

Printed and bound in the United States of America

2 4 6 8 9 7 5 3 1

*To Emma, Ben, Sam and Jake,
who (along with Suzanne) keep me fighting*

*... and to political warrior Carl Gillis,
who I miss, still.*

CONTENTS

INTRODUCTION	KICKING ASS ... or, how I became the Prince of Darkness	1
CHAPTER 1	STAND BY YOUR AD ... or, if you are going to do the time, you may as well commit the crime	17
CHAPTER 2	DAISY AND MR. SAGE ... or, how to make mud stick	41
CHAPTER 3	DAMN SPOT ... or, how to make an effective political ad	67
CHAPTER 4	OPPO ... or, how to demonize the opposition in a few easy steps	93
CHAPTER 5	BARNEY, SPIDERS AND DIRTY TRICKS ... or, how to seize the moment by doing silly things	125
CHAPTER 6	THE NEW COWBOYS ... or, how to use a phone (or a modem) to reach out and beat someone	151
CHAPTER 7	INK-STAINED WRETCHES AND WRETCHESSES ... or, why all political journalists must die	185
CONCLUSION	CAMPAIGNS MATTER ... or, Kinsella's tips on how to survive the next election	213
	ACKNOWLEDGEMENTS	225
	BIBLIOGRAPHY	231

INTRODUCTION

KICKING ASS
... or how I became the Prince of Darkness

> "IT'S HARD FOR SOMEBODY TO HIT YOU WHEN YOU'VE GOT YOUR FIST IN THEIR FACE." JAMES CARVILLE

Tip O'Neill, the Speaker of the U.S. House of Representatives for a decade—and a successful politician for a lot longer than that—knew his way around a political axiom. Some of the many truisms he bequeathed to the political classes include: "Never speak of yourself in the third person"—something certain regal and viceregal personages more than occasionally forget. And: "Never get introduced to the crowd at sporting events"—unless, of course, a tidal wave of boos and catcalls is your cup of tea. And, also, his trenchant phrase: "Any jackass can kick over the barn."

Well, not quite.

While denizens of the corridors of power will often suggest, with a straight face, that negativity is unnecessary, and unpleasant, and something that requires no special skill or knowledge, these same

INTRODUCTION

spinmeisters also know that the truth lies elsewhere. They know, deep in the fetid recesses of their tiny hearts, that negativity and nastiness works. They also know that the practitioners of these dark political arts are a unique breed. While they may indeed be jackasses, they are the only category of jackasses capable of knocking down political barns. Other jackasses merely bray at the barn doors, uncertain about how to get the job done.

I think I know a little about knocking down barns. Along with having acted as an assistant to Canada's current prime minister, and along with the days and nights I have spent advising political campaigns in many provinces and regions, I have, I confess, dabbled in these dark political arts. I have helped to lead so-called "quick-response" teams—groups of politicos who respond to attacks and, where necessary, initiate them. I have crashed political rallies with activists dressed up like chickens (to mock party leaders who refused to participate in debates); I have assisted in the creation of television ads depicting lying politicians as Pinocchio (with the nose growing each time a fib is recalled); and I have even arranged to fly a bottle of polluted water by helicopter, at a cost of many hundreds of dollars an hour (to be used as a prop in a pro-environment speech by a candidate). In the process, I have also been described as the Prince of Darkness.

As near as I can tell, the first person to call me the Prince of Darkness (to my face) was Alex Pannu. Pannu is a bright lawyer from Vancouver who, way back when, was an assistant to a former minister of national defence, Kim Campbell. In spring 1993, I was working as a political assistant to Jean Chrétien, leader of Her Majesty's Loyal Opposition. At the time, Campbell was running for the leadership of the governing Progressive Conservative Party, which she was almost certain to win. That spring I was a member of a small group of Liberal staffers doing our utmost to make life utterly unbearable for Campbell, attempting to link her to assorted scandals, leaking damaging material to reporters and

INTRODUCTION

generally depicting her in the most unflattering light possible. It was rewarding work.

As we settled ourselves in some chairs at a committee room in the East Block, waiting for Campbell to come and speak to the parliamentary committee on defence about yet another mess at the department, Pannu approached me. "You know what we're calling you, don't you?" he said, grinning. "We're all calling you the Prince of Darkness." After Pannu retreated to his side of the room, one of the young Liberals working with me leaned over and whispered: "Wow! The Prince of Darkness! Is that cool or what?"

In political circles, people often privately react like that. They think take-no-prisoners politicking—the kind you would expect a Prince of Darkness to practise—is, indeed, cool. When appearing on televised pundit panels, or when being quoted by the print media, they know that it is not a good idea to sound too enthusiastic about hardball politics, however. So they will make soothing noises about the need to "do politics differently," and to avoid "the old politics," or what is being lately called "the politics of personal destruction." They make these disclaimers because they know it is what the voting public wants to hear (even if it isn't what the voting public necessarily believes, but more on that later). Watching them, you would think such politicos seldom would utter a discouraging word about anyone.

But that's not true, quite frankly. Political people love nasty battles with their adversaries, and people who vote love to watch. That, in short, is what this book is about: even if no one wants to admit it, negative politics work. This book is also about how negative politics is done—about "going neg," to use the phrase popular among politicos.

Before I became the Prince of Darkness, I was a University of Calgary law student and a part-time newspaper reporter on the police beat. On weekends, I would earn a few extra dollars at the *Calgary Herald*. Most of the time, I would sit in the newsroom and listen to the

INTRODUCTION

police radio. Whenever a drugstore was robbed or someone was murdered, I would hop in my battered old Gremlin and speed out onto Calgary's freeways to learn more. If the car crashes I heard about over the police band were sufficiently spectacular, I would also file stories about them, and my news editor would almost always assign a photographer to take pictures. When there wasn't very much else going on in the news world, we would run photos of the car crashes.

Whenever we did that, I was reminded of two things. First, you could publish a fistful of photographs of African children starving to death, corpses floating alongside an overloaded Indian ferry, or the bombed-out wreckage of someone's home in a war zone, and no one would call in to complain. If they cared, they sure weren't saying anything about it to us.

Second, if you ran a photo of a car crash involving locals—without bodies, of course—you'd better darn well make sure you had someone around the newsroom to handle the calls of complaint, because you'd get plenty. Subscribers would call in to declare, loudly, that we were insensitive, and ghoulish, and beneath contempt. They would call to cancel their subscriptions. But here's the funny thing: whenever I was out at those accident scenes, scribbling away in my notepad, I noticed that everyone making their way past the orange pylons and the traffic cops—and I mean *everyone*—would slow down to take a long hard look. Every once in a while, I'd see them fumbling for a camera, so that they could take some pictures, too.

Later on, when I got involved in full-time politics, I remembered this car-crash thing. With a straight face, folks will insist they do not like it when political parties, or newspapers, involve themselves with life's unpleasantness. They will tell pollsters they disapprove of those sorts of things. They will heap opprobrium on the perceived wrongdoers. But, believe me: ten times out of ten (and when they think no one is looking), they will slow down and take a look. Political consultants—the smart ones, anyway—

INTRODUCTION

know that. To mangle a phrase used by Dick Morris, one of the smartest political strategists ever to walk the earth, it's a mutually reinforcing deceit. Political types say they don't like doing the tough stuff—but they do. And voters say they aren't influenced by tough stuff—but they are.

They are, they are.

I was nine years old the first time I got involved in a political campaign. A neighbour of ours in Kingston, Ontario, was running for reeve, so I created some handmade lawn signs for him. I even wore one of his buttons to class; I don't recall if my grade-three classmates at Our Lady of Lourdes Elementary School thought I was weird for doing that, but I forgive them if they did. It *was* kind of weird.

My dad is a doctor, and he spent a lot of time doing medical research, so we lived all over the place. As a grade-school kid in Texas, I knew, and still remember, the Pledge of Allegiance. In Quebec, as a youngish teenager, I was transfixed by the debate over sovereignty. Later on, in Alberta, where my family has been settled for a quarter century, I typed out letters to the editor, castigating Western separatists and anti-bilingualism nutbars. It wasn't until 1989, however, that I decided to get involved in politics as a full-time job. In Ottawa, the seat of government, so to speak.

In that year, a debate was raging about the Meech Lake Accord, a package of constitutional amendments conjured up by then–Prime Minister Brian Mulroney and the provincial premiers. Lots of people were enthusiastic about the accord, but I wasn't one of them. I thought it stunk. As a young lawyer, toiling as a litigator at a smallish Ottawa Valley firm, I thought the notion of sticking a phrase like "distinct society" into the constitution of Canada was just plain wrong. Nobody in a position of power seemed to know what it meant, but they were certainly ready to move heaven and earth to get it in there. I was suspicious

INTRODUCTION

when they refused to get the phrase defined, in advance, by the Supreme Court of Canada. That suggestion was deemed un-Canadian, and would needlessly humiliate Quebec, I read somewhere.

To hell with that, thought I. So I started combing through the classifieds to find a politician to represent my point of view.

I didn't have far to look. In the very next office tower, at another Ottawa Valley firm, Jean Chrétien, formerly a senior Liberal cabinet minister, was also practising law. He wasn't wild about the Meech Lake Accord, either. Every once in a while, I would see him lined up at the sandwich bar located between our respective buildings. He didn't send out his secretary to get his lunch; he'd just stand there, along with me and the other lesser mortals. When he paid for his sandwich, he'd sit at a table on his own, eating it. I liked that. Like most voters, I am not partial to snobs or elites, and Jean Chrétien wasn't a snob. He wasn't a member of the elites, either, but, as I later learned, he knew how to get them to do what he wanted.

When it looked as though Chrétien was going to seek the leadership of the Liberal Party of Canada, I called up his pint-sized adviser, Eddie Goldenberg. A lawyer himself, Goldenberg was also next door, working down the hall from Jean Chrétien. I told Goldenberg I could write a little, and I wanted to volunteer. He was knocking at my door before I had a chance to hang up the phone.

Throughout 1990, while I continued to practise law, I helped out on different things for Jean Chrétien's leadership bid—speech writing, letter writing, policy-making, you name it. It was a lot of fun. Sometimes, Chrétien would ask me to sit in on meetings he had with various Liberal members of Parliament. They would discuss the Meech Lake Accord, or free trade, or taxation, or whatever was hot. I was always too nervous to say anything, but I sure did plenty of listening.

I came out of those meetings with a lot of respect, and a lot of loyalty, for Jean Chrétien. In politics, as in life, I value loyalty: I give it, and

INTRODUCTION

I expect it. I "bleed it," as one Tory friend recently told me, and I guess that is true—I tend to stick with my chosen candidate, even when the cause is hopeless. If someone violates my trust, I never forget it, or forgive it. If someone takes a swipe at someone on my side, I hit them back, twice as hard. It's how I am with all of the politicians I am proud to have supported: the federal Liberals' Allan Rock, the former governor general Roméo LeBlanc, Gordon Campbell, Dalton McGuinty, and others.

Some people in the media have called my loyalty to Jean Chrétien a lot of wild-eyed fanaticism, but that's fine with me. They didn't sit in on those meetings in his law offices, and see what a truly remarkable guy he is. The Liberal leader has an intimidating grasp of political strategy, and he has held most of the major portfolios in government, but you will never hear about any of that from him. Chrétien taught all of us who worked for him one rule: undersell and overperform. In politics, it's one of the rules worth remembering.

Now, it's not as if I was his buddy or anything. I was, in truth, an employee. But over the years, the Little Guy from Shawinigan tends to grow on you. He made me *proud* to be his employee. As a consequence, don't expect this book to be neutral on the subject of Chrétien. With the possible exception of Reform Alliance leader Stockwell Day—I cannot resist giving him a hard time—I try to give everyone a fair shake herein. But I am a Chrétien partisan. So be forewarned.

After he won the Liberal Party leadership in June 1990, Chrétien used the oldest line in the world to get me to work for him. "You can be a lawyer anytime," he said. "But how many chances do you get to work on Parliament Hill, and have some fun?" I became his special assistant, which meant I wrote speeches for him, helped out on the daily Question Period ritual and did whatever needed doing. And what needed doing, most days, was digging up the goods on the government of Brian Mulroney.

Back when I was a reporter at the *Calgary Herald* and the *Ottawa Citizen*, I loved investigative journalism. To me, poking through stacks of

INTRODUCTION

documents for something sensational, or spending weeks trying to get someone to speak to me, was a lot more interesting than attending a press conference and writing down what everybody else did. In my investigative days, I staked out cemeteries at midnight to spy on satanic cults, had neo-Nazis stick rifles in my chest and chased Libyan terrorists around Washington. When I went over to the political side, I simply carried on doing investigative work, but I had a different publisher. I continued to sift through documents; I continued to try to learn everything I could about Chrétien's opponents. If I found out something that the media had missed—something that was unhelpful to the political fortunes of the Mulroney Tories—I would make certain that the media found out.

In politics, one half of the job, give or take, is trying to do some good. The other half is kicking the living shit out of the other guy.

Friends (and foes) tell me I'm good at the second half of that formula. I don't know about that. I do know, however, that if you don't ever do the latter, you'll never get a chance to do the former.

In the beginning there was North Vancouver, a prosperous, tidy federal electoral district situated between the Lion's Gate Bridge, Deep Cove, Burrard Inlet and a bunch of mountains to the north. The most populous urban riding in Western Canada, it was blessed with natural beauty and a median income in excess of $60,000 per annum. Engineers and nurses abounded. Two children per. Dogs in abundance.

This was the riding in which I decided to try for public office—a lawyer, writer, former political assistant in faraway Ottawa and unreserved optimist about my political chances as the Liberal Party candidate in the June 1997 general election. No Grit had won the riding in some twenty-two years, but I was equipped with a sling filled with mildly favourable poll results and the latest demographic data from Statistics Canada.

INTRODUCTION

Weeks later, following a drubbing at the polls of (to me) biblical proportions, I emerged from a dark political wilderness, thinner, older, wiser. In my aching hands—the ache being a product of too many robust handshakes and door-knockings—I clutched the Political Commandment, scrawled on the back of an oversized chloroplast campaign lawn sign. The Commandment would serve to guide future candidates through the inhospitable political climes carrying the name North Vancouver. And maybe a few other ridings, too.

Herewith, the first publication, anywhere, of the Political Commandment: KICK ASS.

On a sunny, pleasant afternoon in mid-May 1997, I am bounding along a residential avenue in Lynn Valley, a neighbourhood near the centre of the riding of North Vancouver. Children are frolicking happily on the lush lawns, birds are chirping in the abundant trees: chirp chirp chirp. Two energetic volunteers and I are engaged in a political canvass. Most often, a canvass involves a candidate loping from one split-level to the next, knocking on doors, ringing bells, soliciting support and perhaps, just perhaps, finding that most cherished political asset: a committed Liberal homeowner, willing to offer his or her property for a big lawn sign.

The suburban stillness and calm is broken. Leaning out of a second-floor window above his manicured lawn, painted driveway and shiny pickup truck is a fellow in his forties, with slurred speech and a neck of reddish hue. "I WOULDN'T VOTE FOR THAT LIBERAL BASTARD IF THERE WERE TWO OF HIM! HE'S A SLEAZY SON OF A BITCH WHO WAS PARACHUTED HERE BY THAT FRENCH BASTARD CHRÉTIEN! GET OFF MY FUCKING LAWN, YOU PIECE OF SHIT!"

I turn to one of the volunteers on the North Vancouver Liberal campaign, and say, "Another undecided. Seems like a really nice guy."

The Parachute Issue had reared its tousled head for approximately the millionth time that day. I sigh, straighten my tie and jog on to the next doorway.

INTRODUCTION

For the record: I came to be in Vancouver, in 1995, because I got a nice job offer. My family and I—indulgent spouse, months-old daughter—came to be in North Vancouver, specifically, because it was a nice area. Nice schools, nice neighbourhoods, nice place to live. Nice.

Having worked as an assistant to Jean Chrétien, and a chief of staff to a cabinet minister, I was dimly aware, prior to the move westward, that the North Shore's two federal ridings were represented in Parliament by two illustrious members of the Reform Party. One had called aboriginal Canadians "spoiled children," who deserved to be treated as such. The other, against whom I eventually ran, had somewhere stated that minorities "get everything they want, to the detriment of the people paying the bills." I did not know much else about the place. I did not, however, move to North Vancouver from Ottawa to run for the Liberals. I ran for a seat in Parliament—after a lot of reflection, and after my spouse attempted to have me committed for a psychiatric evaluation—because I thought I would be not bad at it, and certainly because I believed I would be better than the incumbent.

These simple facts, however, did not interest assorted blowhards at radio station CKNW or the local rag, the *North Shore News*, who knew better. CKNW's resident shouters assured listeners that I had been "parachuted" into the riding, without first spending a few moments to call me to determine if the opposite might be the case. The *News*, meanwhile—a thrice-weekly publication that has achieved notoriety for its pride in publishing a septuagenarian Holocaust-denying columnist, who calls gays "dirt" and immigrants "a cancer"—was the chief proponent of the Parachute Issue. At every opportunity, the *News* shrieked that I was, in fact, *sans doute*, the product of a backroom Liberal Party conspiracy. A parachutist, to wit, dropped into the riding by faceless Grit manipulators to subvert democracy and defy the voters.

A lot of the time, truth matters not in a political campaign. All that mattered was that sundry dough-heads at a noisy radio station and a vulgar little tabloid said a lie was true.

I thought that I knew much of what there was to know about politics, but I made a mistake. I assumed that if I simply *told* registered voters that I was *not* a parachutist, and, additionally, that I was not plotting to force gun control, bilingualism, tax hikes and gay marriages on the unsuspecting burghers of North Vancouver, then all would be fine. Simply tell the truth, over and over. Big-o mistake-o.

The *North Shore News*, CKNW and their ilk were not terribly preoccupied with this particular truth. They were interested only in jamming Reformers into Parliament like so many cords of firewood. It did not matter that I was not a parachute candidate. It did not matter that I had a big (too big) mortgage, or a job, or a B.C. driver's licence. It did not matter that my family had been resident in Western Canada for a heck of a lot longer than the Reform Party incumbent, an immigrant from New Zealand. What mattered was pummelling the Liberal candidate, by hook or by crook.

I forgot the Political Commandment that counts the most: KICK ASS. Instead of fighting back, and aggressively countering the fabrications, I decided to play nice. Instead of hitting back, fast and with facts, I turned the other political cheek. Voters aren't interested in hardball politics, I declared to no one in particular. "I am not a parachute candidate," I murmured to myself. "I mean, if I was a parachute, wouldn't I have demanded a riding where our side actually had *won* at some point in the past couple decades?"

It did not matter, none of it. In campaigns, all that matters, most of the time, are the impressions formed by voters. And voters in North Vancouver had formed the impression that their Reform Party stalwart—a one-time Western separatist the Canadian Press referred to as "elfin"—was the better choice. I picked up 18,514 votes, considerably more than the New Democratic Party (NDP) and Progressive

INTRODUCTION

Conservative candidates' combined total. But the Reformist elf won big, with 26,749 votes.

I lost the election and, soon after, was obliged by necessity to pull up stakes and head back to the Godless East. My family and I had spent two years in British Columbia. Along the way, I made many friends, fell in love with North Vancouver (I still miss it, truth be told), and I relearned a valuable lesson. And that is: KICK ASS. As per the Political Commandment, the rule is always to get tough, or get lost. Always.

If this book is a good idea—you'll have to judge that for yourself—I can't claim credit for it. The idea for this book came out of discussions with my agent, Helen Heller, and my editor, Anne Collins, who are pretty smart. Both of them would listen to me ramble on about how and why tough politicking works, and the tools employed to "go neg," and they would both say: "You may know about all of that stuff. But most people don't know about it, and they might be interested to read about it, too." So I decided I would give it a shot.

Some of my political friends were surprised by that. "Why give away any secrets?" they asked me. I'm not giving anything away, I told them. I'm trying to make the case for an unpopular cause, namely, that negative politics work.

In writing this book, I tried to do a few things. First, I wanted a book that would appeal to what I usually refer to as "real people"—not political scientists, or political journalists, or political consultants. All of those political people already know that so-called negative campaigning works. Real people don't, or, at the very least, they don't like to admit it.

Second, I didn't want the book to be full of comments from political consultants who lose campaigns. I wanted winners. That is why I sought out the likes of James Carville, Haley Barbour and Dick Morris. There is nobody more persuasive on the subject at hand—namely, that it is right and proper to get tough in campaigns where the stakes are high—than someone who has run a few tough, and winning, campaigns. They know what they are talking about.

Third, I wasn't interested in burning anyone. Appearances to the contrary, I have friends in every political party. I happen to know that consultants are notoriously paranoid—"I've been right, and I've been paranoid, and it's better to be paranoid," as the former Richard Nixon speech writer William Safire put it—and they aren't likely to be candid if they suspected that they were about to be subjected to a political immolation in this book. Still, I figured I could get them to tell me interesting stories about backroom intrigue without them simultaneously blowing their political careers to tiny little bits. I wanted the book to be entertaining and, hopefully, a little informative, and I needed their help to do both.

The first three chapters in the book are about political advertising. That may seem like a lot, but it isn't, really. In modern political campaigns, parties spend most of their money on advertising because that is the only way they can speak directly to voters. Nothing matters as much in a campaign, not speeches, not press releases, not events, not glossy brochures. A lot of time is taken up with ensuring that political advertising is done right, because the media, who predictably resent that political parties are going around them to get to voters, subject such advertising to an unholy degree of scrutiny. As a result, "negative" advertising, which, to be honest, isn't negative at all, but is simply a political ad that critiques some part of the other side's platform, is usually the most accurate political communication you will ever see. In every election since the dawn of time, the media have screamed and hollered about what they call "negative" political advertising, and that's fine. Political parties need to be kept honest, and the media helps to keep them honest. But these three chapters, like the whole book, take the position that, in a democracy, it is perfectly okay for one side to characterize

INTRODUCTION

the choices offered by the other side in critical terms. People who suggest otherwise are being disingenuous, or they are just plain wrong.

There is also a chapter in the book about what political consultants like to call "oppo." Opposition research is all about scrutinizing the public record of one's adversary, and letting people know about things which he or she would prefer to keep off the front pages. Most often, but not always, the fruits of one's oppo efforts are intended for what is called "earned media" (advertising you don't have to pay for, and the media are the ones who do it for you) and not paid advertising. In a campaign, oppo teams scrutinize anything said or done by their principal opponents, and respond to it critically and factually. If they do a good job, an oppo team can inflict serious damage to an opponent's campaign.

Another chapter, "Barney, Spiders and Dirty Tricks," deals with the crazy things political consultants, and their clients, do on the campaign trail. In politics, getting noticed is never an easy thing. In a twenty-four-hour-a-day, seven-days-a-week, 500-channel media environment, it is tougher and tougher to get a message in front of the people who count—the voters. This chapter talks about the stunts (or, as the pious prefer, dirty tricks) that campaigns employ to do just that. The chapter dissects, at some length, a stunt I pulled on national television during the 2000 federal election, and why I did it. Along with the challenges created by media gatekeepers, there is another hurdle to get over, too, namely, the fact that most people's lives are busy, and few of them have time to pay a lot of attention to politics anymore. Death-defying (or just funny) political stunts are one way to get their attention and hold it.

I have devoted an entire chapter, "The New Cowboys," to two important parts of any campaign, although one of them is a relatively new addition. This chapter takes a hard look at polling, and tries to argue that public opinion research is not as benign as pollsters would have us believe. It is, instead, another communication tool that campaigners use to influence voters. The second half of this chapter examines the latest addition to modern political artillery, the Internet. The World Wide Web has yet to achieve all that it probably will in future political campaigns. But it has already made a huge impact as a fundraising and recruitment tool, and it is a formidable means of getting out some damaging oppo, as well.

Whether they like it or not—and mostly, they don't—political consultants can't ignore the news media. The final chapter provides some pointers about how to live with, if not necessarily control, coverage of one's candidate or cause. Even though I was a reporter myself, I long ago abandoned the view that journalists and their editors are scrupulously non-partisan and solely motivated by the public interest. They're not, believe me. But reporters and editors still play a role—sometimes important, sometimes not—in influencing the choices voters make when they reach for a pencil in a balloting station on election day.

At the end of the day, this book is mainly about elections, and elections are mainly about choices. In any election campaign—with the time so short and the stakes so high—it is not just *acceptable* to critique an opponent's public record. It is, in fact, the right thing to do.

Take it from the Prince of Darkness: KICK ASS.

CHAPTER ONE

STAND BY YOUR AD
... or, if you are going to do the time, you may as well commit the crime

Saturation Plaza, as it was known, was a long and narrow room tucked away in a corner of the 1993 national Liberal campaign headquarters on Laurier Avenue in Ottawa. On folding tables lining the cluttered perimeter, there was a battery of computers that permitted its occupants—the "Task Force," they called themselves—to track electronic broadcasts, and even reporters' unedited news footage transmitted by satellite dishes located in different parts of the country. Widespread use of the Internet was still some years away, but the denizens of Saturation Plaza had contracted with a small Ottawa-based company to supply digitized clips of election coverage within hours of broadcast.

Tacked to a large board on one wall, near maps of Canada, Task Force members had collected dozens of unflattering photographs and cartoons of Kim Campbell, the leader of the Progressive Conservatives.

Every morning, someone would be sent to a nearby convenience store to anonymously fax one of these photographs to the national Conservative campaign office, just a few blocks to the west. Usually, an embarrassing quotation or unhelpful poll result would be appended to the fax, to render the Tory troops as dispirited as possible.

Against another wall, occupying every inch of available space, were large filing cabinets containing every published statement Campbell had ever made. Each of these quotations had been entered into a huge database, along with their source and date of publication. The database allowed Task Force members to quickly access embarrassing or contradictory comments made by the Conservative leader. When printed off, the quotations could be faxed to reporters in need of what the Task Force blandly referred to as "opposition research." Sometimes, the faxes were sent anonymously; most often, the reporter knew who was sending them but agreed to keep the Liberals' identities confidential. Whenever a reporter's published story used a quote taken from the Task Force's database, it too would be clipped, copied and filed. The unhelpful quotations had been extensively used in no less than three books published about the newly minted Tory leader in the spring of 1993.

Perched precariously on the tops of the filing cabinets were three large televisions equipped with built-in videocassette recorders. One of the televisions was permanently tuned to CBC Newsworld, at that time the only Canadian twenty-four-hour news source. Task Force members watched Newsworld a lot—from about 5 a.m., when the first of them entered the office, to approximately 3 a.m., when local news coverage of British Columbia candidates had been broadcast and dissected. In the dying days of the seven-week-long campaign, when it became apparent that the Liberals had wiped out their Tory rivals, Newsworld's *Fashion File*, featuring leggy supermodels on catwalks, became a particular Task Force favourite.

The room's windows looked down on Laurier and were mirrored. In this way, visitors to Saturation Plaza could not be photographed from one of the buildings on the other side of the street. For weeks, curious journalists had been attempting to learn who made up the Task Force, and what they did. But the members of the Task Force did not give interviews. Anyone who did would immediately be fired. In the view of those who ran the national Liberal election effort, talking about the campaign's inner workings—the "process" stuff, as political consultants call it—was verboten. Voters want to hear about issues, the Grit campaign managers believed, not minutiae about the inner workings of a political office.

The Task Force was, in effect, the Liberal Party's quick-response team for the 1993 election campaign. Modelled on the group that James Carville and George Stephanopoulos had led on behalf of U.S. presidential candidate Bill Clinton, the Task Force was designed to do two things before and during the election: one, respond promptly to opponents' partisan attacks; and, two, promptly initiate partisan attacks when needed. Unlike Carville and Stephanopoulos's group, the Canadian effort was comparatively small, made up of less than a dozen people. I know all these things because I was on the Task Force.

With one exception, all of the members were assistants to Liberal members of Parliament or senators; all but two were male, in their twenties or thirties. Among these were Bruce Hartley, who would go on to be legislative assistant and executive assistant to the future Liberal prime minister; Phil Goodwin, who would later help to prepare the prime minister and cabinet for the daily Question Period; Frank Schiller, who, following a stint at the London School of Economics, would toil as a high-level lobbyist; Marc Laframboise, who would come to occupy senior policy posts in different ministries in the new government; Randy McCauley, who eventually became the prime minister's press secretary; Joslyn Higginson, who quickly joined the exempt staff of the minister of public works and government services; Joan Lajeunesse, who became personal assistant to the minister of national defence; and, most significantly, Roméo LeBlanc, the leader of the Task Force, who would eventually become Canada's Governor General.

Unlike subsequent efforts in 1997 and 2000, the Task Force did not show up on any flow charts depicting the 1993 federal Liberal Party campaign. Members did not attend public meetings. They did not speak to reporters, usually, unless all agreed that the journalist in question could be counted upon to keep his or her mouth shut. Within the campaign itself, Task Force members interacted with only a handful of people—campaign bosses John Rae and Gordon Ashworth, and select pollsters and advertising executives. Only one of the Task Force operatives, Bruce Hartley, communicated directly with the leader's campaign "tour" as it criss-crossed Canada.

In later election campaigns, groups like the Task Force became *de rigueur* in all of the political parties, and usually referred to themselves as "war rooms." Some operatives, like me, became well known in the media as campaign warriors. But in 1993, when the concept was relatively new, and therefore controversial, the Liberals preferred to keep the whole thing quiet. So we did.

Saturation Plaza got its name from the title of an album by the rock group Urge Overkill, and was suggested by Marc Laframboise. All of the Task Force members agreed that the name accurately described what they did: saturate the media, directly or indirectly, with messages that buttressed the Liberal campaign themes, while simultaneously depicting the Conservative government as tired, inept and callous. The Task Force's members had been engaged in political guerrilla warfare for many months, since late 1992, attacking their Tory opponents with a barrage of leaks, stunts and advertising. But by the middle of October 1993, life had become considerably less hectic. Various polls revealed a 15-percentage-point Liberal lead over the Tories, while pundits were suggesting that a Grit majority government was imminent. At Saturation Plaza, therefore, one or two Task Force members could occasionally be observed playing video games on their computers.

On day 38 of the 48-day national-election campaign, those of us who made up the Task Force—and the rest of the Liberal Party's campaign team—were snapped back to attention. Late on a Thursday evening, while a few of us were still around campaign headquarters, CBC Television reported that the Conservatives had prepared two attack ads on Jean Chrétien, which were to start airing the next night, a Friday. When the story aired, one could almost hear jaws dropping. No one had known this was coming.

According to David McLaughlin, who acted as Kim Campbell's senior political and policy adviser during the 1993 federal election, the Tories' earlier attempts at campaign ads had been "decidedly curious [and] ineffective." They showed a seated Campbell speaking into the camera about some of her policy positions. Each ad concluded with a tag line: "It's Time." What this meant, or was intended to achieve, was unclear to most everyone, including Conservatives. In *Poisoned Chalice*, his 1994 dissection of the failed Conservative campaign, McLaughlin noted: "[The tag line] said nothing to voters, thereby confirming the essential vacuousness of the campaign. In that sense it too was reinforcing, confirming the worst impressions voters were concluding about the Tories."

The new ads were different—very different. Using photographs that had been taken at Liberal campaign events just a few days before, the advertisements featured Jean Chrétien's face in close-up. In each, Chrétien's facial paralysis—acquired when he was young—was prominent. While the photographs flew past, unidentified voices could be heard criticizing the Liberal leader. "Does this look like a prime minister?" the ad asked, before the closer: "Think twice." One of the anonymous voices, belonging to a woman, said: "I personally would be very embarrassed if he were to become the prime minister of Canada." It was clear that the woman was referring to Chrétien's facial paralysis.

As the CBC news item on the new Tory ads was broadcast, two dozen Liberal campaign managers and directors crammed into Saturation Plaza to watch, including John Rae, Gordon Ashworth, Roméo LeBlanc and all the members of the Task Force. When the ads were finished, there was silence in the room. Then a couple campaign staffers angrily cursed the Tories. Deb Davis, an organizer who had been a Chrétien partisan for many years, burst into tears.

No one knew quite what to say. It was possible, certainly, that the Progressive Conservatives had just committed ritual political suicide on a historic scale. There was also a possibility, however, that their ads, like most political campaign ads, had been rigorously tested in focus groups and had been found to be effective at some strategic level. (Much later, in fact, it was reported that the principal instigators of the spots—the Conservatives' pollster Allan Gregg and Tory advertising executive Tom Scott—had played them for focus groups without encountering any criticism.)

Could such an approach work? Could an apparent appeal to prejudice win votes? John Rae called for a brief meeting to discuss what to do. As the meeting convened, Senator Roméo LeBlanc seemed to be grinning behind a newspaper.

Sleep, if it happened at all, was altogether brief for the members of the Task Force that night. Very early the next day, many of them were huddled around a table in the Liberal campaign's cluttered main conference room. They scanned newspapers and drank coffee and did not speak much. Without exception, the Conservatives were being excoriated in the media for their decision to produce and broadcast the attack ads. Editorial commentary, from coast to coast, was uniformly negative. In the avalanche of press criticism that followed, veteran *Globe and Mail* writer Kirk Makin spoke for many of the pundits:

With the supposed *crème de la crème* of advertising people and pollsters at their disposal, the Tories have managed to step in every cow flap in the field . . . The notorious Conservative ad showing Jean Chrétien's face frozen in contorted positions has won hands-down as the most bone-headed act of the election campaign. In 30 seconds of symbolism, the Conservatives seemed to confirm what disaffected voters have been telling anyone who will listen for weeks: politicians have no scruples. Politicians will do anything to get elected.

Toronto advertising executive Jerry Goodis, meanwhile, was one of many called upon by reporters to analyze the Tory spots. Goodis, a Liberal, said: "[The ads] show contempt for people's intelligence. Canadians have a sense of fair play, a cultural difference that makes them recoil at things like this, even if they don't like the other person."

Campaign attack ads had become relatively commonplace in the United States since 1988, when the Republicans' George Bush destroyed the Democrats' Michael Dukakis with a series of brutal spots. In Canada, however, attack ads were seen far less frequently. Around the conference table at Liberal campaign headquarters, the Task Force knew that the Conservative ads had introduced a dramatically new dimension to the 1993 federal election campaign. (The Grits knew the power of such ads because they had produced a few negative spots themselves for the 1993 campaign. One, using material provided by the Task Force, attacked the Tories' decision to purchase billion-dollar helicopters. Another simply contained footage Frank Schiller had dug up showing Kim Campbell and Brian Mulroney embracing. Neither of the ads were ever broadcast.)

At first, the Task Force did not know how, exactly, to react, or whether they should react at all. Once the newspapers, clippings and broadcast summaries had been digested, there ensued a quiet debate about tactics. All of the Task Force members were ardent Chrétien loyalists, and all were angered by the nature of the attack on their leader. One group wanted to hit back, hard, and unleash some of the material that had been saved for what Roméo LeBlanc had called "a rainy day"—documents detailing several new Tory mini-scandals, most of them involving patronage appointments. Another group, no less angry, wanted to wait and see what happened; it was particularly important, they noted, that nothing be done until Jean Chrétien could comment on the ads. He would be doing so later, during a campaign stop in New Brunswick or Nova Scotia.

Whatever approach was taken—hit 'em hard and hit 'em low, or wait and see—all of the residents of Saturation Plaza were nervous. The Canadian media were climbing rhetorical heights to condemn attack advertising in general, and the Tory ads in particular. That was to be expected. But Task Force members also knew that attack ads were not used because politicians enjoyed being figuratively crucified by the news media; they were used because, often, they *worked*.

The Conservative campaign spots mocking Jean Chrétien were desperate, and despicable, and destructive. On that point, all of the Task Force members assembled around the conference table agreed. Before any decision could be made on what to do about them, however, the Liberals needed to know whether the ads could harm the party's upward momentum. There was a very slim possibility that the two 30-second spots were the political equivalent of a Hail Mary pass. Or, it was possible (probable, even) that the Tories possessed polling data showing that, in the eyes of one segment of the electorate that had been drifting away from them, the spots were effective. Early on that Friday morning, just hours after the first broadcast of the ads on the CBC nightly news, nobody knew for certain: no one had any polling data yet. (There was already an unconfirmed rumour, however, that popular support for the Conservatives had "spiked" upwards after the CBC item was broadcast.)

"We are in an ugly, ugly place, here," said one Task Force member, sounding morose. There was silence.

Roméo LeBlanc observed the debate between the youthful members of his team without comment, occasionally cupping his hand behind one ear to compensate for some hearing loss. LeBlanc played many roles in the Task Force: leader, sounding board, father figure. We were devoted to him. Unlike other politicos—such as one Liberal campaign communications manager, who had more than once taken credit for LeBlanc's initiatives—the bilingual New Brunswicker was humble and quiet. He rarely lost his temper. His quick-response team, meanwhile, was usually aggressive and highly partisan. Daily, one of LeBlanc's roles involved lowering testosterone levels around Saturation Plaza, and he was uniquely qualified for the task. A veteran member of the House of Commons and the Senate, LeBlanc had held a number of senior cabinet posts, and he had been press secretary, for four years, to prime ministers Lester Pearson and Pierre Trudeau.

When the debate appeared to have run its course, LeBlanc held up two fingers. "Two things," he said, arching his eyebrows. "First, we cannot be seen to be manipulating all of this. Canadians are very mad at the Tories, and we cannot risk them getting mad at us, too. They do not want to see us taking political advantage of this situation. Secondly, we need to remind them—without it looking like we are reminding them—that these Tory ads are un-Canadian. We need to take them to a place, a room, where they look around and say: 'I don't like where I am.' Do you understand what I am saying?"

"I think I do," I said. I waved a stack of pink message slips. "These are just a few of the messages our volunteers at the reception desk out front have been getting. People are plenty pissed off. And the ones who are calling in aren't just Liberals—a lot of them are Tories. Most of them are Tories, in fact. It's like they are calling us to confess, so we can give them absolution."

"Um, I have a bit of a confession to make," said Frank Schiller. "McCauley and I called Tory headquarters already, and said we are concerned citizens—which we are. And the woman who answered sounded really, really frazzled. She said they've been getting calls all night. And she indicated that a lot of them are from Conservatives."

"There you go," I said. "There you go. We don't need to respond with outrage and indignation, or anything like that. We just need to make sure that our friends in the media get these." I waved the pink message slips around.

The Task Force discussed ways to ensure that the names and numbers of angry Canadians were disseminated to the news media. In that way, the story would largely take care of itself. The strategy, in effect, was to let the Tories' error kill the Tories; there was no need to "pile on," as someone said. Some of us would contact media in Ottawa; some would notify reporters travelling with the Liberal leader; and some would find the press contingent travelling with Kim Campbell, so that she could be peppered with questions when she emerged from her hotel room. LeBlanc approved the plan, then went off to tell John Rae and Gordon Ashworth what his team hoped to do.

The Task Force members made their way back to Saturation Plaza, but I stopped to scan the Canadian Press (CP) newswire machine, clattering away in a corner. There was story after story about the Chrétien "face" ads, as they were starting to become known. While tearing off sheets containing CP stories about the Conservative-ad backlash, one of the receptionists approached me. A man was holding on one of the lines, she told me, and he said he wanted to speak with someone in charge. "He says he is a senior Conservative."

"I'm not in charge of anything," I said. "But then again, I doubt he's very senior."

"I'm not sure about that. He says his name is Sinclair Stevens."

I dashed back to my desk, located a notepad and a pen and signalled for quiet. Sinclair Stevens was first elected to the House of Commons back in 1972, and re-elected in every contest that followed until, as minister of industry in the government of Brian Mulroney, he became enmeshed in a nasty conflict-of-interest scandal. He resigned from cabinet in 1986, and did not run in the 1988 election that saw Mulroney returned to power with another big majority. Stevens, a lawyer, had a reputation for being tough and partisan. The notion that he would be calling a Liberal Party office for anything—even the time of day—was, well, incredible.

I went through the preliminaries with the caller, trying to determine whether it was a prank call. The eyes of a few Task Force members widened when I said "Mr. Stevens." The voice on the other end of the line certainly sounded like Sinclair Stevens. After being assured—falsely—that he was speaking to someone in a position of authority in the Liberal campaign, Stevens said that he was outraged about the CBC report about the Conservative ads.

"We have received many calls about the ads, Mr. Stevens," I told him. "Many of the calls are from Tories, too."

"Well, I think they are terrible, and I want Jean to know that there are some of us who weren't consulted about them, and we condemn them," he said. He went on like that for another couple minutes, saying that he wanted the Liberal leader to know that he disagreed with what had been done.

"Do you think you could put that in writing, Mr. Stevens?" I asked him, going for broke. "Mr. Chrétien is on the road, as you know, but I could personally ensure that a letter from you gets to him very quickly."

There was a long pause. In Saturation Plaza, there was no sound. Finally, Stevens said, "Yes. Yes, I think I could do that. What is your fax number?"

At 3:12 p.m. that afternoon, the Honourable Sinclair Stevens's letter arrived at Saturation Plaza, from his home in King County, Ontario. I read it aloud to the Task Force members, some of who were punching the air in victory. Stevens wrote:

> Dear Jean,
>
> As a life-long Conservative, I am embarrassed at the tone of certain PC TV ads being currently run which attempt to depict you in an unfavourable light. This is beyond the bounds of decency and in my opinion should have no place in our democratic system. Certainly, as a 26-year member of our Queen's Privy Council, of which you also know I am a member, you deserve better. I have written to the Prime Minister, Kim Campbell, and requested that she immediately apologize to you and cause the offensive ads to be withdrawn forthwith. During my years in the House of Commons, when we were often on opposite sides of an issue, I found you to be an aggressive combatant but always fair. That is why I find it so reprehensible that certain current campaigners would discard years of tradition in their attempt to make an unfair point. It is a reflection not only on the Progressive Conservative Party, but on the institution of the Parliament of Canada itself. Such ineptitude and contempt for traditional decent behaviour is shocking. I only hope you will get a decent apology.
>
> Sincerely yours, Sinclair Stevens.

Saturation Plaza erupted in cheers as I made my way to the fax machine. Cover pages had already been made up.

An hour after Sinclair Stevens's letter to Jean Chrétien appeared on a fax machine at the Liberal Party's campaign headquarters, the Conservatives conceded that they had made a terrible, terrible mistake.

Speaking at an impromptu press conference in the lobby of the Hilton in Quebec City, where she had just met with a newspaper editorial board, Kim Campbell declared that the ads would be immediately stopped. "I would apologize to Mr. Chrétien and anyone who found them offensive," she said. The words seemed grudging, and anything but heartfelt. Campbell turned away from a stand-up microphone to return to her hotel suite, reporters shouting questions at her back. Upstairs, she broke down in tears.

According to David McLaughlin, her apology came after a "hellish" Friday morning. There had been calls to Campbell from assorted cabinet ministers, demanding that the ads be pulled. One of them, Public Security Minister Doug Lewis, issued a press release to that effect. Tory candidates across the country swamped the PC campaign staff with angry phone calls. Lawn signs were actually being returned by long-time Conservative supporters.

Initially, at least, the Conservative campaign's stalwarts elected to ride out the storm. A sheet called "Lines on the ads" were issued to candidates. "Our ads focus on the very questions we have been asking Mr. Chrétien for the last three months," the document stated. "We are simply raising questions about leadership—questions that Canadians themselves are asking. The photographs are not the issue—they are no different than the cover of the most recent *Maclean's* magazine, and were taken in one day last week. Our new radio ads ask the same questions in the same manner." Real Canadians had been used in the spots, the "Lines" document noted, and not actors.

In the space of a few hours, the "face" ad controversy mushroomed. A disabled member of the Alberta legislature had filed a complaint about the ads to the Canadian Human Rights Commission on the grounds that they "exploited a disability." A spokesman for the federal broadcasting regulator, the Canadian Radio-television and Telecommunications Commission (CRTC), confirmed that the advertisements were being investigated. The Task Force, meanwhile, had obtained a copy of an internal memorandum of the Telecaster Committee of Canada, a watchdog that scrutinizes all television commercials to ensure that they contain no "portrayals likely to be offensive to the majority of viewers." According to the memo, issued to networks and stations across Canada, the commercials "may be offensive to some viewers as they may be interpreted as a personal attack on Jean Chrétien. These spots may be seen as ridiculing Mr. Chrétien's facial paralysis and we have received complaints from viewers and member stations. You may therefore wish to view these commercials prior to airing." That memo, too, was recirculated to the news media by the Task Force.

For many members of the Task Force, seeing the ads withdrawn was not enough. They wanted the Conservatives to be utterly crushed—to lose any of the few seats in which they still had a fighting chance. Said one member: "Those sons of bitches want to humiliate our guy? Well, we'll fucking humiliate them."

Because he knows a thing or two about politics, Jean Chrétien, like Roméo LeBlanc, also knew it was important to approach the issue of the Progressive Conservative's two 30-second spots with great care. So, when he appeared at a campaign stop in New Brunswick, Chrétien said: "It's true that I have a physical defect. When I was a kid, people were laughing at me. But I accepted that, because God gave me other qualities and I'm grateful." The crowd erupted in cheers and applause; the Tories' humiliation, at that point, was complete.

Some years later, Allan Gregg sits in his cluttered office on Avenue Road in Toronto, a block or so north of the Four Seasons Hotel and the Royal Ontario Museum, his feet on his desk, remembering.

"The weak link for Chrétien was economic knowledge, and representing Canada abroad," he says, words spinning out of him at a pace that reflects the exceedingly smart person that he is. "Those are always tough for an Opposition leader. So we sent a photographer out to a Liberal rally and got a bunch of pictures. And I remember talking to Tom Scott, and saying these are the ones we've chosen. We chose them because they weren't particularly flattering, but they also weren't particularly awful. There were worse ones we could use, and there were better ones we could use. We thought those ones were really typical."

When the two 30-second spots were put together, Gregg and Scott showed them to a focus group. "Lo and behold!" says Gregg, laughing. "The response was really good. Really good." He pauses. "The story, which you can believe or not believe . . . " He trails off, shaking his head, scratching at his beard.

It is apparent that Allan Gregg does not have many fond memories about his work on the 1993 Progressive Conservative federal election campaign, and no one can blame him for that. After all, he had experienced many more wins than losses until that point in his political career: more than fifty campaigns, most of them victories. An Edmonton native, with a bachelor's and a master's degree from the University of Alberta, Gregg was drawn into Tory politics when pursuing a Ph.D. at Carleton University in Ottawa in the 1970s. He had long hair, and he swore a lot, and he dressed like a member of a rock band, but he won a job at the Research Bureau of the Opposition leader on Parliament Hill. He was, more than anything else, very smart.

Within three years of his arrival on Parliament Hill, Gregg was number three in the Tories' campaign hierarchy. His understanding of the intricacies of public opinion polling techniques, along with how to make use of polling data to craft effective campaign communications, and strategy, and tactics, made him unique in Canadian politics. The Liberals had their own pollster, Marty Goldfarb, and their own media manipulators, such as Roméo LeBlanc, but no one else had a pollster and a media manipulator embodied in a single person. Gregg helped Conservatives win elections, federally and provincially, time after time.

He went on to found multimillion-dollar companies like Decima Research and Public Affairs International, but the events of the fall of 1993 stuck with him like an unwanted house guest. Years later, Conservatives continue to blame the Chrétien "face" ads for a large part of the 1993 election rout, where they saw their 169-seat parliamentary majority reduced to two seats. Years later, many of those same Conservatives also blame Gregg—and Tom Scott, and senior campaign strategists John Tory and Tom Trbovich—for what happened.

There is a pause, so I ask Gregg The Question, still unresolved after so many years. In her best-selling book, *Time and Chance*, Kim Campbell called the spots "completely unintelligent" and "disgusting," and suggested that Gregg and his colleagues were "obtuse" to have developed them in the first place. She emphatically denies that she had seen them in advance, let alone approved them. So, I ask, did Gregg and Tom Scott and the others actually conspire to put the ads on the air without Kim Campbell seeing them, or any of her senior campaign staff, or anyone else? Did he do that, as other Tories have alleged?

He looks as if he is about to spit. "I talked to Kim Campbell *that* morning, *that* morning that they went on the air," he says, his finger stabbing the air for emphasis. "The whole campaign group saw them. Everyone. What was never anticipated by any of us was that the allegation would be made that we were making fun of Chrétien's face. When you think about it, when you actually stop and think about it, and you assume for a second that I, and John Tory, and Tom Trbovich, and Tom Scott are stupid, and that we're all bad people. And we're sitting around a table and we're 21 points behind the Grits, and we go: 'You know what? You know what will really work? Let's make fun of the guy's face!' Fuck!" He laughs, long and hard.

"We would never do that in a million *years*! We just never anticipated the reaction we got. It never came up in any of the focus groups—at all. But once the allegation was made, holy shit *la merde!*"

In the messy aftermath, the pundits clamoured to be the first to suggest that the Chrétien "face" spots were unusual, unexpected and unwelcome, and a decidedly American approach to electioneering. It hadn't happened before in Canada, they claimed, and it would almost certainly never happen again. But the pundits, as is often the case, were wrong about one thing: while the now-infamous spots were probably unwelcome, and comparatively unusual, they were decidedly not unexpected. Senior Liberals, at a July 1993 meeting in a conference room in the Opposition leader's offices in Ottawa with party ad agencies Vickers and Benson and BCP Strategy-Creativity, anticipated that the Tories might resort to personal attacks on Jean Chrétien. It was at that meeting that BCP chairman Yves Gougoux suggested a series of ads in Quebec that would attempt to use gentle humour to acknowledge that, while Chrétien may not be a matinee idol, he was admired and trusted by Canadians.

The BCP spots, by their existence, acknowledged that a minority of Canadians—very, very stupid Canadians, one might say—had reservations about Jean Chrétien's leadership because of the way he looked or spoke. In three television spots conceived long before the Tory television ads rocked the 1993 election campaign, for example, BCP's creative team had featured a large photograph of Chrétien alongside a unique message in French: "Funny face. Yes, but what vision." Another one read: "Funny wrinkles. Yes, but what insight." The BCP ads, in a sense, perhaps anticipated the Conservative attack, and "inoculated" the Liberal leader against ridicule over a physical defect.

Earlier than that, in 1991, a study conducted by the Royal Commission on Electoral Reform and Party Financing concluded that tough negative ads would almost certainly become an ongoing feature of future Canadian elections. The study noted:

> Throughout our interviews with party strategists and advertising agency executives, we were struck by the number of respondents who remarked, unprompted by our questions, that the 'old rules' about what was permissible in campaigns, particularly in campaign advertising, had been shattered. While not dismissing obvious sins of past campaigns, a number of those whom we interviewed felt that they had been dealt low blows in the last campaign, and at least some looked forward to settling the score. According to one respondent, 'We never believed anybody could stoop that low. We were wrong. We'll shoot first next time!'

Ironically, the Tories "face" spots were, along with being objectionable to many people, probably unoriginal. In September 1968, in the United States, the Democratic Party's advertising team produced a spot called "Heartbeats," to support the effort to elect Hubert H. Humphrey and Edmund Muskie, and defeat the Richard M. Nixon/Spiro Agnew Republican ticket. In the ad, a camera pulls back to reveal a single, simple question: "Agnew for Vice-President?" In the background, an unidentified person is heard—according to the spot's storyboard—laughing "uncontrollably." The tag line to the ad read: "This would be funny if it weren't so serious." Twenty-five years later, Nixon speech writer William Safire called the spot "the most distasteful, unfair and audience-insulting commercial" he had seen in years.

Unlike the Americans, who regularly eradicate entire forests to produce analyses of advertising used in their election campaigns, Canadians have been relatively silent on the subject. American academics, columnists and television analysts endlessly poke through the entrails of political spots, in some cases even running regular "Ad Watch" features in newspapers, to determine the reliability of claims made in campaign commercials, but Canadians usually do not. One exception came six years after the 1993 election, when a group of Ontario and Quebec professors dispassionately dissected the television advertising campaigns of the Liberals, Conservatives, New Democrats and Reformers in that campaign.

In their slim study, the professors, mainly from the universities of Laval and Windsor, examined all of the advertising broadcast during the 1993 campaign. According to the rules promulgated in the Canada Elections Act, partisan ads were permitted only for the final four weeks of the campaign period, with no advertising allowed on the day before voting, and election day itself. The Tories were the most enthusiastic advertisers: their spots account for thirty-five of the fifty-seven English-language ads run by the four major parties contesting the 1993 election. The PC commercials ran 230 times, which meant that the Tories took up nearly 50 per cent of the political advertising broadcast time. The Liberals came next, with eleven different ads, almost all of which ended with Jean Chrétien saying: "I have the people, I have the plan. We will make a difference." The Grit contributions were televised 123 times, giving the party 26 per cent of the overall total. The New Democrats ran nine ads on eighty-one occasions, many of them very negative; four of the spots, called "Angry Voices," were shot in black and white, and showed various Canadians literally yelling about health care, patronage, free trade and unemployment. Despite their third-party status, the NDP telecast percentage was not far behind that of the Liberals, at 17 per cent. The nascent Reform Party, meanwhile, broadcast two ads on democratic reform and fiscal responsibility, ending with the tag line: "Reform—now you have a choice." The French-language campaigns of the Tories and the Grits were more evenly matched, with the former producing eleven spots, and the latter sixteen; overall, the Liberals were "on air" in Quebec most often, with 40 per cent of the total political telecast time, compared to the Conservatives' 35 per cent.

Most of the parties' English-language ads ran on the CBC—with 72 per cent of spots airing on the public broadcaster, while a puny 28 per cent could be found on its private sector rival, CTV. The vast majority of the ads produced by all of the parties were the same—nearly two-thirds of them were 30 seconds in length. The remainder clocked in at a minute or two.

And what did the academics think about the Chrétien "face" spots? Two of them, Laval University communications professor André Gosselin, and University of Windsor political science professor Walter Soderlund, interviewed a number of partisans to assess the damage caused by the ads. Long-time Conservative Bill Neville claimed they cost his party more than fifty seats. A New Democrat strategist, Michael Balagus, estimated that the spots defeated Tory candidates in more than two dozen ridings. "Whatever the likely number," note Gosselin and Soderlund, "the decision to run these two ads has to rank as the single greatest blunder in the history of advertising in Canadian elections."

A blunder was made, there can be no doubt. The public and media outcry was too loud and too outraged to pretend otherwise. But was the blunder the running of ads, as Gosselin and Soderlund (and many others) believe, or was it that the ads were pulled so quickly?

In elections, and in Canadian elections, in particular, voters make choices based upon a variety of factors. A 1988 survey conducted by *Maclean's* magazine, for example, identified six: media coverage (51 per cent); televised leaders' debates (45 per cent); local candidates' meetings (31 per cent); television commercials (26 per cent); leaders' activities (24 per cent); and published polls (23 per cent). In light of these facts, and in light of the fact that voters, once they start paying attention to a race, are very smart indeed, it is more than possible that Canadian voters were aware that the Tories had made an exceedingly risky move. And it is equally possible that Canadians were also aware that the Tories were aware that the "face" spots were high risk. So voters in the 1993 federal election, being smart, waited to see what the Conservatives would do about all of this risky business. Would Kim Campbell's team, having gone negative, tough it out and stand by their ads? Or would they somehow implicitly, or explicitly, admit that the spots were a mistake?

The arguments for keeping the ads on the air were simple enough. One, the damage had been done, and those who did not like the ads had quickly vented their spleens. There was little to lose by staying the course. Two, ad hysteria is nothing new, and the media love to write pious editorials condemning negative advertising. But research data shows, time after time, that while voters say they do not like such ads, voters remember them, and are motivated by them. Three, in an election campaign, acknowledging a major error, not merely an innocent stumble, but a gargantuan misstep, often suggests to voters that a political party cannot be trusted to govern competently.

The arguments for pulling the Jean Chrétien "face" ads were also straightforward. One, the negatives evidently far outweighed the positives; after all, even Conservative candidates were taking to the air to condemn them. Two, Chrétien had, in Allan Gregg's own words, "brilliantly" counter-punched with his comments in New Brunswick, and thereby deflated any benefits the spots could offer. Three, and most compellingly of all, pulling the ads was simply the right thing to do. The political discourse had, in the view of a lot of people, been demeaned by a pair of poorly executed television commercials. In politics, criticizing an opponent's public policy record is fine. Criticizing their physical appearance is not.

In the end, and contrary to the Parliament Hill mythology that developed in the years that followed, neither the Liberal Party nor its Task Force quick-response team single-handedly stirred up public outrage against the ill-fated Conservative attack ads. The Tories did that all by themselves. By making the ads in the first place—or by yanking them off the air—the Conservative Party did itself irreparable damage. On that last point, all agree.

Allan Gregg's long-time friend, Hugh Segal, certainly feels that the bigger mistake was *admitting* a mistake. For decades, Segal was a key player, and a brilliant one, in the backrooms of Ottawa. From the time he was a Conservative Party activist in university in the late 1960s, to when he became a staff member for Ontario Conservative Premier Bill Davis and federal Conservative leaders Robert Stanfield and Brian Mulroney, Segal has been at the epicentre of Progressive Conservative Party politics. After an unsuccessful run for the party leadership in 1999, Segal has busied himself as the conservative panellist on assorted television political programs, and as Resident Fellow at the School of Policy Studies at Queen's University in Kingston, Ontario. He has also authored a number of books about politics.

In one of them, *No Surrender*, Segal recalls the Conservatives' ill-fated 1993 election campaign. On the "face" ads, he remains defiant, writing: "Far more unflattering pictures of Chrétien had appeared in *Maclean's* magazine and other places." Moreover, he notes, the Liberal Party's own Quebec advertising agency had devised a billboard campaign featuring Chrétien's face and the slogan: "Strange-looking forehead. But reflect on what's inside." Says Segal: "I was angry about the decision to pull the ad. It was the kind of ad a campaign crew uses if it both tests well in research, and there is no other choice. It should have run its course for a few days... Tory numbers started to trend upward when the ads hit; clearly, it was working ... Even if the ads were a mistake, pulling them that way was a bigger mistake."

Allan Gregg agrees with his old friend's assessment. The nightly polling numbers, he says, showed a perceptible rise in support for Kim Campbell's Conservatives. "Our tracking the first two nights, before they were pulled, saw us spike up," he says. "We went from twenty-one points down, to eleven down, and then ten, on the two successive nights. That's hard to read a lot into, but it's something."

The mistake made in political campaigns—Canadian, American or British—is not in "going negative," Gregg insists. The mistake, he says, is getting spooked about having done it: "When they pulled those ads, it confirmed every bad suspicion that people had—that we were venal and stupid, and therefore completely unworthy." He shrugs. "I just went home. I went back to my hotel, packed my bag, went to the Ottawa airport and went home."

The moral of the story? The moral of the story, he agrees, is a simple one: stand by your ad. "Yep, that's right," Gregg says, escorting me to the door. "Stand by your ad."

CHAPTER TWO

DAISY AND MR. SAGE
... or, how to make mud stick

It begins quietly, with a little girl. She appears to be standing in a field somewhere, with some trees and branches visible behind her. The wind is blowing. It is warm enough for the child to be wearing a sleeveless top and a pair of shorts. She has long, straight hair, with bangs to just above her large eyes, which are preoccupied as we meet her. She can be no more than three or four years old.

She is a holding a flower—a daisy. In a child's singsong voice, the little girl is counting the petals as she removes them from the daisy. "One, two, three, four, five," she says so softly she can barely be heard. She gets her counting wrong, as young children sometimes do: "Seven, six, six, eight, nine, nine..."

And then she stops and looks up, startled and apparently frightened. Abruptly, a man's voice, very loud, echoing as if amplified through a loudspeaker, starts to count. As he does so, the camera moves closer and closer to the little girl. "Ten, nine, eight, seven, six, five, four," he says, and all that can be seen are the child's eyes, which are afraid. "Three, two, one . . ." The shot moves into the dark centre of her eye.

Then, there is an explosion—a huge, lingering explosion—and the child's iris is filled with a grainy image of an atomic bomb being detonated. As the mushroom cloud reaches upward, filling the sky, another voice is heard: the voice of Lyndon B. Johnson, president of the United States.

"These are the stakes," he says in the flat idiom of Texas. "To make a world in which all of God's children can live, or to go into the dark." Pause. "We must either love each other, or we must die."

The screen goes black, and a few words appear in white: "VOTE FOR PRESIDENT JOHNSON ON NOVEMBER 3." Then the last voice-over: "Vote for President Johnson on November 3. The stakes are too high for you to stay home."

Most of those who have seen the spot that came to be known as "Daisy" agree: it was, and remains, the most powerful piece of political advertising in history. Some say it marked the beginning of negative political advertising, but that is wrong on two counts. First, the genre of political communications it represents—that is, tough but accurate criticism of one's political opponent—is hardly new. It reflects, in fact, some of the oldest campaigning there is. Second, it is not accurate to dismiss Daisy as "negative." The spot has a kind of poetry about it and, visually, it is beautiful.

It is also wrong to suggest that Daisy belongs to the same category of advertising as the Chrétien "face" ads. The Tories' 1993 spots were all about a man, and had really nothing to do with policy. Daisy, on the other hand, did not mention once the name of President Johnson's opponent, but it was all *about* a policy: nuclear deterrence.

As a paid advertisement, it ran only once, on the evening of September 7, 1964. But Daisy profoundly altered modern electoral politics, and the way in which political messages are communicated. Almost four decades later, it can still send shivers up the spines of seasoned political campaigners, the ones who claim to have seen it all. More than Ronald Reagan's 1984 "Morning in America" spot; more than George Bush's 1988 "Willie Horton" attack ad, Daisy was, and still is, the best.

On the night it ran, during *Monday Night at the Movies*, Daisy's effect was immediate. Within moments, recalled former Johnson press aide Bill Moyers, the White House switchboard lit up with hundreds of calls from those who wanted to protest the ad. Moyers even fielded a call from his boss, who also sounded irate. "Jesus Christ!" Johnson yelled at Moyers, who was part of the team that had produced Daisy. "What in the world happened?"

"You got your point across, that's what happened," Moyers replied.

There was a lengthy silence. "Well, I guess we did."

They most certainly did. Other networks started to run the ad as part of their news coverage—for free. One Republican senator complained to the National Association of Broadcasters. The chairman of the Republican National Committee, Dean Burch, filed a formal objection with the Fair Campaign Practices Committee, stating that Daisy amounted to "a libel against the Republican nominee," Senator Barry Goldwater. More than 1,300 people called the Republicans, or G.O.P., to register their objections to Daisy, including, allegedly, a Virginia mother who said the spot had reduced her four-year-old to tears before bedtime. "This horror-type commercial is designed to arouse basic emotions and has no place in this campaign," wrote Burch, who was only half-right: yes, Daisy had been carefully designed to stir up basic emotions. But the message Daisy conveyed certainly *did* belong in the 1964 U.S. presidential race, because the stakes were very high that year, indeed.

Arizona's Barry Goldwater scared people. Even before he won the Republican Party's presidential nomination at the Cow Palace in San Francisco in July 1964, the hardline conservative had alienated many Americans, and even members of his own party, with statements and allies better suited to the Wild West than a national election effort in a pluralistic democracy. In May 1963, while the U.S. war effort in Vietnam was escalating, Goldwater told an ABC news program that, if one wished to expose arms supply routes to Viet Cong guerrillas, then "defoliation of the forests by low-yield atomic weapons could be done." His ruminations caused an international uproar. In October 1963, Goldwater horrified Americans by claiming that the nuclear bomb was "merely another weapon." In 1964, he voted against the Civil Rights Act, thereby earning the enthusiastic support of the Ku Klux Klan and the white supremacist John Birch Society. He disavowed the support of neither.

At the Republican convention in San Francisco—which Norman Mailer described, memorably, as "murderous in mood, [where] chimeras of fascism hung like fogbanks"—Goldwater had not done much to relieve himself of the extremist mantle. Near the conclusion of his acceptance speech, he said: "I would remind you that extremism in the defence of liberty is no vice! And let me remind you also that moderation in the pursuit of justice is no virtue!"

To the Democrats managing Lyndon Johnson's campaign, among them Bill Moyers and Jack Valenti (who would later achieve distinction as a powerful Hollywood lobbyist for the Motion Picture Association), Goldwater had built himself a gallows, strung up a noose and placed his head within it. By attacking Goldwater, they were merely granting the Arizona senator his desire for electoral euthanasia. The advertising campaign they conceived was easily the toughest in U.S. history. It was also, the Johnson team fervently believed, a valuable public service.

The parentage of Daisy is claimed by many. It seems clear, however, that the person most responsible for the spot was a New York City adman named Tony Schwartz.

Though Schwartz was from New York, he was far removed from Madison Avenue, home to the advertising agency establishment. In the brownstone where he lived with his wife and two sons, he built a soundproof recording studio, filled with top-of-the-line cameras and editing machines. He was a bit of a curiosity to the Madison Avenue types, many of whom had long and enduring relationships with the Republican Party. Schwartz had, for example, an interest in recording children at play, and in what he called "the world of numbers." Long before Daisy would change a presidential campaign, Schwartz said, he "wanted to do a record essay on numbers without any narration, just the world of numbers. I saw a book that IBM put out, called *The World of Numbers*, and I thought, I would love to do a record to go with that... The most complex use of numbers was the countdown on the atom bomb or a rocket blast-off. The simplest use of numbers was a child counting from one to ten. I started fooling around with [that]."

By the summer of 1964, the advertising firm of Doyle Dane Bernbach (DDB) had been retained by the Democratic Party as their agency of record for the forthcoming presidential campaign. Moyers, Valenti and the DDB admen had resolved to go negative against Goldwater from the start of the campaign, reminding Americans about his extremism and fondness for the nuclear option. A DDB producer who had worked with Tony Schwartz asked him to come to the firm's Manhattan offices, without telling him why.

In an interview from his home—Schwartz rarely travels anywhere because he is agoraphobic—he remembers the genesis of "Daisy." Born in New York City in 1923, Schwartz is not as young as he used to be, but his memory is very sharp.

In his soft New York accent, he tells his story: "A political ad is about things that are important to the people, at the time the election is taking place. The Daisy ad was an interesting thing, the way it came about. I went down to [DDB] and the producer held up Johnson's picture, and said: 'Would you work for him?' I said yes." He laughs. "They asked me to do the sound for six or seven spots for Johnson, and I said okay."

The Democrats and the DDB team wanted a spot to emphasize the fact that, as president, Goldwater's finger would be on the nuclear "button." Schwartz told them he had just what they were looking for. "I told them I had it all done already. I had done a Polaroid spot for Doyle Dane Bernbach with my nephew, counting up to ten and getting all mixed up as kids will at his age—four or five," he recalls. He had also produced dozens of spots and radio essays for WNYC, the New York affiliate of National Public Radio. In one of them, he had an idea. "I added [to the spot featuring his nephew] a countdown from a rocket blast, and a bomb sound going off. And then I had an announcer say, 'In a world of nuclear weapons, we have to have a strong United Nations.' So I took that, and played it for them. They flipped. Find a child, I told them, picking the petals off a daisy. And I'll produce it."

The little girl—four-year-old Bridget Olsen, whom DDB found through a city talent agency—was filmed with her flower while walking near the Henry Hudson Parkway north of the city. "The Democrats and DDB gave me five hours of Rose Garden speeches by Johnson," Schwartz says. "They had a script, and they had a little section they had marked off, which they liked. So I listened to all of the five hours of tape, and found the section. I listened to it. It had no emotion, and I didn't like it at all. So I just went through the whole thing again, and found this piece that I liked. 'These are the stakes...' And I used that."

While not as many Americans saw Daisy as Schwartz or the Democrats would have hoped—most were watching NBC that Monday night—many later claimed to have seen it, or had it described to them. A surprising number insisted, to Schwartz or others, that Barry Goldwater had been named in the spot. Schwartz is vehement on this point: "We never mentioned Goldwater. The type on the end said vote for President Johnson and so on. But Goldwater's name was *never* mentioned in it. Now, for years, this was called the beginning of negative political commercials. But it wasn't."

The unforgettable words that LBJ spoke, as it turns out, were not the president's, or Bill Moyers's, or Jack Valenti's. They belonged to the British poet W. H. Auden. "It turned out he wrote a lot of the Rose Garden speeches," Schwartz says, amused. Years later, members of the Auden family tracked down Schwartz and asked him how the New York City adman had persuaded the poet to write for a political commercial. He laughs at the memory, but Auden himself, apparently, had not been amused. A White House speechwriter had appropriated the stanza from Auden's most famous poem, "September 1, 1939," written about the growing storms of war. When Auden finally saw Daisy, he was livid. "I pray to God that I shall never be memorable like that again," he said, giving orders that the poem not reappear in any collections of his work.

Schwartz says he thinks he knows why Daisy worked: it played on the public's belief that Goldwater favoured the use of nuclear weapons, while LBJ did not. When the commercial came on, people asked themselves: "Whose finger do I want on the nuclear trigger? The man who wants to use them, or the man who doesn't?"

Daisy, in this context, was not really a negative political spot at all. It was an advertisement about choices. It highlighted, in dramatic terms, the difference between Johnson and Goldwater on the nuclear question, and asked voters to make a choice. The way in which the choice was laid out—stark militarism versus a little girl with a flower—was, without a doubt, maddening to partisan Republicans. But, stripped down to its core facts, Daisy was not inaccurate. Goldwater *was* more willing to consider the deployment of nuclear weapons. He and his fellow G.O.P. members may not have approved of the fact that Johnson had chosen to emphasize that point of difference. But it *was* a point of difference. And voters *were* entitled to be told about it.

Elections are about choices. And Tony Schwartz was, one might say, merely suggesting that one choice was infinitely better—infinitely safer—than the other.

In his book *The Responsive Chord*, Tony Schwartz suggests that Daisy was effective—despite the controversy, despite the expressions of outrage—because it stirred up powerful emotions, unarticulated emotions, among those who saw the spot. "The best political commercials are similar to Rorschach patterns," wrote Schwartz. "They do not tell the viewer anything. They surface his feelings and provide a context for him to express those feelings."

Feelings were in ample supply after Daisy was broadcast, just that once, on September 7, 1964.

Barry Goldwater's mistake was to underestimate the power of the spot, which had become the talk of the nation. At first, he dismissed Daisy as "weird television advertising." Two weeks later, however, Republicans, including Goldwater himself, apparently, had woken up to the significant damage done to their campaign by Tony Schwartz, a little girl and a flower. Desperate, they hauled Dwight D. Eisenhower out of retirement to prop up Goldwater's faltering presidential hopes. In a hurriedly-produced sixty-second spot, Eisenhower and Goldwater were filmed chatting. Goldwater says: "Our opponents are referring to us as warmongers." Says Eisenhower, looking barely indignant: "Well, Barry, in my mind, this is actual tommyrot."

Goldwater aficionado and former actor Ronald Reagan also stepped forward to provide a filmed speech to assist Goldwater. Reagan's speech, called "A Time for Choosing," was masterful, and it even attempted to throw back at the Democrats some of their own dark imagery. Said

Reagan: "You and I have a rendezvous with destiny. We can preserve for our children this, the last best hope of man on Earth, or we can sentence them to take the first step into a thousand years of darkness."

It was not insignificant, perhaps, that the Democrats and the Republicans were making essentially the same allegation against each other—that the future was at peril in the presidential race. But it was the Democrats (or, more accurately, Tony Schwartz) who understood that, on television, the picture of a child was worth far more than any of Ronald Reagan's words. In politics, that basic proposition has not been challenged since: pictures equal emotion, which equals power. Words do not equal pictures.

When the results came in, early on November 4, 1964, Lyndon Baines Johnson had won by a landslide. Barry Goldwater, meanwhile, barely won his home state, by less than 1 per cent. Out of fifty states, the Republican nominee took only six. Daisy had won.

A book lover, a Virginian and the son of a Methodist minister, Thomas Rosser Reeves does not seem the likeliest of candidates to have conjured up modern political advertising. In *Reality in Advertising*, published in 1961, he describes himself as "a licensed pilot, a skilled yachtsman, a collector of modern art, a Civil War buff, a musician and the writer of short stories." Sporting bow ties and hornrimmed glasses, smoking cigarettes incessantly, he also wrote novels and poetry and once acted as captain of the United States chess team. In his early days, Reeves hoped to be a lawyer. The Great Depression, however, forced him out of the University of Virginia, and he became a reporter for the Richmond *Times-Dispatch*.

Of his many interests and avocations, it was for advertising that Rosser Reeves became known, and, in particular, advertising that used the new medium of television to revolutionize political campaigns. Tony Schwartz would create a genre, but it was Reeves who created the medium.

Until Rosser Reeves came along, political salesmanship was a primitive process. Candidates for national office were obliged to submit themselves to gruelling, months-long campaigns—travelling great distances by train, hollering themselves hoarse from makeshift platforms, grasping innumerable hands at innumerable rallies and occasionally making use of radio to broadcast lengthy speeches listened to by only a few. In 1948, the year Harry Truman won the U.S. presidential race, Truman himself estimated that he had "travelled 31,000 miles, made 356 speeches, shook hands with half a million people, [and] talked to 15 or 20 million in person." Truman was unenthusiastic about other, more modern approaches to communicating with voters: "My own experience is all personal contact," he declared. In the 1948 campaign, the Democrats had produced just a single advertisement to be used in movie theatres or television. At a post-victory press conference, when a reporter asked Truman whether television had assisted his campaign, all the other journalists erupted in laughter.

It would not be very long before people like Rosser Reeves would be doing the laughing. The 1948 U.S. presidential campaign represented the final hurrah of so-called retail politics: campaigning door-to-door, vote by vote, with little or no attention paid to mass communication techniques. In 1951, transcontinental cable led to the quick formation of national networks in the United States while, in Canada, the Canadian Broadcasting Corporation announced plans for the debut of a national television service. By the following year, more than 20 million television sets were to be found in homes in North America, particularly in urban areas clustered along the Canada–U.S. border. A lot of votes lived in those homes.

Much of the earliest television programming on privately owned networks—*I Love Lucy*, *The Milton Berle Show*, *The Ed Sullivan Show* and so on—was sponsored, and ultimately controlled, by advertisers. Programs carried names like *Camel News Caravan* or *Texaco Star*

Theatre, and featured lengthy ads only from those companies. One Madison Avenue advertising executive, frustrated by the restrictions placed on the new medium, promoted the fact that advertising rates dropped dramatically in the broadcast minutes sandwiched between the sponsored programs. The executive—a young Rosser Reeves, who had abandoned Virginia for the big city—told his clients that they could use those minutes to reach as many households as Texaco or Camel, but at a fraction of the price. Developing shorter, memorable ads he and others called "spots," Reeves became rapidly known as an adman who could deliver cost-effective messages that produced results.

Reeves was indeed effective. Some of his advertising milestones remain well known many years after the fact. There was: "Certs breath mints—with a magic drop of retsyn." And: "How do you spell relief? R-O-L-A-I-D-S." And: "Wonder bread helps build strong bodies in eight ways." And, perhaps most memorably of all: "M&Ms melt in your mouth, not in your hands."

For a quarter of a century, Reeves worked at the Ted Bates Agency, where he was known as the "Prince of Hard Sell." His view of advertising was unromantic. To Reeves, too many agencies were preoccupied with the development of advertising that won industry awards but did little else. He said: "Let's say you have a million dollars tied up in your little company and suddenly your advertising isn't working and sales are going down. And everything depends on it. Your future depends on it, your family's future depends on it, other people's families depend on it . . . Now, what do you want from me? Fine writing? Or do you want to see the goddamned sales curve stop moving down and start moving up?"

The advertising Reeves produced ultimately stressed simplicity, clarity and repetition. (One of his spots for Fleischmann's, for example, mentioned the words "corn oil margarine" no less than seven times.) To Reeves, it did not matter that a commercial was interesting or not. In his view, early television audiences were captivated by the new medium, and were therefore very likely to see and hear an agency's spot. What mattered most, then, was not the interest level an ad generated, but its effectiveness. Anything that detracted from a commercial's selling message, such as a clever visual or graphic, was a scene-stealer—what Reeves called a "video vampire." Originality and prettiness were simple distractions, he argued, that had been conjured up by egocentric advertising copywriters who placed creativity over selling the client's product. On one occasion, when challenged on his tough approach to advertising, Reeves replied: "No, sir. I'm not saying that charming, witty and warm copy won't sell. I'm just saying that I've seen thousands of charming, witty campaigns that didn't sell."

Reeves called his no-nonsense advertising philosophy the USP—the Unique Selling Proposition. In *Reality in Advertising*, Reeves writes: "Advertising is the art of getting a unique selling proposition into the heads of the most people at the lowest possible costs."

There were three components to the USP. The first was that the ad must make "a proposition" to the customer being targeted. The message needed to be more than words, or a catchy phrase, or a colourful graphic. To Reeves, it needed to say to the consumer: "Buy this product and you will get this specific benefit." The second requirement of USP was, as the name implies, uniqueness. It had to be able to make a claim about the product or service that the competition could not. The third USP component was likely the toughest. The proposition needed to be strong. It needed to be one that could motivate masses—in the television age, that meant millions of potential consumers—to purchase what was being sold.

In the early 1950s, using modern advertising techniques to market political candidates on television was not merely new, it was unprecedented. Earlier on, radio had been used in the campaigns of the likes of Franklin D. Roosevelt; being confined to a wheelchair, FDR used his mellifluous broadcaster's voice to great effect with his Depression-era fireside chats. But Harry Truman possessed a raspy twang, unsuited to radio. And, like Truman, many politicians in the U.S., and in other places, were suspicious of television. In fact, most advertising agencies were still unsure how to make effective use of the new communications medium.

The Ted Bates Agency, where Rosser Reeves started working in 1940, was different. The Bates team had been involved with television advertising from the start, when few TV sets had meant few sales. But, before long, the agency's knowledge of the fledgling medium started to pay dividends. Said Reeves: "We discovered that this was no tame kitten. We had a ferocious, man-eating tiger. We could take the same advertising campaign from print or radio and put it on TV, and, even when there were very few sets, sales would jump through the roof. It was like shooting fish in a barrel."

Reeves, a Republican, took his enthusiasm to Thomas E. Dewey, governor of New York and the Republican's challenger to Truman in the 1948 race. Reeves argued that the contest would be a close one. If the Republicans saturated key markets with effective Dewey spots, he argued, they would win. Dewey, who was referred to derisively as "the little man on the wedding cake"—a stiff and formal person—sniffed at Reeves's ideas, stating that they were "undignified." He went on to be clobbered by Truman.

By 1952, when Truman's term was at an end, the Republicans were less quick to dismiss Reeves. Since 1948, television's growth had been explosive. Even Thomas Dewey, in his 1950 campaign for re-election as governor of New York, had changed his tune. Assisted by advertising executives at Batten, Barton, Durstine and Osborn (BBDO), Dewey agreed to participate in an eighteen-hour marathon of talking, wherein voters from across the state would stand before television cameras and ask him questions. His ability to answer questions in detail, and to speak extemporaneously, not to mention the fact that he was prepared to answer literally hundreds of questions for eighteen hours, won him re-election.

Rosser Reeves, and his revolutionary ideas about television and politics, started to seem less revolutionary. The first to come and pay obeisance was, fittingly enough, the Republican Party. Madison Avenue ad agencies had, from the outset, a pronounced Republican tilt, partly owing to the party's local and statewide successes. Moreover, and more significantly, perhaps, many of Madison Avenue's corporate clients were run by businessmen who were committed followers of the G.O.P. So, in the summer of 1952, when Reeves was summoned to the Racquet Club on Park Avenue by a group of Republican businessmen, he was unsurprised. Truman had earlier decided not to seek re-election, and the Republicans desperately wanted their candidate, General Dwight D. Eisenhower, to win.

The businessmen told Reeves that the Democratic candidate, Illinois governor Adlai Stevenson, had a great slogan: "You never had it so good." The Republican campaign of Eisenhower, meanwhile, offered a line that was less inspiring: "Time for a change." Could Reeves think of something better? "Ike doesn't need a slogan," Reeves told the businessmen. "He needs a strategy."

Reeves told the Republican businessmen that Eisenhower should make use of television spots. Recalled Reeves: "These [businessmen], they didn't know an advertising spot from Alpha Centauri, so I explained the whole theory." Reeves told the men that television was "so powerful that it's changing the whole media structure of the world," and that politics should not be immune from its effects. Nor could it be.

The businessmen were intrigued. Money would be no object, they told him. Go and develop a strategy for Eisenhower in the coming presidential election. Over a weekend, Reeves and an associate produced two memos for the Republicans. One of the memos, stamped "CONFIDENTIAL," remains a fascinating document, and represents the first known attempt by a Western political party to address the powerful challenge represented by television. Titled "Program to Guarantee an Eisenhower Victory," the three-page, double-spaced memo uses language that, until that point, many of the Republican mavens and money men had never seen before. The enthusiasm it contains is almost childlike, but there can be little doubt that Reeves was ahead of his contemporaries. The memo reads:

> The betting odds may be even—some pollsters may say it's in the bag—but don't forget what happened in '48. Look at the number of electoral votes the Democrats now confidently claim—293 (266 needed)—and look at the number the Democrats concede to the Republicans—a probable 78. Complacency and wishful thinking will not elect Ike. His top advisers know it is going to take plenty of work; lots of money; plus something new—something EXTRA AND SPECIAL. This program may well be it—so read carefully.

In the same breathless, enthusiastic tone, the memo goes on:

> Is *there a new way of campaigning* that can guarantee a victory for Eisenhower in November? The answer is: 'Yes!' It is not a theory. It has been tried, tested and proven in local elections. Now for the first time this method is ready for national treatment, ready for Ike... WHAT IS THIS 'NEW WAY OF CAMPAIGNING?' This new way of campaigning, in essence is a new use of what advertising men know as 'spots.' A spot is a 15-second or one-minute announcement on radio—or a

20-second or one-minute announcement on television. Most people do not know the power of spots. However, here are the cold facts. THE HUMBLE RADIO OR TV 'SPOT' CAN DELIVER MORE LISTENERS FOR LESS MONEY THAN ANY OTHER FORM OF ADVERTISING. Let us repeat that. THE HUMBLE RADIO OR TV 'SPOT' CAN DELIVER MORE LISTENERS FOR LESS MONEY THAN ANY OTHER FORM OF ADVERTISING.

Reeves goes on to discuss the financial advantages offered by the use of spots placed strategically between sponsored shows featuring stars such as Jack Benny, Eddie Cantor and Fred Allen as well as Edgar Bergen and Charlie McCarthy. ("YOU GET THE AUDIENCE BUILT AT HUGE COSTS BY OTHER PEOPLE," Reeves gushed.)

The same summer, Reeves had spoken with public opinion pollster George Gallup about which issue was most important to Americans. Without hesitating, Gallup answered that there were three: corruption, taxes and the ongoing Korean War. True to his USP credo, Reeves preferred just one issue, but Gallup insisted there were three. So Reeves concluded his with a section headlined:

WHAT DO THE SPOTS SAY? Plenty! However, they all touch on just three problems—the 'big three' which the largest number of people are worried about: 1. Corruption in government. 2. High prices and high taxes. 3. War! In these spots, Eisenhower identifies himself as one who fully understands the problems of Mr. and Mrs. America (which is 50 per cent of the battle in winning people's confidence). He sits down in

> personal interviews with people in all walks of life—cab drivers, schoolteachers, office and factory workers, housewives, etc. It is a way of having a big 'TOWN MEETING'... but letting 60,000,000 people hear all the questions and answers! This intimate, informal 'spot' technique is ideally suited to [Ike's] warm personality.

While Eisenhower's campaign manager was skeptical, as was the national chairman of Citizens for Eisenhower-Nixon, Rosser Reeves's determination overcame all Republican resistance. Closeted away in a hotel room on Fifth Avenue for weeks on end, Reeves scrutinized Eisenhower speeches, spoke to Gallup some more and typed out a total of twenty-two scripts. In mid-September 1952, Reeves and Eisenhower met for the first time at a film studio in Manhattan. At the start, Eisenhower resisted Reeves's approach. "To think an old soldier should come to this!" he remarked at one point. But Ike eventually succumbed to the adman's blandishments. The Republican nominee was persuaded to abandon his glasses, and read Reeves's scripts off cue cards bearing giant-sized letters. In time, Eisenhower was racing through takes, while Reeves typed up seventeen more scripts in another room. (Eisenhower, warming to the task, apparently even wrote one himself, but no one seems to be able to recall the subject.) In all, forty were written and filmed, featuring Eisenhower briefly answering a question.

The questioners, mainly tourists, were rounded up and filmed over a couple of days outside New York's Radio City Music Hall. Reeves wanted Americans who were not actors—real people, wearing their own clothes, asking questions in their local accents. The tourists were filmed reading questions from cue cards. Later, the tourists' questions, and Ike's answers, were spliced together, to magical effect. Each spot started with a slide that read: "EISENHOWER ANSWERS AMERICA."

In one particularly brilliant spot, a dark-haired woman asks: "The Democrats have made mistakes, but aren't their intentions good?" Replies Eisenhower: "Well, if the driver of your school bus runs into a truck, hits a lamppost, drives into a ditch, you don't say his intentions are good. You get a new driver." In another, which succinctly addressed George Gallup's advice, a man in a plaid shirt says: "General, the Democrats are telling me I've never had it so good." Says Ike: "Can that be true, when America is billions in debt, when prices have doubled, when taxes break our backs, and we are still fighting in Korea? It's tragic and it's time for a change." Another featured an elderly woman wearing a hat who says: "You know what things cost today. High prices are just driving me crazy." Says Eisenhower, who at that point likely did not frequent too many grocery stores: "Yes, my Mamie gets after me about the high cost of living. It's another reason why I say, it's time for a change. Time to get back to an honest dollar and an honest dollar's work."

The Ike spots, which cost $60,000 (the price of a few seconds' broadcast time in today's campaigns) were revolutionary and radical. When word leaked out about the ad campaign, however, the Democrats did what all political parties would later do when queried about an opponent's advertising: they went into attack mode. George Ball, executive director of Volunteers for Stevenson, attacked the Republicans' use of Madison Avenue "high-powered hucksters." Sniffed Ball: "[The Republicans are attempting] to sell an inadequate ticket to the American people in precisely the same way [advertisers] sell soap, ammoniated toothpaste, hair tonic or bubble gum."

In an advertising industry publication in early October, Ball said: "They have all the money, but no candidate . . . Found with this dilemma, they have invented a new kind of campaign—conceived not by men who want us to face crucial issues of this crucial day, but by the high-powered hucksters of Madison Avenue." Stevenson himself picked up on the theme, stating that the G.O.P. was showing "contempt" for the intelligence of the American people. In their criticisms, there was no doubt that the Democrats were partly right. Reeves, in fact, privately admitted as much: he *was* attempting to sell Ike in the manner that toothpaste was sold, although doing so could hardly be labelled "contemptuous" of the voter. Condescension and contempt, after all, do not sell toothpaste: good messaging does. In the end, Democratic pieties did not matter much. Unfortunately for Ball and Stevenson (whose comments actually spurred a number of large contributions to the G.O.P. to finance the ad campaign), and unfortunately for the Democrats (who fatally misunderstood, or underestimated, the power of television), Rosser Reeves's TV theories won the day.

His theories were durable, too. Even when the Republican ticket was later beset by trouble—when vice-presidential candidate Richard Nixon was accused of benefiting from a "secret" fund to supplement his income, with his wife, Pat, receiving a mink in the bargain—the adman's formula was employed to devastating effect. (The Democrat charges were true, but also somewhat unfair: most political party leaders receive stipends and allowances from their partisan fundraisers.) In his "Checkers" speech, Nixon knocked the Democrat allegations out of the proverbial ballpark. Looking straight into the television camera on September 23, 1952, Nixon said: "My fellow Americans, I come before you tonight as a candidate for the vice-presidency and a man whose honesty and integrity have been questioned." Nixon described what he and his wife owned, then said: "Pat doesn't have a mink coat. But she does have a respectable Republican cloth coat, and I always tell her she would look good in anything."

Nixon could have stopped right there, having utterly vanquished his adversaries. But he went on: "One other thing I probably should tell you, because if I don't, they will be saying this about me, too. We did get something, a gift, after the nomination. A man down in Texas heard Pat on the radio mention the fact that our two youngsters would like to have a dog. Believe it or not, the day before we left on this campaign trip, we got a message from Union Station in Baltimore, saying they had a package for us. We went down to get it. You know what it was? It was a little cocker spaniel dog, in a crate that he had sent all the way from Texas—black and white, spotted, and our little girl Tricia, the six-year-old, named it Checkers. And you know, the kids, like all kids, loved the dog. And I just want to say right now, that regardless of what they say about it, we are going to keep it."

Dwight D. Eisenhower and Richard M. Nixon won the election with nearly 60 per cent of the vote. Rosser Reeves, who died in January 1984, was characteristically modest about his own achievement, calling the Ike spots "only an interesting footnote to history." Said Reeves: "It was such a [Republican] landslide that it didn't make a goddamned bit of difference whether we ran the spots or not."

Others beg to differ. Lynda Kaid is director of the University of Oklahoma's Political Commercial Archive. The archive contains more than 55,000 political commercials, in film, audio and videotape, reaching back to 1936. Nearly two-thirds of the university's holdings are simply unavailable anywhere else. Kaid has probably seen more political commercials than anyone else on the planet, and has this to say about Rosser Reeves: "His work was enormously important—for its groundbreaking nature. Reeves realized that television spots could overcome selective exposure, thus ensuring that Democrats and Republicans would be exposed to Eisenhower's political messages.

"His intuitive sense about this was later borne out by some of the earliest empirical work on political television advertising. Reeves was also successful in using the spots to achieve a softening of Eisenhower's cold military image, helping to reshape his appeal into the warm fatherly figure Eisenhower is remembered to be."

When they are periodically polled on the issue of negative advertising, Canadians, like Americans, are of almost one voice. They insist that they do not like it. A November 1988 Canadian Gallup poll, for example, noted that 60 per cent of Canadians expressed opposition to "political advertising which criticizes another party's policies and leaders." This finding, Gallup asserted, was consistent across economic, regional, educational and linguistic divides. It does not appear, however, that Gallup probed a related, and more salient, question: namely, do critical campaign ads work? Even if Canadians profess to dislike them, do they not recall such ads more readily? Why has there been so much critical campaigning in recent decades, if voters say they aren't paying any attention, and claim that they are unmoved by it?

In the only recent study of the issue, three Canadian professors of political science and communications examined the issue at length; their findings are part of a volume that makes up the 1992 report of the Royal Commission on Electoral Reform and Party Financing. In their essay, titled "Negative Political Advertising: An Analysis of Research Findings in Light of Canadian Practice," Professors Walter Romanow, Walter Soderlund and Richard Price noted that there is, indeed, an increasing amount of negative advertising filling the airwaves. But why is there so much of it, the professors queried, if it is allegedly so harmful to a candidate's prospects?

The answer, they concluded, is undeniable: in Canada, as in the United States, "negative advertising works." There are two reasons for this. First, television is an emotional medium, and emotional messages work best with voters. "With too much information around," the professors wrote, "our senses are overloaded and advertisers have turned away from information-imparting ads to an approach that 'goes for the gut,' appealing to core values... Negative ads are crafted in the best dramatic tradition: they contain characterization (implicit or explicit), plot and conflict." Second, they wrote, negative ads work because they are negative: "Simply put, negative information is more powerful in crystallizing decisions than positive information. In politics, it is said, 'mud sticks,' and negative ads are the way in which seeds of doubt about an opponent are introduced and negative perceptions are reinforced."

In Canada, as in the United States, negative campaign advertising is nothing new. "Historically," the professors added, "negative or attack ads... have played a significant part in the ad campaign tactics of the three major parties."

In his seminal 1993 work on the relationship between Canadian politicians and Canadian reporters, *Scrum Wars*, author Allan Levine emphatically agrees. Levine recalls that aggressive partisanship has always characterized Canada's public life. "In a world defined by whether one was a Grit or a Tory," he writes, "it was usually good business for a newspaper to identify with one side or the other." Among other things, well-behaved newspapers—that is, ones that propped up the ruling party and brutally derided the opposition—were the recipients of lucrative advertising contracts, and a loyal readership. In some cases, politicians such as Sir John A. Macdonald actually invested their own monies in the partisan journals. For the better part of a decade, for example, Sir John A. worked with a group of followers—unsuccessfully, as things turned out—to establish a pro-Conservative newspaper to counter the debilitating effects of the Liberal *Free Press*. And in the 1860s, Canada's first prime minister actually contributed $5,000 of his own money to help launch the *Daily Telegraph* in Toronto but, ironically, the paper ended up being one of the Conservatives' most ardent critics.

With political parties relying upon newspapers for partisan support, and in some cases owning them, there were not many compelling reasons, in the late 1800s and early 1900s, to spend more money on expensive advertising campaigns attacking one's partisan opponents. As Canadian newspapers grew increasingly independent, however, this changed. It gradually became necessary for politicians and their advisers to develop their own communications vehicles, and not simply rely upon partisan broadsheets. The transition does not appear to have been difficult. The Liberals and the Conservatives threw themselves into vicious advertising campaigns with unrestrained enthusiasm.

The first use of wide-scale negative campaigning in Canada can be seen in the 1935 general election, with William Lyon Mackenzie King representing the governing Liberals, and Richard Bedford (R.B.) Bennett leading the Conservatives. Both parties made some use of partisan newspapers, as they had done in the past; and both parties continued to make use of campaign posters featuring highly unflattering caricatures of King and Bennett. But the Tories, as things turned out, were the first to recognize the power of the new medium called radio.

The Conservative negative ad campaign had been the idea of Earl Lawson, a party organizer and Toronto member of Parliament. Relying upon a researcher named R. L. Wright at the Toronto agency of J. J. Gibbons Limited, Lawson first placed tantalizing display ads in different newspapers in September 1935. "Introducing Mister Sage," read the ads. "A shrewd observer who sees through the pretences, knows the facts, and understands the true issues of the present political campaign, discusses the election with his friends..." There followed a listing of the radio stations that would be broadcasting Mr. Sage's ruminations, along with the relevant times. No mention was made that the ads had been placed by the Conservative Party.

The first ad was presented as a dialogue between two actors, the aforementioned "Mr. Sage" and one "Bill." It pulled no punches. In fifteen short minutes, the radio ad alleged that Mackenzie King's Liberals were engaged in threats, blackmail, lies and "slush funds." For those who pine for a time when Canadian politics was more genteel and refined, the Mr. Sage broadcasts make the argument that no such time has ever really existed. In one blistering segment, Mr. Sage tells Bill: "In 1930... I happened to be staying with my brother-in-law in Quebec. Mr. King's henchmen used to call up the farmers and their wives in the early hours of the morning and tell them their sons would be conscripted for war if they voted against King..."

Later in the same broadcast, Mr. Sage notes that King had led his Liberal Party into "the Valley of Humiliation." The character named Bill is blunt: "Slush fund, wasn't it?" Mr. Sage responds: "Yes, Bill—over $700,000—and that's the man who wants to be Prime Minister of Canada. Can you beat it?"

The second broadcast of Mr. Sage's musings took place a few days later, but ran for thirty minutes instead of fifteen. Mr. Sage lived in "a typical home, in a typical Canadian town," listeners were told, and was "our friend and neighbour" and simply a benign "political observer." In this segment, Mr. Sage essentially accused Mackenzie King of being a grasping, dim-witted, self-absorbed, vainglorious liar. In a chat with his wife—presumably Mrs. Sage—the "simple observer" states: "We've only got to take what that Mr. King said about Mr. Bennett... [King] said a lot of things, didn't he, but mostly harm... He doesn't care whether it helps or hinders the people of the country so long as it helps him to be Prime Minister. That's the pity of it: [King] is frightened of losing the leadership... It seems to me he's just like the movie star who is losing her appeal to her public and she's afraid that one of her smarter and better-looking rivals will put her nose out of joint. Mr. King's so fearful, that he does anything at all that he thinks will please the crowd."

Following a barrage of complaints to the Canadian Radio Broadcasting Commission, the earliest of our broadcasting regulators, the Conservatives were persuaded to identify a sponsor of the Mr. Sage attack ads. They claimed that it was only the Gibbons Agency's R. L. Wright, and not the Tories themselves. Outraged Grits continued to complain about the ad campaign, however, so the Tories relented: the sponsors were identified as "R. L. Wright and a Group of Conservatives." As would be the case with every subsequent target of a negative Canadian ad campaign, Mackenzie King did not resist unburdening himself about the Mr. Sage ads: they were "insidious," "libellous" and "scurrilous," he puffed.

Notwithstanding all the *ad hominem* nastiness, the Liberals possessed better chances in the 1935 general election: the Great Depression had dramatically eroded Tory support, and Bennett had become isolated from public opinion. The Grits, moreover, had a better slogan than the Tories—"King or Chaos." The Tories had the mundane "Stand by Canada" (and "Vote Bennett"). The Liberals were also better funded, and King had learned to make better use of the radio medium. (As King was later advised by the first Canadian *spinmeister*, Jack Pickersgill, what mattered most in broadcasting was sound not content. Pickersgill was right.) By 1930, more than 75 per cent of all homes in Canadian urban centres possessed radio sets. So, when the Grit leader aired three FDR-style "talks," he was heard by many, and the broadcasts were well received. An August 1, 1935, *Ottawa Journal* editorial, for example, declared that King possessed "stately diction" and "an excellent speaking voice," and had acquitted himself with "distinction."

Voters, apparently, agreed. Slightly more than two months later, R. B. Bennett was drubbed by Mackenzie King—173 Liberal seats, compared to the Conservatives' 40. But Mr. Sage, while ineffective in attracting votes, was not forgotten by the newly elected Liberals. In his final campaign address in Ottawa, the *Citizen* reported on October 14, 1935, a fiery King declared that Mr. Sage–style campaign attack ads would be outlawed: "I will do all in my power to see to it that no man in future generations has to put up with that sort of thing through a medium over which a Prime Minister and his government has full control."

King may have won the election, but, as subsequent events, and Canadians campaigns, would demonstrably prove, his battle to purge the airwaves of negative political ads was a lost cause before it even got started. Following 1935, nasty campaign advertising became as all-Canadian as hockey and *Anne of Green Gables*.

CHAPTER THREE

DAMN SPOT
... or, how to make an effective political ad

Harrington Lake has a fabled name, but it does not look like much. It is a nice old wooden home—a cottage, really—with two storeys and an unobstructed view of one of the prettier lakes in Gatineau Park, north of Ottawa. Down the steps near the front door, there is a small boathouse. It is a quiet retreat, but it could not ever be described as posh, or extravagant.

In 1959, John Diefenbaker paid a visit to the place, at the urging of friends who thought it would serve him as an excellent country home. Believing that Diefenbaker needed some persuasion, his friends spoke to the property's caretaker, and told him to ensure that Diefenbaker went fishing and, should he go fishing, also to ensure that he caught a trout. The Dief did go fishing, and he caught a fish, too. Soon after, the federal government acquired Harrington Lake.

Since then, all of Canada's prime ministers (and the Queen, who rested her head there in the fall of 1977) have stayed at Harrington Lake. The one who was most taken with the place was Pierre Trudeau, who went there as often as he could with his three sons. In the woods to the south of the house, Trudeau and his children had a secret spot where, some speculate, they buried a bottle containing a poem. Not long before his son Michel died in an avalanche in British Columbia in 1998, Trudeau and his boys returned there for a last time, to hike through the woods and find their secret cache.

Even now, with the exception of the presence of the Royal Canadian Mounted Police (RCMP) at a roadblock a few minutes' drive from the house, and also in a clapboard building near the estate's small parking lot, there is little about Harrington Lake to suggest it is a prime ministerial residence. It is for that reason, partly, that thirty or so people descend on this retreat one autumn Sunday in October 2000: it is a quiet place to prepare some political spots without having to worry about nosy journalists. Anyone who tries to get near, after all, must first get past the Mounties. The Liberal Party of Canada has rented the estate for the shooting of the commercials.

The election call is just a few days away. Most of those present are technicians, brought there by Vickers and Benson, the Toronto advertising agency that has prepared political spots for the Liberal Party of Canada for as long as anyone can remember. Representing V&B, as it is called, is its president, John Hayter, and its chairman, Terry O'Malley.

Also gathered at Harrington Lake, and loitering outside, taking in the view, are a number of Chrétien political loyalists: John Rae, the manager of all of Chrétien's prime ministerial election victories; Francie Ducros, Chrétien's director of communications; Patrick Parisot, Chrétien's special adviser and one of his closest confidants; Chrétien's long-time executive assistant, Bruce Hartley; Jean Carle, Chrétien's former director of operations; myself; a couple of pollsters with the Pollara agency; and a young adman from Western Canada, Leon Macrae, who does not wish to give his real name (for reasons he declines to discuss).

Of all of those present, Macrae is the least known, which is how he prefers it. Wearing a borrowed sweater (he had forgotten how cold Ottawa can get), a pair of chinos and a bemused expression, Macrae hangs at the edges of the V&B people, or the Chrétien people. Everyone is waiting for shooting to begin. Macrae occasionally scribbles in a notebook, or squints through his dusty glasses at a monitor the technicians have set up in a mud room. He does not say much, but when he does, he has the undivided attention of those who are directing the day's events—Rae, Hayter and O'Malley.

Despite his youth (he is still in his thirties) and despite the fact that he is largely unknown to the tightly knit Chrétien crowd (apart from me, who recommended him to various senior Liberals a few months earlier), Leon Macrae is unique in Canada: he is an adman who understands politics. In the United States, the species is comparatively commonplace, but Canada has no one like Leon Macrae. Here, there are plenty of advertising people who think they understand politics, but do not. There are also far too many political people who believe they know how to do advertising, but do not. Macrae has attracted the attention of the people who help to run one of the most successful political franchises in the world. That is not easy to do.

The political advertising work done by Macrae's agency, which operates in both Canada and the United States, is recognized as some of the best around. In the U.S., he takes on only Democrats as clients; in Canada, only Liberals. Like most politicos, he knows that clients do not make use of consultants who represent both sides of the ideological divide; consultants are generally only liberal, or only conservative, and they must stick with their team.

Recently, the trade magazine of political consultants, *Campaigns and Elections*, gave an award to Macrae's firm for "the best political TV commercials." The *Chicago Tribune* has called his work "creative," while the *Washington Post* has declared that voters "love" the spots Macrae and his colleagues produce. In the United States, his clients have included mayors, judges, congressmen, senators, the Democratic National Committee, and the Bill Clinton and Al Gore campaign of 1996.

Macrae was born in the Prairies in 1961. He will not say much about his family, other than to mention that they still live in Western Canada, and that "they still vote Liberal." In his youth, he was that rarest of political commodities—a Grit who lived in the West. By the time he was in his twenties, Macrae was doing advertising in the United States. He was good at writing ad copy, but he was interested in doing more. "I was in advertising," he says, "but I had always been tremendously interested in politics. That's what I wanted to do."

Before he established his own firm with a well-known U.S. media consultant, Macrae had been a senior strategist and producer with a huge political communications outfit in Washington, D.C. The firm is one of the U.S. capital's oldest political Democratic communications firms, representing senators Paul Simon and Bill Bradley, Congresswoman Geraldine Ferraro and a number of high-profile lobby groups. Following his move to the United States, Macrae counted a number of prominent U.S. politicians among his clients—senators Dianne Feinstein and Bob Kerrey, as well as Congressman Dick Gephardt. During one memorable campaign in the late 1980s, Macrae even relocated to Panama, where he assisted in the electoral effort to dislodge General Manuel Noriega. The campaign did not work, and Noriega was relieved of his post by 24,000 U.S. troops in December 1989.

Macrae is passionate about political advertising, and about what it can mean to people's lives. He reacts angrily to suggestions, often made by his colleagues in the advertising world, that political issues can be sold in the same manner as soap or toothpaste. "The difference between a decision about the future of your country, or your state, or your province, and what you are going to have for breakfast, is obvious," he says. "Some people may say political advertising is like selling soap, but it's not. That's a crazy, insulting suggestion. Political advertising is about making important choices."

What Leon Macrae is good at—very, very good at—is depicting those choices, through advertising, in tough terms. That's not negative advertising, it's informative advertising that does not hesitate to offer criticism where it's deserved. And informed criticism is what election politics is all about.

The morning air is crisp and clear, and the scenery is beautiful, so Macrae, the Chrétien people, and the senior V&B creative team stand outside the house, waiting. On the driveway, there is a large white 18-wheeler, containing klieg lights, cameras and recording equipment. Over some of the ground-floor windows, technicians have affixed screens to make the sunlight seem more diffuse inside. Before long, there is a commotion: word has been received that Chrétien and his RCMP escort will be arriving in a few minutes. The advertising and political people move quickly into the house and assume their positions.

Moments later, Chrétien steps out of his car, wearing a Gap shirt, a sweater and a pair of slacks. A big man, with an easy manner, he waves at familiar faces. After a bit of glad-handing, he heads into the house to get to work. While a woman applies makeup to the prime ministerial face, Chrétien chats about the recent polls with an aide. Then John Rae brings Leon Macrae into the room and Chrétien reaches over to shake Macrae's hand. "Hello there, young man," he says. "Thank you for your help. What do you think of our chances?"

Leon Macrae gives a toothy smile. "Oh, I think they are very, very good, Prime Minister."

Macrae sits on a chair in the cramped garage at Harrington Lake, writing. His desk is a few planks laid atop a pair of large boxes. He is oblivious to the RCMP officers and staff buzzing around him as he squints at a sheaf of spot scripts. The text for one, called "Canada," is on a single sheet, in large print. It reads:

> Canada is a great nation. Built on Liberal values. Freedom...justice...sharing...tolerance. Today, Canada can be a leader in a new world. What is most important for me, Jean Chrétien, is that each and every Canadian can take their place in this new world...without ever losing sight of our fundamental values. We have a bright future. It is up to us to achieve it.

The spot script is for what is referred to as a "thirty"—as in, a thirty-second-long advertisement. In political advertising, the early days of a campaign are made up of a lot of thirties, in order that a candidate may present one or two ideas or issues. (Some candidates with a lot of money, like Ross Perot in the 1992 U.S. presidential election campaign, may even employ sixty-second spots.) Once the campaign is up and running, it is possible to run a cluster of "fifteens" on single issues that are important in the race.

Macrae scowls at the text, which has not been written by him. Repeating some of the phrases aloud, he extracts a pen from his jacket and starts scratching out words and sentences. The first to go is "nation"—the word is one that Americans use, but English Canadians do not, explains Macrae. It is also a word favoured by Quebec separatists to describe their province, and he knows that no one in Canada wishes to discuss the Quebec issue for a long, long time. So "nation" becomes "country."

The sentence fragment about "Liberal values" is the next to go. That phrase sounds like Liberals believe the country can only be defined in the context of their own value system. "Arrogance" is a word the opposition and the media are throwing around a lot to describe the Liberal decision to call an election before the end of its four-year electoral mandate. So "Liberal values" is also excised, and becomes: "Because of the values we all hold—freedom, justice, tolerance, sharing."

The next sentence, about Canada being "a leader in a new world," sounds too ephemeral, too vague. He writes: "In today's world, we must be even more of a leader. But we have to do it together." He chews on the end of his pen and looks disapprovingly at what he has written. "New world," he says. "What the fuck is that, new world?" He sighs. The "together" sentence is important. One of the key messages of the anticipated Liberal election campaign is inclusion; it is a strong but subtle way of distinguishing itself from the right-wing opposition in the Canadian Alliance. Macrae and others want to depict the Alliance as an extremist group with a hidden agenda—an agenda that includes fat tax breaks for millionaires but little for middle or moderate-income Canadians.

The next section, too, ends up completely rewritten. "We can never make a choice that says some Canadians are more important than the rest. Every Canadian must take their place in this new world. If we stay true to our values, then we ensure that every Canadian wins." Macrae squints at this last part, reads it aloud to a couple of political people standing nearby. The changes he has made are the product of his own experience about what works, and what does not, in political advertising. Most of all, however, the changes reflect the results obtained in focus groups held in different Canadian cities just a few days earlier. Each one of the phrases and concepts has been rigorously tested because, as Macrae knows, the writer of the spot may find a phrase funny, or powerful, or somehow effective, but the viewer—a potential voter—may hate it. So testing an ad, both before and after production, is essential. Before the Liberal leader sees the text, later in the day, Macrae and Terry O'Malley will have changed it again.

All day will be spent with Jean Chrétien, rehearsing half a dozen spots like "Canada." The text will be run over a transparent teleprompter, placed directly over the camera's lens so that the prime minister will not be looking offscreen when he speaks. On that day, and in the days that follow, Leon Macrae's pen will fall on some other scripts, too—these ones much tougher than those being filmed at Harrington Lake. One spot, also filmed with Chrétien facing the camera and called "Not A Toy," was never broadcast. It reads:

> Stockwell Day and his Reform Alliance party want to do something very dangerous for this country of ours. Mr. Day wants to take your federal government out of your health care. He wants to give control of it to the provinces. This could lead to a have and have-not health care system in which some Canadians simply could not afford to get sick. This is totally unacceptable to me and to the Liberal Party. On election day, tell Stockwell Day that your health care system is not a toy to be played with. In our Canada, everybody must win.

Originally, all of the critical scripts referred to the Liberal's principal adversaries as the Canadian Alliance. In so doing, however, we were effectively going along with the opposition's attempt to re-brand itself as something kinder and gentler. Macrae and I therefore lobbied for the name that was ultimately used: the "Reform Alliance." Our adversaries' former name, the Reform Party, recalled their past, which, many Canadians felt, was characterized by policies that were intolerant and mean (for example, opposing Sikhs wearing religious symbols in the RCMP, or preventing changes to Canada's ethnic culture). Thereafter, in Liberal circles, the party became and remained the "Reform Alliance."

The spot also focused on what Macrae and others felt was a major tactical error by Stockwell Day: a few weeks earlier, the Reform Alliance leader had sent a strangely worded letter to the provincial premiers. The letter's tortuous structure permitted an interpretation that Day favoured a wholesale withdrawal from health care by the federal government. It would be a theme the Liberal campaign would return to many times in the fall election.

Another toughly worded thirty-second spot, written for shooting at Harrington Lake, was called "Not That Difficult." Again featuring the prime minister, the script read:

> Stockwell Day and I see the issue of tax relief in this country very differently. With his proposed flat tax, Mr. Day would have a country in which the interests of a few take priority over the well-being of the many. I see another option. I see a country in which tax relief benefits you and your friends and your neighbours. I see a tax relief program where everyone is better off. If that is more like the Canada you see, vote Liberal on election day. In our Canada, everybody must win.

The notion that Day and his Reform Alliance were proposing a flat tax—which, as every economist knows, disproportionately benefits the rich—is one that a few of us had been propagating for many weeks. At their glitzy policy platform launch a few weeks earlier at Conestoga College in Kitchener-Waterloo, Day had gone to great lengths to emphasize that his party had abandoned its previous single-tax-rate stance. It now had two marginal tax rates, he said. While some might have felt it unfair to continue labelling his tax plan a "flat tax," Macrae and I were of the view that we were not in the fairness business. Judges dispense fairness; in a political campaign, we dispensed facts that said a lot of good things about our side and a lot of bad things about the other side. Day could call his plan whatever he liked, but we would continue to call it a flat tax that favoured the rich. And we did. The spot, as written, did not make it to television, but its basic theme was used in other Grit campaign communications that fall.

There were other such tough spots, some of which were filmed, some of which never made it past the ideas stage. One of Leon Macrae's very best spots never made it to television. I had found out that in 1994 Stockwell Day had purchased a revolver at an auction to protest the Liberal government's plans to introduce a gun registry and better gun control laws. When I told him this, Macrae's eyes lit up. He got to work. The spot he quickly wrote was called "Example." Alongside a photo of a handgun like the one Day bought, and alongside newspaper headlines documenting that Day had, in fact, done what we said he did, Macrae found an actor to read his script, as ominous-sounding music played in the background.

> While Canada's Liberal government was protecting our families with gun registration, Stockwell Day had a different idea. He bought a handgun. In fact, the Reform Alliance wants to scrap gun registration altogether. No wonder the gun lobby is working so hard to end gun controls and elect

them. What kind of an example is that? Ask yourself: does Stockwell Day's Reform Alliance speak for you?

Despite the fact that the spot was not used by the Liberal Party's campaign, Leon Macrae's devastating tag line—"Does Stockwell Day's Reform Alliance speak for you?"—was repeated hundreds of times, at the conclusion of other spots about health care and gay rights. Those spots, and that rhetorical question, helped the Liberal government win re-election.

The consumer drives the complexity of commercial-making, and in politics, that "consumer" is the voter. In days of old, advertisers were content to develop a single, simple spot, which they would run repetitively and for a lengthy period of time. This all changed when advertising executives realized that viewers were easily bored, and were tuning out. Making political spots that were creative, and therefore memorable, became essential. Spots are too important to be left to chance: they provide the means for political parties to do what U.S. consultant Dick Morris calls "an end-run around the media."

The news media, which resent political spots as trespassers on their territory, dramatically changed the way in which politicians advertised their wares. These days, pollsters such as Environics have produced detailed studies showing that North Americans now obtain most of their information about public affairs from ninety-second television news items. To the distress of newspaper journalists, television watchers actually regard news broadcasts as far more reliable, more accurate and more timely than the print medium. These same viewers therefore see nothing wrong with basing a decision about who to vote for on watching a thirty-second political ad. For political consultants, television offers them all that they need: a larger audience than newspapers, an immediate emotional impact and a tolerable level of credibility.

In the early days, prior to 1966, most political advertising was shot in black-and-white film. When videotape became available as a format in the 1970s, political consultants did not flock to it, believing that it had a low-budget appearance. What they wanted was emotional immediacy, and videotape did not provide it. Filmed images were softer and, like the motion pictures that continued to make exclusive use of it, film seemed larger than life.

The spots themselves take on different formats. The "talking head" type features a politician speaking, clearly and directly, to the camera. For charismatic candidates, like Jean Chrétien, Bill Clinton and very few others, such a format can be highly effective and relatively inexpensive to produce. One of Leon Macrae's Democratic colleagues is Dane Strother, a funny and outgoing former newspaper reporter who now produces political spots for a living. At a June 2001 gathering of political consultants in Washington, D.C., Strother endorsed these simple one-on-one spots as among the best approaches for appealing candidates. "Look, voters vote from *here*," he said, jabbing a finger in the vicinity of his heart. "Not from here!"—he pointed at his head. "They want to vote for someone they'd like to have dinner with, not someone who is going to give them a dissertation about policy."

Another type of spot is called a "streeter"—average people are interviewed about the issue or issues a campaign team has identified as important. In one such streeter prepared for the last federal election, a number of Albertans are seen speaking about health care, and what they fear the Liberal's political opposition will do to it. The spot's effectiveness can be measured in the response it produced, with the Opposition leader Stockwell Day denouncing it as "lies" and demanding repeatedly that it be withdrawn. (It wasn't.) Scott Howell, one of Dane Strother's (and Leon Macrae's) southern U.S. Republican opponents, thinks this type of spot is the most effective. Running through some of the spots he has produced for winning campaigns for far-right Republicans such as Jesse Helms, Howell says that to catch the attention of "your average Joe and average Mary" streeters can't be beat. "It works so much better if you get real people to tell a real story. It's a pain in the ass to extract it out of them—it takes a lot of time—but it works."

A third type of political ad depicts the candidate in action. One series, used by respected Democratic senator (and unsuccessful vice-presidential candidate) Lloyd Bentsen, showed the veteran U.S. politician fishing with his grandson, and helped to get him on the ticket in 1992. Another spot of the genre, showing an athletic-looking Stockwell Day jogging before delivering an earnest health care message, was judged unsuccessful by media critics because it seemed contrived. (As a means to "introduce" the newly elected Reform Alliance leader to Canadians, I felt, as did a few other Liberals, too, that it was not bad.)

Spots making use of actors are sometimes used, but they are both costly and risky. Hiring an actor or two is much more pricey than simply running some scrolling text, and it's risky because reporters regularly (and properly) submit political ads to rigorous "reality checks," and sometimes learn about things that are embarrassing. A much-seen spot developed by the Ontario Ministry of Natural Resources in the early 1980s, for example, promoted the environment with a man paddling in a canoe on a beautiful lake. The problem was that the canoeist, who was named, wasn't who the ministry said he was—he was an actor. An enterprising reporter from the *Toronto Star* ferreted out his identity. Fortunately for the Ontario government, the actor turned into a very effective spokesman for environmental issues.

"Compare and contrast" spots, which were used with devastating effectiveness by the Ontario Progressive Conservative Party in 1996, when it came from behind to beat the thought-to-be-unbeatable Ontario Liberals, are a favourite of many campaign consultants in

Canada and the United States. The spots typically feature a split-screen checklist or comparison, highlighting no more than two or three issues. Ontario Premier Mike Harris's advertising whiz kid, Jaime Watt, used compare and contrasts—or, as he refers to them, "T-bars"—to hammer Ontario Liberal leader Lynn McLeod on issues such as "workfare" (they're against it, we're not) and employment "quotas" (they want them, we don't). Recalls Watt: "I'm very proud of the T-bar ads we did in 1996. Mike Harris will do this, Lynn McLeod will do this. I liked those ads for three reasons. One, those little suckers—which we made for a couple thousand dollars in the studio, in a few hours—did an awful lot of damage. Two, when I presented the idea, I was completely derided for not being creative. But those ads have produced all sorts of imitators in Canada. And, three, it's not about winning the entire war, it's about getting a message across. We had time and money pressures, but those ads got our message across more than the Liberal ads did—which were visually beautiful, but essentially without meaning." The point worth stressing, here, is that, notwithstanding what media cynics sometimes claim, content counts. The best political ads contain clear, digestible facts, not just spin. Compare and contrast spots are effective because they are designed to relate, in simple terms, one or two pieces of information of interest to voters.

A final type of political spot is a favourite of Leon Macrae—scrolls. In scroll spots, text runs up or across the television screen, usually accompanied by a narrator reading the words. For the November 2000 election campaign, Macrae produced nearly a dozen scroll spots, for use nationally or in regional markets. In one dramatic spot broadcast late in the campaign, Macrae developed a script based upon news clippings I faxed to him. The news stories—one a July 1986 *Calgary Herald* story, the other an August 1997 *Edmonton Journal* story—recounted Stockwell Day's views on gays and lesbians. In the fifteen-second version, a narrator speaks over ominous-sounding music: "As a Member of the Alberta government, Stockwell Day said that gays and lesbians were not 'condoned by God.' He fought to override the Charter of Rights, to make it legal to discriminate against gays and lesbians. Does Stockwell Day's Reform Alliance speak for you?" In the thirty-second version, the fact that Day was opposed to abortion—even "in the case of rape or incest"—was added to the scroll spot, to drive home the point that Day's party was extreme. The abortion spot helped to elect Liberals in Vancouver and Edmonton, where the races were tight.

No matter what type of spot is used, all must grow out of the central message or messages of the campaign. Spots are tactical, and should never confuse, contradict or "step on" a campaign's communication strategy. As such, the spots need to be as simple as they are memorable. Simplicity, all agree, is essential: when a candidate has a minute or less—sometimes a lot less—to present an idea, the idea cannot be difficult for voters to understand. In every instance, the idea, whether a positive about one's own candidate, or a negative about one's opponent, must be derived from a solid foundation of research.

Using focus groups and "dial" groups (in which a representative sample of voters literally use dials to indicate approval or disapproval of what they see on the screen), research must determine two things. First, which messages are effective. And, second, whether the messages have been effectively communicated. Although they were universally ridiculed by the media, the spots developed by the Progressive Conservatives in the November 2000 election—spots that parodied the old "K-Tel" ads (notorious for loudly hawking the latest Top 40 hits), and featured an announcer loudly recalling alleged Liberal "lies"—tested well with focus groups. The Tory K-Tel ads called Jean Chrétien a liar, repeatedly, and were therefore seen as highly negative. But because the spots used humour to make their point, the Tories escaped the sort of backlash stirred up by their 1993 "face" ads.

The other key requirement is that a political spot be memorable. To be memorable, campaign consultants need to recall that television is a visual medium, and that the best political spots are therefore stories told with pictures. It is not enough to simply say it, you have to show it, too. In one health care spot Leon Macrae developed to critique Alliance health care policy, he showed tear sheets of different headlines from newspapers, all of them suggesting that the Alliance wanted to privatize, or otherwise destroy, the Canadian health care system. Another important element of making a spot memorable is repetition. Generally, consultants agree that a spot must be seen at least three times to be remembered.

All of this is not without its costs, of course. Taping with a one-person crew (that is, someone acting as cameraperson and director) can run up to $2,000 a day. A two-person crew, the second person usually being a sound technician, nearly doubles the cost. Studio postproduction can cost up to $500 an hour; digital editing, which is used more and more frequently, can approach nearly $800 an hour. Stock music can cost a few hundred dollars per spot; special effects add hundreds more per hour. Narrators will charge up to $1,000 a spot; makeup artists up to $700 a day. And duplicating the final, produced spot will cost up to $50 a tape for each thirty-second tape. Producing a very basic spot, then, can cost $5,000. Then there's the more expensive prospect: buying time for it to be seen on air.

Is it worth it? Given the gargantuan price tags involved, should politicians opt for different ways to reach voters?

Dick Morris, for one, asserts that a good political spot should appeal to the heart and the head. It presents viewers with a problem that the viewer identifies with, and then it presents a solution. In his book, *The New Prince*, Morris, a senior adviser to Bill Clinton before a sex scandal forced his ouster, calls political advertising a way to "manage the dialogue." Writes Morris: "In today's politics, paid television advertising is, by far, the most effective way to win the issue debate at the core of a political race... Today's sophisticated electorate sets high standards for what will move them in a political commercial. A good ad should function on two levels: the rational and the emotional... Each ad must overcome public skepticism and tap into a deep reservoir of hope that animates our people." It is a weighty assignment for any political ad-maker, but the good ones, like Tony Schwartz and Thomas Rosser Reeves, have learned how to do both.

Sprawled on a chair at Harrington Lake, four or five spots in the can for the federal election campaign that is just a few days away, Leon Macrae agrees with Morris. "This is how you move people," he says. "You can introduce a candidate to people in two days—to everyone you want, and with the same message for all of them. You can do that, while tons of old-fashioned field political work, or something like that, couldn't hope to equal those kinds of results in a year. You need to get people's attention. And these damn spots do that."

Just *making* a political spot, as noted, requires skill and money. But so too does the other part of the process; the part where a campaign decides when, where and why to put the spot in a voter's living room. The part where the campaign buys "time," and places a spot on a voter's TV set.

The office of Tobe Berkovitz, tucked away in a bland, four-storey building fronting on Boston's Commonwealth Avenue, and not far from the Massachusetts Turnpike and the Charles River, is a very crowded place. From the ceiling to the floor, the Boston University professor has jammed hundreds of videotapes of political spots, along with stacks of books about campaigns, consultants and commercials. Here and there, Berkovitz has affixed buttons and banners from different campaigns—John F. Kennedy's, Jimmy Carter's and many others.

Berkovitz stretches out, propping his running shoes on his crowded desk. With lots of dark hair, an unlined face and a genial manner, Berkovitz does not look like a man who is just past 50, or for that matter, like someone who is considered one of the smarter political ad buyers in the United States.

He comes from Connecticut, and he got his start there in 1974, doing a fifteen-minute free-time film for Tony Discepelo, an independent candidate running for Congress. Berkovitz had been teaching television production and broadcast studies at the University of Connecticut when he got the call from the aspiring congressman's campaign staff. "We were essentially slaughtered," he says. "But the film I did for this guy—that was pretty good." When 1978 rolled around, he was living in Michigan, and helping out Carl Levin, then the president of Detroit's city council. A long shot, Levin was seeking a seat in the U.S. Senate. His team hired Tobe Berkovitz to be its advertising coordinator.

Berkovitz knew enough about television to teach, and he knew how to read a poll. He also, as things turned out, knew how to read a television ratings book. "I just worked as [Levin's] in-house media buyer," he says. "And, lo and behold, Levin won. Knocked off a guy who had a couple decades of experience, a real senior senator." In the simplest terms, he placed Levin's spots on and around the TV programs most favoured by the voters Levin needed to reach. There is no point, Berkovitz says, in placing spots at times when nobody will see them, or at times that primarily attract voters who are already voting for your candidate. They need to be seen by the voters called "persuadables."

By 1980, Berkovitz had moved again, this time to Washington, D.C. He worked on Capitol Hill for Democrats, and he toiled as a media buyer for a trio of Democrats seeking seats in the Senate. Two of them were Arizona's Morris Udall, and Ohio's John Glenn. Notwithstanding that 1980 was the year that Ronald Reagan swept to the presidency, and liberal Democrats were being toppled across the political landscape, Glenn and Udall were elected. Berkovitz, one of those credited with the Glenn and Udall wins, was on his way up.

In those days, he says, there were not many political consultants. No more than two dozen, he estimates, certainly not the hundreds of consultants and consultancy firms now found in every corner of the United States. "In the seventies, people said to me: 'Well, what are you doing?' and I'd tell them I was working as a media consultant. And no one would know what the hell I was talking about," he recalls. "It wasn't the era of the James Carvilles and all the superstar consultants. There was a small group of people who did this sort of work, but you were really talking about a dozen Democrats and a dozen Republicans and that was it."

In 1985, Berkovitz met one of those top-rung Democratic political consultants, Ken Swope. Swope is an award-winning writer and strategist who has led successful campaigns against clear-cutting in the western United States. He is a committed believer in political advertising, and has suggested that good advertising, and a good ad buy, can turn around a twenty-point deficit in the polls in less than a week. Swope and Berkovitz struck an informal partnership, and have been consulting on Democratic campaigns ever since. Says Berkovitz: "Most often, the media buyers are sort of backroom people, and the consultants are front-room people. Sometimes they will trot out their media buyer at a political meeting, but most often they won't. It's ironic, really, because [ad buy] is where most of your campaign's money is going. If you do it efficiently, then it's going to be good. But if you're not doing it efficiently, then you're going to end up wasting a fair amount of money." Not just Berkovitz feels this way. John Rowley is another Democratic Party ad-buy expert, from Nashville. Speaking at that June 2001 Washington gathering, he said, "Candidates and campaign managers will spend hours and hours debating whether we should say 'should' or 'must' in a script. And then, when it comes to the media buy, they just forget about it." On the importance of political ad buying, Rowley stated: "Television is a thermonuclear weapon. There's a lot of waste with a thermonuclear weapon, but it gets the job done."

In 1996, Tobe Berkovitz wrote a short guide called, simply, "Political Media Buying." The paper ended up in literally dozens of places on the Internet, and is widely known in U.S. political circles. While it is only eleven pages in length, the guide has been tremendously influential in a number of U.S. campaigns. In his paper, Berkovitz defines political media buy this way: "The goal of media buying in an election campaign is to reach a defined target audience in the most efficient and economical way possible." To ensure that the media buy is done the right way, it is essential that the political campaign—its candidate and its consultants—are very clear about six elements.

The first order of business, Berkovitz says, is the development of a media plan that works. When buying ad time, consultants focus on what are called GRPs—"gross rating points." GRPs, he writes, "are the sum total of ratings achieved for a media schedule." To figure out how much a campaign's media buy is going to cost—and in Canada and the United States, it is safe to assume that as much as 80 per cent of a campaign's spending will go to ad buy—consultants multiply GRP by CPP, or cost per point. It sounds confusing, but it is not: "The general rule of thumb is 100 GRPs means the average TV viewer sees a commercial once. Therefore, 500 GRPs should expose the average viewer five times to the commercial."

In the United States, if the media buy is "spot"—that is, in a regional media market—then 500 GRPs is usually enough to influence what Berkovitz calls "the voting decision." In a national media buy—called a "network" placement—about 300 GRPs is considered about right. (In the closing days of a campaign, some consultants argue for GRPs of nearly 2,000.)

In the United States, a network buy during the newsmagazine *60 Minutes*, or *Prime Time Live*, or *20/20*, can cost as much as $200,000. That may sound pricey, Berkovitz concedes, but there are shows that are even more expensive. When *Murphy Brown* was on-air, he says, placement of a spot could cost up to $335,000, while one during *Friends* was $400,000. Says Berkovitz: "It's expensive. A million bucks—if I'm running in a rural part of Iowa—hell, with a million bucks, I'm going to do okay. But in New York, a million bucks? Great, that's a week [of buy]. Now what do we do?"

The second important element of a good media buy plan is timing. Since few candidates can afford to advertise from the start of the campaign through to election day, different "patterns" of advertising are commonly used. A "continuity pattern" airs spots at a single GRP level throughout the election. One of the dangers associated with such an approach, he warns, is that a continuity pattern does not take into account the sorts of disasters that befall every campaign, such as candidates saying something embarrassing, or issues unexpectedly attracting public interest.

A "pulsing" pattern is what the name implies. A campaign team may, to use Berkovitz's term, "heavy up" a buy at the start and end of an election, and do less in between. The idea, he says, is to ensure that "the weight and timing of the advertising is matched with the political objectives of the campaign." A "flighting" pattern, meanwhile, sees advertising going on and off the air. It allows a campaign to save precious funds and respond to issues only when a response is truly needed.

A third important element is the target audience: whom does the campaign wish to reach with its advertising? Without exception, the demographic that a campaign wishes to reach, and influence, is identified by a campaign's pollster, and can vary significantly at different times during a campaign. For example, if a tax message (which is usually most popular with men) is not effective, then a campaign may wish to consider a switch to an education or health message (which are typically much more appealing to women). Women are just as susceptible to tough ads as men, Berkovitz explains, but an ad buyer needs to be sensitive to when, and where, an ad is placed. Says Berkovitz: "What are you running in the six o'clock newscast—lots of burn, slash and attack advertising. Maybe, earlier in the day, during the soaps, you want to be a little kinder and gentler—and a little more emotional and warmer."

Point number four is geography. Called variously the "Area of Dominant Influence" or the "Designated Market Area," these geographic regions are served primarily by clusters of broadcasters within the area. Broadcast planning and spending, Berkovitz says, are built around these regional clusters. Once polling is analyzed, "weighting" is done, meaning that an advertising budget is divided between the different geographic areas a campaign is trying to influence. Weighting forces a campaign consultant to determine which areas have priority, and to spend accordingly.

The "media mix" is number five in Berkovitz's list. In his view, and in the view of the vast majority of campaign professionals, television is the "prime medium for delivering the campaign's advertising message." Many more people watch television than read newspapers, and the people who watch it tend to come from diverse demographic categories. Notwithstanding the eye-popping costs mentioned above for placing a spot during television programs like *Friends*, Berkovitz argues that "on a cost-per-point basis, television is excellent for reaching overall audience."

Every broadcast day is divided into sections called "dayparts." Advertising is then purchased for programs that fall within the dayparts. The "early-morning" daypart is principally filled with local news, network news and information programs; these reach opinion leaders and high-interest voters. Next is the daypart actually called "day," and which is filled with syndicated talk shows, game shows and soap operas. This part of the broadcast schedule is watched mainly by women, with little education, between the ages of 24 and 54.

The "early fringe" of the late-afternoon daypart is made up of syndicated talk shows, sitcoms and tabloid television. Again, the main audience is women who have no post-graduate education. The "early-news" daypart is important; it comprises local and network news, and reaches better-educated viewers likely to vote. The "access" daypart is next, with syndicated sitcoms, game shows and more tabloid TV. It has high ratings and is cost-effective for media buy; the types of viewers vary, but is considered to be rich in potential voters. The "prime" daypart has high ratings as well as varied demographics and is what Berkovitz calls a "premium audience." Late news is the next daypart, and reaches highly educated people who can be counted upon to vote. The final daypart, "late fringe," has a wide audience and is made up of late-night talk shows and syndicated sitcoms. (The importance of these shows shouldn't be underestimated either: in the 2000 presidential campaign, both George W. Bush and Al Gore did shows with the likes of Jay Leno and David Letterman, because an increasing number of voters are getting political information from these sources. In May 2001, Jean Chrétien was persuaded by his assistant, Charlie Angelakos, to appear on CTV's *Mike Bullard Show*.)

Radio has a far smaller audience, but also must be considered in the "media mix." It has its advantages: it is far less costly than television, and it is better targeted to certain audiences. MOR—middle-of-the-road—stations attract the 35-and-over audience that political candidates need to win. News and information radio stations are also efficient at attracting likely voters. Talk radio, which is usually right-wing ideologically, can boast a loyal audience that is highly motivated in elections. Contemporary hit radio and varied rock formats attract a younger audience that is less interested in public affairs and often does not vote. For political parties, the daypart segment with the largest radio audience is "AM drive," reaching workers and commuters; following that, midday also has high ratings, among people at work and at home.

Cable television, called "narrowcasting" by some, has become an important ad-buy consideration in the past decade. John Rowley notes that "at any given time, half the people are not watching the big networks. Cable is a complementary medium, but it's not the primary place to deliver your message." Even the cable programming that attracted the largest audiences ever—CNN's coverage of the O.J. Simpson trial—never equalled the total for the average U.S. network newscast, Rowley notes.

Commercial formats are the sixth and final element of a good media buy plan. "The 30-second spot is the workhorse for campaign advertising," Berkovitz writes. "On television, 60-second spots are an effective way of communicating a deeper message to the voter, but cost twice the amount... this means that only half as many rating points can be purchased for 60s." Often, consultants are obliged to buy thirty seconds of air time to show two fifteen-second spots back-to-back. They are forced to do so because television stations and networks, these days, do not have many other advertisers developing fifteens.

Media buying has changed dramatically in the past two decades, Berkovitz says. "In the old days, they used to talk about counties and precincts and districts. But now you're talking media markets. Two years ago, we did a race for a governor in Rhode Island. I love doing Rhode Island, because you buy Providence and you get to carpet bomb the whole state. It's not cheap—we spent about a million bucks—but we were running commercials by the pound because it's a nice clean media market."

Canada has its share of political ad-buy geniuses, too. The Liberal Party relies heavily upon the smarts of Toronto's Gordon Ashworth, while provincial and federal Tories have retained Jaime Watt many times. On average, U.S.-based media buy consultants like Tobe Berkovitz will receive up to 15 per cent of the costs of the advertising they place, which can be very significant. Along with placing spots, media buyers will review invoices received from broadcasters, to ensure that their candidate is getting what they paid for. They attend to the paperwork of the buy and monitor whether spots are actually broadcast when, where and as often as desired. Simultaneously, buy consultants will track the placement and frequency of an opponent's spots, and any third-party organization seeking to harm their candidate.

Generally, ad-buy experts will try to purchase air time far in advance of an election. In Canada, with election dates unknown to all but the prime minister (federally) or a premier (provincially), this is hard to do. In the United States, with fixed election dates, it is easier. But its predictability does not make it cheaper; in fact, the reverse is true. Broadcasters seldom, if ever, provide ad-buy discounts to political campaigns. Says Berkovitz: "The stations are obviously trying to maximize what they can get out of you. They certainly all play at the edges and they don't cut you any slack. It's important to remember, though, that [in the United States] we are buying in the fourth quarter. That's the most expensive time of the broadcast year."

The decision to go neg with an ad buy should not, most agree, come at the start of an election campaign. Particularly in the case of "challenger" campaigns—that is, campaigns attempting to dislodge an incumbent, popular or not—it is important to first define one's candidate. Let the voter see the candidate at work, with family. Let them hear a little about the "issues" that motivated the candidate to run. It generally takes a few days for these issues to become defined in the public's collective consciousness, and for the public to decide where they stand themselves. At that point, and only at that point, is it safe to start deploying toughly worded issue advertising.

The time of day a so-called attack ad runs requires a lot of thought, too. These types of spots generally have two effects: they either persuade a voter to vote against one's opponent, or they persuade the opponent's committed voter to essentially do the same thing by staying home. Detailed demographic data is therefore required to figure out when the target audience—the audience one wishes to stay home, for example—is most likely to see one's spot. Evaluating the data, and making these decisions, is tricky, most consultants agree, and can make or break a campaign.

Despite all of the apparent complexity of ad buying, and despite the political risks associated with it, Tobe Berkovitz is modest about what he does. Walking me to the door of his office, he shrugs. "You know what? I don't think media buying is that big a deal. It's really just tinkering at the edges. It's about when do we go on, how strong do we go on, that kind of thing. But I'm not sure that media buying wins or loses campaigns. It just contributes to it." He pauses. "But I guess you can say that you don't want to screw it up."

CHAPTER FOUR

OPPO

... or, how to demonize the opposition
in a few easy steps

In the dark, mysterious, arcane, misunderstood world of opposition research—called "oppo" by its practitioners, and "character assassination," usually, by those unhappy political candidates who are on the receiving end of it—James Carville is godlike.

During the 1993 Canadian federal election campaign, for example, the Liberal Party of Canada assembled its own small oppo team. In the long room that served as the nerve centre for the Liberals' opposition researchers, atop a battery of televisions and video machines, was a photograph of James Carville. Below the photo, someone had inscribed, in big, black letters—"GOD."

Many years later, God—who is bald, lanky and possessed of squinty eyes—sits in his office on South Washington Street in Alexandria, Virginia, a posh suburb of Washington, D.C. He laughs uproariously when he is told that a group of young Canadian politicos regarded him as their deity and "shamelessly" copied his formula for political success.

"Well, surely it wasn't a shameless copy," he says in a Louisiana drawl so thick he is barely understandable.

When I assured him that we Canadians stole as much as we possibly could, then brazenly claimed to have originated the idea, Carville lets loose with another whoop of laughter. "Well, fuck," he says. "If y'all had been original, you would've never gotten into politics, right?"

Right. Like the New Orleans rhythm and blues that he loves, which trades on a limited number of beats and a finite catalogue of chord progressions, James Carville knows that, in modern political campaigns, there aren't many original ideas. Empty chairs at all-candidates' debates, volunteers wearing chicken suits chasing around candidates, waving colourful props on television, using pop culture analogies in "spin" lines—all have been done to death. If a voter has the impression that he or she has seen something, or that he or she has heard something before, he or she usually has. Political campaigns are notable for many things, but new ideas are not typically among them.

James Carville, however, is not merely notable for his friendship with Bill Clinton, or for his success in guiding political campaigns around the globe, or even for the fact that his own wife, a Republican spinner of note, named Mary Matalin, calls him "serpenthead." He is not merely notable because he is, in his own words, a "pamphleteer, raconteur and Democratic party animal." He is not merely notable because he refers to himself, on national television, as "the Ragin' Cajun" or "Corporal Cue Ball," the latter appellation referring to the fact that he is, to paraphrase the words of Joseph Conrad, not just bald, but impressively bald. No: James Carville is notable because, in 1992, he and a small group of other Democrat whiz kids elevated oppo to an entirely new level. In that year, Carville used oppo to change history, and elect his candidate to the post of president of the United States—a candidate who, just a few months before, everyone, except Carville, had considered to be unelectable.

That, in a nutshell, is why scrappy political operatives around the planet regard him as God.

James Carville was born in October 1944, appropriately enough, in Carville, Louisiana. It was, he says, a "one-stop-sign town," about a half-hour's drive from Baton Rouge, and it bore the name of his grandfather, who had been its one-time postmaster. Carville's father, also a postmaster, ran the local general store, while his mother, called Miss Nippy, sold World Book encyclopedias door-to-door so that she could put her eight children through college. Which she did—all of them. James, an altar boy, was the oldest.

While still a student at the all-boys Ascension Catholic High School in nearby Donaldsonville, young James Carville became involved with his first political campaign, for Price LeBlanc, a car dealer seeking a seat in the Louisiana state legislature. LeBlanc called himself "the Trading Country Boy," and his Elvis-inspired campaign slogan was the refreshingly honest "I Want You, I Need You, I'll Work for You." Along with passing out LeBlanc's pamphlets to locals, Carville would, like every young volunteer to every political campaign, put up his candidate's signs by day and tear down the opponent's signs by night. James Carville recalls that he put his heart into that campaign, but Price LeBlanc still lost.

After high school, in 1962, Carville enrolled at Louisiana State University, where he flunked out. Having come from an all-boys Roman Catholic high school, Carville admits that he was much more preoccupied with his social life than with his studies. He spent very nearly every weekend hundreds of miles away from school, carousing with his buddies in the wild Texas border town of Laredo. The rest of the time he chased coeds. After he racked up too many Fs, LSU asked Carville to occupy himself elsewhere.

Being Catholic, and being accordingly guilt-stricken, Carville immediately sought to expiate his academic sins with a stint in the Marines. Given that the United States was then at war with Vietnam, and itself, Carville's decision to enlist could easily have been one of his last. But the young Louisiana Democrat remained stationed at Camp Pendleton in San Diego, toiling as a regimental food supply corporal, and thereby avoided combat in Vietnam. By 1968, he was out of the Marine Corps and back at Louisiana State University, where he took night courses to complete his undergraduate degree. Since he was a talker, he was talked into attending law school because, his relatives reasoned, lawyers get paid a lot to talk too much.

For a time, Carville laboured as a litigator with a Baton Rouge firm called McKernnan, Beychok, Screen and Pierson. He was there for six years. His mother, for one, says "he was the worst lawyer in the world." During that time, Carville recalls that he was happiest when helping out on local and statewide campaigns. He helped one of his firm's partners, Jerry McKernnan, in a race for a spot on the public service commission. Carville also helped another lawyer at the firm, Mary Olive Pierson, in a bid to become a judge. Both McKernnan and Pierson lost. His chosen candidate to become governor, "Bubba" Henry, lost too.

But James Carville had the bug—the political bug. In 1980, he quit the law and went to work for a political consulting firm, and finally racked up some wins, one in a congressional race and another in the Baton Rouge mayoralty race. He was happy, and he was starting to attract attention as a smart political operator.

By 1982, he was running a successful Democratic Senate campaign in Virginia, nursing a slender lead as the race entered its final days. And then he made a mistake. When his candidate committed a gaffe, essentially by saying that it was "too bad" if young Americans did not like providing

Social Security support to older Americans, Carville chose to play it safe. Even though the Republican opponent seized on the blunder, Carville decided against responding, against hitting back. On election day, his candidate lost to the Republican side by a single percentage point. It was a political lesson Carville would not soon forget, and the lesson was simple: never leave a charge unanswered.

In that same year Carville headed farther north. For very little money, and for not very long, Carville toiled for U.S. Democratic presidential candidate Gary Hart in Washington, D.C. When the money ran out, Carville headed home to Louisiana, and waited for his phone to ring. Eventually, it did: in 1983, Lloyd Doggett was seeking the Democratic Senate nomination in Texas, and he asked for Carville's help.

Doggett was far behind his two opponents in the nomination race—"about a gazillion points," Carville recalls. But the Ragin' Cajun, as Doggett's people came to call him, threw himself into the race. When one of Doggett's opponents derisively referred to him as a "Little Leaguer," Carville leapt on the remark. He took Doggett to small towns across Texas, where he would hold press conferences on Little League baseball diamonds. As smiling youngsters in baseball uniforms would crowd around him, Doggett would cheerfully admit to being a Little Leaguer, and then declare that the "Big League" insurance companies, banks and utilities already had enough representation—in the form of Doggett's principal opponent.

Later on in the campaign, Carville discovered that the front-runner, a Texas state senator, had taken few, if any, firm positions on any public policy issue. He pounced again. The Doggett campaign's speech writer, Paul Begala (Carville's future business partner) produced a text stating that only Doggett had "the guts" to stand up against special interests, and for schoolchildren and civil rights. Carville suggested a change. Guts, he told Begala, was "gross" imagery. He said to use "backbone" instead.

The "backbone" theme proved as beneficial as the Little Leaguer stunt. Holding up a plastic replica of a human spinal column at every stump speech he delivered, Doggett declared: "This is what I have that my opponent doesn't have: a backbone. I'm going to take this backbone to Washington so I can stand up for the voters of Texas." Doggett went on to do what had been considered impossible: he beat the front-runner. That done, Carville and Doggett turned their attention to the runoff race for the Democratic nomination.

Doggett's next opponent, a congressman, was calling for beefed-up border patrols, to keep out Mexicans seeking to enter the U.S. illegally. His position was a very popular one. When Doggett tried to oppose the congressman's policy using facts and logic, his opponent merely grew more popular. "We tried to argue emotion with intellect," Carville wrote later. "That didn't make a dent. The head has never beaten the gut in a political argument yet, and I doubt if it ever will."

So Carville deployed his research staff to find out what the congressman had said about the issue on the floor of the House, and what bills he had introduced to toughen border patrols. After poring over stacks of paper, the opposition researchers had located precisely nothing. Carville, therefore, decided to hold a press conference.

Doggett stood beside an easel draped in velvet. "Now we are going to show you everything, every word, that my opponent has ever said about the question of immigration, until his pollster found it in a poll, about eight weeks ago." He dropped the veil to reveal a blank slate, containing nothing. "The truth of the matter," Doggett continued, "is that my opponent is a single-issue candidate on a single issue that he has never done a single thing about." Doggett beat his last remaining opponent, and secured the nomination to become the Democratic candidate for senator. It was a huge, heady victory.

In the general election, Doggett faced off against a formidable foe—Republican Phil Gramm. It was 1984, at the height of Reagan-mania:

Carville and everyone working for Lloyd Doggett knew they faced a gargantuan uphill climb, but they also knew that they had a fighting chance. And then, disaster struck. The press learned that Doggett had attended a fundraiser at a San Antonio gay club featuring "Frankie the Banana Queen and Mr. Gay Apollo." Doggett accepted money—$354 in all—from those in attendance, thus attracting the attention of reporters around Texas and around the globe, and thus abruptly ending his dreams of a Senate seat. And James Carville returned to part-time lawyering and consulting in Louisiana.

In 1986, Carville got a break. A three-time loser, Bob Casey, was running for governor of Pennsylvania, against William Scranton III, a moderate Republican with pro-choice views and scion of one of the state's most prominent families. Casey was a strong-willed anti-abortion Irishman, the son of a coal miner; Scranton practised transcendental meditation and had campaign money to burn. Being broke and unemployed, Carville did not hesitate to take the job Casey was offering, but this time he knew he had to win.

By October 1986, following six weeks of hard work, James Carville and the Casey campaign team had helped to narrow Scranton's lead with a lot of aggressive campaign messages and some good oppo. For example, Scranton was the son of a popular former Pennsylvania governor, but Carville's team quickly established that he had a poor attendance record as lieutenant-governor. So Carville developed a take-no-prisoners tag line for their advertising: "We gave him the job because of his father's name. The least he could do is show up for work."

After a few weeks of back-and-forth nastiness, Scranton threw Carville and the Casey campaign a curve ball: he held a press conference to renounce all negative campaigning. No more attack ads, no more cheap shots, just sunshine and light. The trick had the desired result. Scranton was the beneficiary of lots of glowing press coverage and editorial commentary, while Casey looked like a crass practitioner of "old politics," digging around in the dirt with the help of his opposition researchers. Following a candidate's debate, where Scranton appeared modern and Casey appeared anything but, Casey lost eight points of support—in a single night. There were only nine days left until Election Day.

To the chagrin of voters everywhere, plenty of politicians make pledges that are promptly discarded after they secure office. By the time they are sworn in, politicians are beyond the voters' immediate reach. When one makes a promise in a campaign, however, it is axiomatic that the promise needs to be kept while the campaign is ongoing; electoral retribution, after all, can be immediate and decisive. William Scranton III forgot this axiom.

Notwithstanding his solemn vow to reject anything smacking of negative campaigning, Scranton's Republican team sent out 600,000 letters describing Bob Casey as a "crook." He threw around a few other insults, too, but "crook" caught everyone's attention—as a flagrant violation of Scranton's promise to avoid negative campaigning. Once he had a copy of the letter, Carville orchestrated day after day of press coverage hammering the front-runner for his flip-flop. Scranton's lead started to shrink. The weekend before voting day, Carville approved the development of a spot that remains infamous in Pennsylvania political lore—the unforgettable "guru ad." In the commercial, Scranton is quoted praising transcendental meditation, while viewers are shown a photograph of the Republican candidate in college, wearing hippie-style clothing and sporting a head full of scruffy hair. A sitar twangs in the background. Without explicitly mentioning drugs, the spot suggested to voters that Scranton was a meditating kook—and, if that were not enough, a druggie.

Carville took a lot of heat for the spot, but shrugs off the criticism. "Since time immemorial, there has been nothin' wrong with coating a tougher message with a bit of fun. You keep your blade in its scabbard, but you still get your point across." He laughs. "Yeah, that's a good skill to have—to demean an opponent in a nice, funny way, you know?"

Bob Casey's Pennsylvania gubernatorial campaign went from an eight-point deficit to a two-point lead in just over a week. Casey had broken into the big time—and so, finally, had James Carville.

One sunny day in the middle of August 1992, when Republicans were gathering in Houston's Astrodome to confirm George Bush as their presidential nominee, I was sitting in the Sparks Street Mall in Ottawa, eating a hot dog.

The mall itself was not much to look at. It ran from the Bank of Canada building in the west, to the War Memorial in the east. In between, there were a handful of banks, a Zellers, a Marks and Spencer store, and more than a few shuttered shops. Along the way, there were also government offices—lots of government offices. In buildings of all shapes and sizes, the government of Canada played landlord to members of Parliament, senators, political assistants, parliamentary employees and, most notably, journalists. Hundreds of journalists and editors and technicians.

The Sparks Street Mall, as a result, was much more than a place to grab a quick hot dog. It was also a place to obtain, or disseminate, or, more than occasionally, manufacture political gossip. During the lunch hour, journalists and political staffers could be seen, here and there, sharing tidbits about who was up and who was down. Sparks Street was no Downing Street or Pennsylvania Avenue, but it had its uses.

At the time, I was 32 years old and special assistant to Liberal Party leader Jean Chrétien. My job description was pretty imprecise. I wrote speeches and also helped prepare members of Parliament for the daily Question Period ritual. Other things I did included approving letters for the Liberal leader's signature, keeping an eye on the direct-mail efforts of the Liberal Party, and just generally stirring up trouble for the

Progressive Conservative government. I loved working for Chrétien. I also loved the fact that I was getting paid by him to attack Tories. To me, there was nothing more satisfying than getting under a Conservative's skin. I would have done it for free.

So there I sat, eating a hot dog, drinking a Diet Coke and reading the *New York Times*. During the Republican convention, there was plenty to read. The Republicans, more recently, bested the Democrats in presidential races. Usually, they were better funded and better organized. In August 1992, the Republicans were about twenty points behind the Democrats, but most of them were not professing to be worried. Four years earlier, George Bush had been about twenty points behind Michael Dukakis, too, but he went on to decisively beat the Democratic candidate. The Republicans claimed that they felt confident. Bill Clinton's "zipper problem" was well known, as were revelations about his past drug use. In fact, Mary Matalin, Bush's political director, and James Carville's then-girlfriend, had referred to Clinton, on-air, as a "philandering, pot-smoking draft dodger." Meanwhile, the G.O.P. was readying itself to appoint U.S. Secretary of State James A. Baker, one of the smartest politicos on the planet, to the post of campaign manager.

Tucked in the middle of all of the *Times*' Republican convention coverage was a little item about the Democrats. The piece noted, with some amusement, that the Democrats were at the convention, somehow, and were faxing reporters information about the G.O.P.'s missteps. In one case, the Democrats were actually responding to Republican speakers *while* they were onstage. *While* they were speaking to the assembled delegates.

That minuscule reference jolted me, like sticking my finger in a wall socket. I read it, then read it again. The Democrats were hitting back at the Republicans before the Republicans could complete their sentences. Nobody had ever done anything like that before. The Democrats, led by James Carville, as things turned out, were taking the political game to an entirely different level. I rushed back to the office to learn more.

OPPO

The Internet didn't really exist in those days, so there would be no research done in a few seconds. The Library of Parliament, which is an extraordinary resource available to MPs, senators and their political staff, was no help at all. With my eyes gleaming, I spoke to the librarians about "quick response" and "opposition research"—phrases mentioned in the *Times* story—and they looked at me as if I was mad. So I had to scrabble together bits of information from my reading of the *Times* and other U.S. media. Who were these Democrats? What were they doing?

A piece from the *Los Angeles Times*, written the week before the Republican convention, revealed that the "quick response" effort was being directed out of Little Rock, Arkansas, where Bill Clinton's campaign was headquartered. The quick-response people had a magical name for their headquarters: "the War Room." To me, the phrase neatly summed up how politics should be conducted—as a bloodless war. The story talked about how "Clinton responded to a criticism of his health care plan by Bush before the President had levelled it." And how the War Room operated twenty-four hours a day, seven days a week, with dozens of people scanning wire copy, monitoring satellite feeds and speaking to field operatives about their political adversaries. And how, as James Carville told the *L.A. Times* reporter, if a charge is left unanswered for even one day, it cannot be effectively answered. That caught my eye.

Another story, from the *Boston Globe* and published just before the convention, was equally tantalizing. Headlined "Attack and counter-attack: Clinton team masters striking back, and hard," the story revealed how the War Room was hammering back at Republican criticisms, up to half a dozen times a day, and "sometimes within minutes of the charge, always within hours." Another War Room representative, communications director George Stephanopoulos, explained that the quick-response team drew upon other parts of the Clinton campaign to do what it did—opposition researchers, press people and field workers scattered across the United States. From what I could glean from my distant perch on Parliament Hill, Carville and his colleagues seemed to have somehow welded opposition research to quick response, creating one hell of a political machine. As far as I knew, no one had done it that way before; certainly, no one had done it as *well*.

Over the next few weeks, I learned that a group of Democratic operatives had indeed gained admittance to the Astrodome, where the Republican convention was taking place. The group, called "the SWAT team," was led in part by Democratic National Committee (DNC) chairman Ron Brown, who, as commerce secretary four years later, would die in a tragic plane crash in Bosnia. Also leading the SWAT team effort was Betsey Wright, Clinton's chain-smoking former Arkansas chief of staff from 1983 to 1990. Wright was the person with the best knowledge of the former governor's record there, and is credited with conjuring up the phrase "bimbo eruptions"—to wit, the not-infrequent appearance of women claiming to have been bedded by the libidinous former governor. (In the movie *Primary Colors*, the fictional account of Clinton's 1992 campaign, Wright is played by a pistol-packing Kathy Bates, but Wright insists that she is not *that* crazy.) Brown and Wright's luckiest break in Houston came when they were handed an embargoed copy of George Bush's acceptance speech by a careless Republican campaign worker. The War Room's oppo team picked through the speech and produced critiques of virtually every line, backed up with facts. The oppo research was then faxed back to Brown and Wright in Houston, who used it to torment Bush and his team during what should have been the convention's most important moment—the acceptance speech.

"We were defending Bill Clinton against the charges of our opponents," says Wright, who is now living a quieter life in the little town of Rogers, Arkansas. Her reputation is that of a fierce political warrior who sacrificed a great deal to assist her friends, the Clintons. She doesn't give many interviews these days. Speaking with an easy southerner's twang, her pet bird cheeping in the background, Wright says being on the ground at the G.O.P. convention in Houston was vital to the Democrats' effort to get Clinton to the White House. "I took two or three people with me and we went down to Houston in order to answer immediately the allegations they would make about Bill Clinton. And we did that."

Every morning during the convention, Wright and her team would gather before journalists at a restaurant not far from the Astrodome to respond to Republican attacks against Clinton and to take a few swipes of their own. Every evening, she would appear on news talk shows to do the same thing. When the G.O.P.'s bosses saw how much coverage Wright's team was getting, they dispatched frat-boy young Republicans to try to disrupt the press briefings, often by banging on the restaurant's plate-glass windows. "It was scary, some days," recalls Wright.

In the summer of 1992, there were plenty of Democrats who were skeptical about Carville, Brown and Wright's operation. To the doubters, it seemed too reactive, too defensive. Why not simply wait to see which Republican charges stuck, and then deal with those? Why respond to an allegation that the media, or the public, would ultimately ignore? "My operation was purely a defensive operation," recalls Wright. "There were just all kinds of scurrilous attacks being made on the state of Arkansas, on the Clinton record as governor and on his personal character. Those were my responsibility to respond to, and to defend.

"You have to respond. And you have to respond immediately, because of the rapid and massive and immediate media situation that exists in the world today. That's just the way it is. And that's what we did in Houston." Wright laughs. "And I can tell you, that was my first and my last Republican convention!"

Notwithstanding the many mythologies that have developed around Carville and Wright's War Room, opposition research is neither new nor glamorous. It is, instead, sometimes boring work that has been done in political campaigns for many, many years.

Two hundred years ago, opposition researchers with the Federalist Party campaign discovered that Thomas Jefferson, the author of the Declaration of Independence, had several mistresses, all of them slaves. The researchers even determined that Jefferson had fathered children with one of the slaves, Sally Hemings. When the Federalists made their charges public, Jefferson never responded. He was elected anyway, and served as president for nearly a decade.

The Thomas Jefferson story is a useful one to remember: while oppo is vital to any modern political campaign, and while it can be devastatingly effective, it should not be the focus of the campaign. It is merely one part of a large and complex campaign organization, drawing together press relations, polling, field organization, debate preparation, advertising and the candidate's retail politicking. At best, an oppo team's damaging revelation will throw an opponent off his or her campaign "message" for a day, perhaps two days. But rarely will it wipe out a strong contender's chances.

Until 1992 or so, not every campaign could afford the sort of oppo team that people like James Carville and Betsey Wright perfected. In local campaigns, particularly, candidates could not find the money, or the technology, needed to do proper opposition research. Some hired private investigators, of course, but these were expensive, and, if voters found out, they could be politically costly, too.

By the early 1990s in the United States, however, oppo started to come into its own. Larry Sabato, one of the most acute observers of the species that calls itself a political consultant, estimates that there was a 200 per cent growth in opposition research firms in the U.S. in this period. Such paid, full-time professional political consultants, as opposed to the ad hoc, decidedly amateurish political consultants that had preceded them, had become a big, multimillion-dollar business. One reason for this was the injection of large sums of cash into the system by aspiring politicians and advocacy groups. Both the politicians and the special interest lobbies needed people who could run effective campaigns in a complex and competitive media environment. A second reason for the huge growth in the number of professional political consultants is, in the United States, at least, a continual election cycle, encompassing a myriad of never-ending congressional, senatorial, primary and presidential races. There was, in short, a market for campaign specialists. A third reason for the burgeoning oppo and political consultant industry were technological advances that enabled the media, and politicians, to do things that had been previously only dreamed of. In the case of politicos, for example, computers permitted even the most modest campaign to develop crucial databases containing information about supporters, as well as information about the activities and statements of opponents.

Despite its successes, and despite the fact oppo is now a component of virtually every large election campaign effort in the United States, Canada and Europe, it is not always popular with the people who ultimately benefit from it. Politicians will often express hesitation, or hostility, about the need to undertake opposition research. James Carville does not accept such objections. "Look," he says, "the best way to do this game is to get all your information, and then get all your information out. The voters deserve more information, you know? We're not in this business to be mean or negative. We're in it to draw distinctions, and to draw distinctions that favour our side. So we just go out and try and be very honest about these distinctions, these differences."

Along with being accurate and factual—in highlighting what Carville calls political "distinctions"—it is also vital that the oppo work be done as quickly as possible. A twenty-four-hour, seven-days-a-week news cycle leaves one with no other choice. These days, he and others note, "opposition research" and "quick response" are now usually mentioned in the same context. One is not very effective without the other.

Carville recalls that the team he headquartered and built from scratch in Little Rock knew that the information they passed on to reporters had to be both reliable and quick. Says Carville: "Well, it was one of those ideas that just kind of grew out of necessity, you know? We have these sort of compressed news cycles now. A long time ago, I would have eighteen war room guys, and one of them would be pecking away on an Underwood typewriter, and the rest of them would come and look over his shoulder. And that was about 80 per cent of what was going on." He laughs. "But now, if you have a political event, the media guys—these guys on CNN and MSNBC and all the talk shows and the columnists—are going to be dying to find out what's going on before it does. So you just got to be on top of everything that is going on, and you got to be on top of everything fucking fast. I mean, that is the whole name of the game now."

Wright agrees with Carville on the need for speed (although the pair often clashed about strategy during that first Clinton presidential campaign): "We had to be in the same news story [in Houston], to try and minimize any damage [the G.O.P.] would try to do. They were just wild with made-up stories. There were Republican people walking all over Arkansas, handing out tens of thousands of dollars to people to make up stories and lie, and we were doing our best to keep up with that. You have to be in the same news story. Otherwise, it gets engraved in the public's minds without your response, and the next day they and the media move onto something else."

Notwithstanding the wishes of their audience, who, market surveys tell us, would much prefer to be informed about public policy issues, reporters love to write about subjects like opposition research and quick response. Because reporters are perpetual outsiders, and because it is frankly easier to produce gossipy campaign "insider" pieces than to write intelligently about policy, reporters cannot resist such stories. To most of them, war rooms smack of Machiavellian, cloak-and-dagger dirty tricks. The reality, however, is much more mundane.

How do oppo types do oppo? Most of the time, by poring over stacks of mundane reports and newspaper clippings. This kind of work is done by studious, methodical political staffers who pay attention to detail. Once something is found—something that is embarrassing, or outrageous, or just plain wrong—it is checked, then rechecked, then saved in a database or a filing cabinet. At the appropriate moment—during an election, usually—the quick-response team will kick into gear. The quick-response types, unlike their opposition research counterparts, are communicators. (Some of them, like me, are bigmouths, too.) Their stock-in-trade is aggressively marketing what the oppo researchers dig up—to reporters, or voters, or whomever is paying attention. Quick-response people throw whatever they can at whatever wall is available, and see what sticks. Their favoured tools are repetition, pithiness and volume. Volume usually works best.

Most of the time, opposition research focuses upon a politician's public life—the votes he or she made in the legislature, the curriculum vitae he or she offered up, the travel costs he or she passed along to the taxpayer. Few reasonable people would argue that an opponent's public record should be exempt from scrutiny. It is one of the principal ways, and sometimes the only way, voters can make informed choices on election day. A louder debate, however, rages about the ethicality of probing a politician's personal life. Is it fair to publicize long-ago bounced cheques, or drug use, or draft dodging? Is it right?

As in most matters political, the answer is that it depends. In the 1992 presidential race, for example, George Bush's campaign warriors were fighting a battle on two fronts. On the one flank were the likes of James Carville and Betsey Wright, emphasizing the negatives in Bush's record and responding quickly to attacks on Bill Clinton's. On the other flank were the crazed, far-right Republican forces of Patrick Buchanan, who was challenging Bush for the G.O.P. nomination. Buchanan, an unpleasant polemicist, was a former speech writer to Richard Nixon and Ronald Reagan. With his "America First" themes, he struck a responsive chord with delegates interested in protectionist and/or xenophobic rallying cries—demands for trade policies that favoured American-manufactured goods over those produced by foreigners.

Bush's opposition researchers did not have to look very far, or very long, to produce evidence, taken from Buchanan's private life, to demonstrate that their opponent was not practising what he preached. Buchanan, they learned, drove a Mercedes-Benz sedan, a European car. Bush's oppo team quickly developed a spot depicting the noisy Republican challenger as an utter hypocrite. No one, apart from Buchanan's puny band of followers, suggested that digging into an opponent's personal life, in this instance, was inappropriate. It was, in fact, the right thing to do. And it worked: after Buchanan showed some early strength in the primaries, Bush went on to decisively beat him.

In developing an oppo file on a political adversary, particularly one who has a long record of public service, there are many and diverse public sources of information. (For the purposes of illustration, and to protect the innocent, I will use examples from the opposition research done by Liberals on Kim Campbell, leader of the Progressive Conservatives in 1993.) The first place to look for material, generally, is a candidate's voting record: many jurisdictions now place the information on-line. It is also considered to be the safest area to probe. Public opinion research consistently shows that how a politician casts a vote—in a legislature, in a committee, or anywhere else—is of great interest to voters.

At this level, opposition researchers are particularly interested in votes that a politician missed. While voters generally will put up with a small amount of incumbent absenteeism—say, missing one in four votes—politicians who miss a lot of votes are potentially exposing themselves to a lot of criticism. Speeches made to support, or oppose, a proposed law should also be scrutinized for a contradiction, or a falsity, or an embarrassment. Sponsorship of a bill or a legislative change are always worth examining.

One of George Bush's most effective political operatives was the late Lee Atwater, and one of Atwater's oldest disciples is Rod Shealy, a rumpled and bearded southern Republican. His tough approach to politics, particularly in direct mail campaigns at the constituency level, has earned him rebukes on the front page of the *New York Times* and even on *Court TV*. But the Republican tactician is unrepentant. "I don't do negative campaigns," he says without irony. "I say that anything that is on the public record, that's not negative." Atwater taught Shealy that the timing and the credibility of the charge are critical when getting tough with an opponent. "It has to be fair game," says Shealy. "And anything that is on the public record, that is about a public official discharging their public duties, is obviously fair game."

To opposition researchers, one of the best sources of material are reversals made on previously held positions—the cherished "flip-flops."

In the 1993 Canadian federal election campaign, the Liberals' opposition researchers catalogued a list of Conservative government reversals, and particularly those of their newly minted leader, Kim Campbell. In a confidential "talking points" document I wrote in September 1993 for use by Liberal candidates, we accused Campbell of flip-flopping on medicare user fees, research and development programs, deficit reduction and a program to assist impoverished groups in their court challenges. But the focus of the document was another reversal: Campbell's decision to cancel an order for seven of fifty multimillion-dollar EH–101 helicopters. For most of the spring, Campbell had repeatedly insisted in the House of Commons that the government was right to spend $5.8 billion on the high-tech machines. But with the economy way down, and unemployment and the deficit way up, the Liberals decided to turn the copter purchase into an election issue. I wrote in the talking points:

> With today's cancellation of part of the copter purchase—one of the largest expenditures of its

type in Canadian history—Campbell portrayed herself as indecisive and desperate and without a coherent plan for governing. For months, Liberals have called upon Campbell and her Tory government to cancel the EH–101 program, and spend money where it is needed—on job creation, on infrastructure, on cash-strapped social programs like medicare... Kim Campbell's election-eve, death-bed semi-repentance on the EH–101s speaks volumes about her desperation, indecisiveness and lack of credibility. It speaks volumes about the decision-making ability of a politician who can say for months how crucial something is, then suddenly decide—when voting day is nearing—that a change of heart will gain an extra few seats.

In the document, I harped upon Campbell's decision-making abilities because secret Liberal Party polling had revealed that the public was uncertain about whether she could be trusted to make the right decisions, and to stick with them. To drive home the point, we dispatched a young Liberal named Fred Gaspar, now a well-connected Ottawa lobbyist, to don a chicken suit and chase Campbell at an Ottawa speech, mocking her for her refusal to publicly debate the wisdom of the helicopter purchase. The Grit chicken was mentioned in most news stories written about the EH–101 "flip-flop."

For opposition researchers, another rich vein of "public record" material is what is sometimes called "résumé inflation." In any campaign, big or small, a smart oppo operative will closely examine an adversary's résumé, to find contradictions, exaggerations or plain old lies. In 1982, for example, long before she would become a household name in Canada, Campbell was a law student, and was seeking an elected position with the Vancouver school board. A *Vancouver Sun* reporter asked Campbell, and all of the other candidates in the race, to provide a short biography and position statement. In part, Campbell's read: "A graduate of the University of B.C. and the London School of Economics, a political scientist, a teacher and third-year law student, Kim is running for her second term on the school board."

While she was certainly a U.B.C. grad, Campbell had not graduated from the London School of Economics. She had received funding from the Canadian government to attend the prestigious British institution, but she never completed her thesis, one of the conditions of her receiving financial support in the first place. Using Access to Information legislation, our team of oppo workers and other Liberals obtained all of the letters authored by Campbell and the government bureaucrats hounding her about her unfinished thesis. We also made certain that the letters found their way into the hands of reporters, resulting in two damaging stories: one, Kim Campbell apparently fibbed about graduating from the London School of Economics. Two, she didn't pay back the money taxpayers provided her to *attend* the London School of Economics. A double play.

Along with voting records and curricula vitae, oppo teams display a great fondness for expense account embarrassments—details about how much an opponent spent on a taxpayer-funded trip, or for staffing a political office, or for office renovations, or for a meal at a ritzy restaurant. Abuse of so-called franking privileges—mailing out tons of political propaganda at taxpayer expense—is also important. Another favourite is voting for one's own pay raise, which all politicians regularly do, or inflating one's pension. In the big scheme of things, of course, with governments and legislatures disbursing billions on all manner of goods and services, such things should not matter much. But with voters, as one wag once put it, political graves are often dug with small shovels. And in politics, as in war and football, it's the small things that kill.

Following Kim Campbell's victory in June 1993 at the Progressive Conservative leadership convention, Liberal war room workers flooded Access to Information bureaucrats with demands for Campbell's expense accounts and travel spending. The Conservative government dragged its feet in releasing any documents. That did not stop the Liberals: they simply pulled out an atlas and calculated how many kilometres Campbell had travelled since her installation as prime minister, and multiplied that figure by the per-kilometre cost the Canadian auditor-general had established for the use of government Challenger jets.

One of the most effective and aggressive Liberal members of Parliament, Don Boudria, was then assigned to make some electoral hay with Campbell's spending habits. In one memorable press release from mid-August 1993, Boudria noted that Campbell had "logged over 40,000 kilometres criss-crossing the country on government jets in a pre-election campaign tour, sticking Canadians with a bill for approximately $1,250,000—and the meter is still running!" Throughout the summer months, Boudria issued press release after press release, and, wherever possible, scheduled press conferences, to complain about the tax dollars Campbell was spending on travel, hotels and meals. The press ate it up. On one hot afternoon, in fact, I even drew an unflattering cartoon of Campbell astride a government jet, alongside the latest costs for using them, and persuaded the satirical magazine *Frank* to print it.

There are other sources of public documents that candidates sometimes neglect to closely examine: court records of bankruptcies and lawsuits (someone sent us nasty affidavit material about one of Campbell's divorces, but we refused to make any use of it, and quickly threw it away); property records (to see who holds mortgages or liens against the property of candidates which, in Campbell's case, was nothing inappropriate or out of the ordinary); and lists of political donors. This latter category is very important in any opposition research effort, and has long been a source of enduring political embarrassment and scandal.

Long before she was appointed minister of national defence by Brian Mulroney in 1993, and long before she had won the Progressive Conservative leadership in June 1993, the Liberal Party's Task Force had carefully scrutinized the names of companies and individuals that had donated money to Kim Campbell during her 1993 campaign to represent Vancouver Centre. One of the oppo staffers assigned to the task, Marc Laframboise, noted that one of the companies that had donated to Campbell shared the same name as a company that had received a lucrative National Defence contract after Campbell became minister. If the two companies were the same, or somehow related, it could have meant a huge political scandal. After many days of investigation, Laframboise determined that the two companies were owned and run by different people. The shared name was merely a coincidence. So we dropped the matter, a little disappointed, but relieved that we had adhered to the cardinal rule of opposition research: just the facts, ma'am.

The Conservatives, who maintained their own oppo/quick-response team during the 1993 Canadian federal election, learned this lesson the hard way.

In September 1993, stories had been swirling about what Jean Chrétien planned to put in his campaign platform, and when he planned to release it. It was dubbed the Red Book by those of us in the campaign, mainly because its covers would be Liberal red, and a vigorous debate had taken place about whether to release it at the start of the campaign (thereby risking that its contents, and news value, would be lost by the end of the race); at the end of the campaign (thereby risking that it would arrive too late to positively influence voters); or, break it up into pieces, and release it at different points in the seven-week campaign (thereby diluting the impact that a single, dramatic release might have). The decision, appropriately, was made by Jean Chrétien—to release all of the Red Book close to the start of the election, on September 15.

A lot of hype and speculation preceded the launch of the Red Book, and the Tories were clearly spooked by it. Lacking any kind of a coherent campaign document of their own, Campbell's campaign made the right decision—to pull out the stops and attack the Liberal platform with every weapon in their arsenal. The Tory oppo team, PC Caucus Services, got to work.

On the afternoon of September 14, the day before Liberal MP Paul Martin and Liberal caucus research bureau director Chaviva Hosek were scheduled to reveal the Red Book in an Ottawa hotel, the Tories struck. They chose the late afternoon because, they knew, it was not too late to get something into the next day's papers and that evening's broadcasts, but it was probably too late for a reporter to properly check out whatever the Conservative war room was offering up. As things turned out, what they were offering up was impressive: a thick blue binder, 102 pages long, couriered to reporters all over Parliament Hill. We were able to intercept a copy by pleading with a friendly journalist.

The blue binder contained a number of out-of-context snippets of speeches by Liberal members of Parliament, policy statements and some press clippings. Campbell's former key election aide, David McLaughlin, describes it best in *Poisoned Chalice*: "Conservative headquarters decided that the most effective focus of attack on the Liberal platform was its putative costs. On the day before the platform was released, PC Caucus Services (the party's research arm) made public its calculations of Liberal promises to date, which they claimed totalled some $22 billion. This pre-emptive strike was designed to knock the Grits off-balance and drive the media questioning of their platform the next day."

But the Tories, as McLaughlin himself admits in his book, made a fatal error. They injected too much spin into their oppo.

The blue binder stated that the Liberals planned to spend "0.7 per cent of Gross National Product for international aid, as soon as possible." That was equivalent to $17.8 billion, by far the largest chunk of the Tories' $22 billion spending figure.

I quickly brought together some of our best campaign people. Speech writer Scott Shepherd reminded everyone that "if we kill the head, we kill the body"—it was essential, everyone knew, that we rebut the international aid claim. Researchers Dan Demers and Mike Pearson noted that the "0.7 per cent of G.N.P." figure was in fact merely a goal, and not a firm commitment. What's more, Demers and Pearson noted, the Liberals weren't the only ones who had pledged this. Both Brian Mulroney, the former Conservative prime minister, and Jean Charest, the minister of the environment, and Campbell's principal opponent in the Conservative leadership race, had told the June 1992 Rio de Janeiro Summit that the 0.7 per cent target was one the Tories supported, too. A quick scan of our 4,000-quote database demonstrated that no less than Kim Campbell, in May 1993, had also backed the Rio target.

Clutching the quotes from Campbell, Charest and Mulroney, I jumped in front of the nearest computer terminal and started typing faster than I have ever done, before or since. Shepherd hovered above me, contributing lines. The heading: "LIBERAL RESPONSE TO THE $22 BILLION TORY 'BIG LIE' DOCUMENT."

"If Kim Campbell and her Conservatives spent as much time trying to repair the damage they have done to the Canadian economy as on their 102-page 'Big Lie' document, we would all be in a lot better shape," it began. "The Conservatives are running scared—and that is why they have prepared a document that responds to a Liberal platform that hasn't even been released yet! . . . The Canadian people won't be fooled by the politics of desperation."

As things turned out, neither was the Parliamentary Press Gallery. The Tory attack had failed, utterly. McLaughlin admitted as much, when he later wrote that our group had "undermined" the Tory war room: "It took [us] weeks to overcome the credibility problem with the media that ensued." After scanning our document, and the Conservative binder, the *Globe and Mail*'s bureau chief, Ed Greenspon, said: "Man, did [they] ever fuck up."

We knew we had scored a coup when, shortly after we distributed our talking points hither and yon, CBC Newsworld's Don Newman held them up, live and on camera. "These are from the Liberals, responding to this," he said, then holding up the blue binder. He grinned almost admiringly. "We got the Liberal response to the Tory document before we had even received the Tory document. Canadian politics, it seems, has embraced the high-tech, quick-response techniques of American politics."

We cheered and clapped each other on the back, partly because we had beaten the Tories, but partly because Don Newman was right. The rules of the game had changed: oppo was here to stay.

Told this story many years later, God—a.k.a. James Carville—gives another one of his patented laughs. "You know," he says, "you may have been a lot more sensitive about your politics in Canada way back when. But, in Canada and everywhere else, the media age has kind of changed things, you know? You used to have a little less aggressiveness in your politics, and a hell of a lot less than in American politics.

"But that's all different now, ain't it?"

Indeed it is. And there is no better evidence of this than the political *contretemps* that came to be known, variously, as "Shawinigate" or the "Grand-Mère Affair."

Like many oppo files, the background to the alleged scandal is complex. On April 16, 1993, a numbered company in which Prime Minister Jean Chrétien's family had a one-quarter interest sold its shares in a Shawinigan, Quebec hotel called the Auberge Grand-Mère. Chrétien made the deal with Yvon Duhaime, a businessman in Chrétien's riding of Saint-Maurice. Six months later, on November 1, 1993—two days before he was to be sworn in as Canada's new prime minister—Chrétien sold his shares in the Grand-Mère Golf Club. These shares amounted to approximately 22 per cent and were again held by his family's holding company. They were sold to Akimbo Development Corporation, which later defaulted on its payment for $300,000. Notwithstanding the similarity of the names, it is worth remembering that the Auberge Grand-Mère and the Grand-Mère Golf Club are separate legal entities.

The controversy, essentially, was about the communications between Chrétien and the Business Development Bank of Canada (BDC), a federal Crown corporation, in which the prime minister supported the extension of a loan to the Auberge Grand-Mère. The parliamentary Opposition and much of the news media, principally the *National Post*, alleged a conflict of interest. Their argument, boiled down to its base elements, was this: Chrétien's interventions on behalf of one business (the hotel) somehow benefited an unrelated business (the golf course) in which he allegedly had an interest (the unpaid debt).

The fact that Chrétien lost thousands of dollars in the deal did not, as things turned out, matter to the *Post* or the Opposition parties. Nor, seemingly, did it matter that the federal ethics counsellor had twice determined that, in contacting the Business Development Bank on behalf of a constituent, Chrétien was acting within his capacity as a member of Parliament. (To underline this point, the counsellor noted in November 2000: "In our constitutional system, one of the most important responsibilities that members of Parliament have is to represent the interests of their constituents.")

To the Opposition and the *Post*, it did not matter that the Royal Canadian Mounted Police determined similarly, following conflict of interest complaints by the leaders of Canada's two conservative parties, the Tories and the Alliance. (In a release, the RCMP stated that there were no grounds for "pursuing a criminal investigation into this matter.") Finally, and tellingly, public opinion didn't seem to amount to much, either: a large Ipsos-Reid survey, conducted after the election and at the height of the supposed scandal, found that more than 80 per cent of

Canadians wanted the Opposition parties to "move on." They did not, and they would not.

"Shawinigate" was a term used repeatedly by the *Post* and Chrétien's political opponents. Unimaginative politicos always append the word "gate" to some noun, hoping that it will become synonymous with political wrongdoing. Shawinigate also became, among other things, an interesting case study in oppo, demonstrating how opposition research and quick response could be effective and, sometimes, ineffective.

Typically, on a political campaign, oppo and quick-response teams work in tandem. Opposition research is done, and the results are handed over to the quick-response unit to be communicated. By the end of the 1990s, oppo and "QR" were done in this way by every political party extant. But in Shawinigate, it was all done somewhat differently.

For starters, the vast bulk of the oppo done in the so-called Shawinigan scandal was conducted by a newspaper, the *National Post*. In its editorials, but also in its "straight" news reporting, the *Post* was unafraid to appear shamelessly partisan and anti-Liberal. In years past, newspaper editors and reporters endeavoured to create the impression—publicly, at least—that they were keeping an open mind about the issues of the day. But the *Post* was uninterested in such niceties. In April 2001, for example, no less than its deputy editor, Martin Newland, gave an on-the-record interview to another publication, the far-right *Report* magazine, in which he baldly stated that a "conflict of interest" had, in actual fact, taken place involving the prime minister of Canada. Officials of the Liberal government, said Newland, streamed into the prime minister's riding "with buckets of cash, pouring it into every orifice [sic] that they could see.... That's not right." To dispel any illusion about the *Post*'s partisan approach to reporting, Newland stated, "We do believe it is a violation of the [conflict of interest] code." It did not matter to Newland, apparently, that the RCMP had concluded that there was no violation.

From the outset of the controversy, in or around 1999, the *Post* was determined to transform the inoffensive Quebec town of Shawinigan into something synonymous with the Watergate apartment complex. For months, *Post* reporter Andrew McIntosh (whose employer, it should be recalled, was suing the prime minister for denying him a lifetime barony) had been a veritable journalistic St. George, charging out to slay the twin-headed dragon of prime ministerial perfidy and misdeeds. To McIntosh's frustration, no doubt, neither the Canadian public nor competing newspapers seemed to give a sweet damn. But the *Post* was undeterred, because, for most of the relevant period, it could count on Canada's two conservative opposition parties, the Canadian Alliance and the Progressive Conservatives, to do its bidding.

Disgruntled former Alliance staffers would later tell Liberals that the *Post* usually supplied the Alliance, under the leadership of Preston Manning or, later, Stockwell Day, with advance notice of the stories McIntosh and others intended to publish about Shawinigate. In this way, the Official Opposition would have sufficient time to prepare the questions it intended to raise in the House of Commons. It also ensured that the *Post*'s hoped-for revelations would receive a parliamentary boost, giving stories with a short shelf-life another day or two on the public agenda. While some of the twists and turns in the Shawinigate story had been the product of actual research efforts by the Tories or the Alliance themselves, it was common knowledge that most of the Shawinigan-related oppo was being done by the *Post*. The quick-response part of the formula, then, became the responsibility of the *Post*'s conservative political allies. (Ironically, the Opposition politician who came to be seen as the most effective was the Tories' Joe Clark, leading only a dozen MPs in the House of Commons; Official Opposition leader Stockwell Day, meanwhile, never seemed to recover from the pounding the Grits gave him during the election campaign.)

One of the *Post*'s greatest strengths, its single-mindedness, soon became its biggest liability. For instance, the newspaper's complete inability to lower the volume on its coverage—each new development, however minor, was accorded front-page treatment, with the size and type of headline reserved for the return of the Messiah or the announcement of Armageddon—alienated other media organizations, which (correctly) sensed that a journalistic vendetta was underway. What the *Post* needed most was the legitimization that another media outlet could give its Shawinigate fixation. For many months, it didn't get it.

The oppo lesson, therefore, is this: take your shot, make it hurt, then move on. If voters sense that a participant in the partisan political process (in this case, amazingly enough, a daily newspaper) is motivated by something other than a desire to illuminate the truth, that participant risks a backlash. In a wonderful bit of phrase-coining, David Corn, the Washington editor of the liberal U.S. magazine the *Nation*, calls all of this "the umbrage gap." During the Monica Lewinsky scandal, Corn notes, public opinion polling showed Bill Clinton's popularity going up, not down. The popularity of the Democratic president's Republican inquisitors, meanwhile, plummeted.

The umbrage gap, Corn explains, essentially means this: voters do not get terribly upset about their leaders' personal failings, simply because they think politics should be a lot more about the people and a lot less about the politicians. It follows, then, that in good economic times, which both Clinton and Chrétien have enjoyed, real people have a general sense of well-being and don't care much (if at all) about the character flaws of the men and women at the top. Even if the *Post* and its conservative parliamentary political mouthpieces had made out a good case in Shawinigate, Canadians, from coast to coast, had scrutinized their oppo and found it lacking. The unwillingness of the *Post* and the Opposition to move on, as a result, started to irritate the voters. The umbrage gap, Canadian-style, stopped the Shawinigan oppo effort dead in its tracks.

But that, regrettably, was not the end of the story. Following the election that saw Chrétien win an unprecedented third majority, many

Liberals were surprised—and despondent—that the *Post* and its political allies were determined to keep the story alive. While disappointed, the Grits did not take long to react. With Chrétien's approval, Francie Ducros continued to lead a post-election war room. Whenever a factual error was made in any Shawinigate story, Ducros, making use of the talents of Chrétien's legislative assistant, John Milloy, and one of her writers, Ken Polk, would respond quickly. She did not bother, for the most part, with editorial commentary; but where an error had been made about the factual record, Ducros would respond in a matter of hours. That, at the end of the day, is good QR. The tactic quickly ensured that those journalists who continued to publish Shawinigate stories would be held to a higher standard. And, once again, polling suggested that Ducros's approach worked: Canadians were fed up with the media's fixation on the Shawinigan stories and had not been persuaded that Jean Chrétien was a crook.

Just as Bill Clinton's fling with Monica Lewinsky rebounded on the Republicans who tried to use it for political gain, Alliance leader Stockwell Day's preoccupation with Shawinigate did him no good, either. Throughout the early months of 2001, Day and his Alliance cohorts laboured mightily in the House of Commons to use Shawinigate to attack Jean Chrétien. And throughout that period, the popularity of Day's party started to slip. Following the two-week Easter break in April, many Alliance MPs returned to Ottawa and openly expressed doubts about Day's capacity to lead. (Most of Day's critics were supporters of Reform party founder Preston Manning, who remained conspicuously above the ensuing fray.)

There were lots of reasons why Day's leadership came under sustained attack by his own MPs: a libel lawsuit in Alberta that cost provincial taxpayers $800,000; Day's apparent willingness to hire a "spy" to obtain further Shawinigate-style dirt on the Liberals; his attack on the integrity of a judge—later hastily recanted—whom Day attempted to link to the Shawinigan file; and a series of other blunders and missteps. But Shawinigate, and the opposition research efforts that produced it, did not help Stockwell Day one little bit. One Alliance MP—who later called for Day to resign and was kicked out of his party's parliamentary caucus—admitted to me that there was plenty of evidence to suggest that the reverse was actually true. "Shawinigate didn't do what it was supposed to do. Constituents told me they were fed up with it, and fed up that Stock didn't drop it," said this Alliance rebel. "And now Shawinigate is faded from memory, but our party is still stuck with Stock." The Alliance bloodletting continued throughout the spring and summer of 2001, while Jean Chrétien's popularity, and that of his government, edged upward.

The final word, here, should go to James Carville, who says he knows a little about Shawinigate. After listening to me describe the latest developments in the file, and periodically letting loose with one of his whooping laughs, Carville says this about those (like the *National Post*, the Reform Alliance and the Conservatives) who persist in going on and on and on about the story: "They made a mistake. You need to *politicize* your political differences, not *criminalize* them. You turn people off if you go too far. Voters aren't stupid, you know?"

CHAPTER FIVE

BARNEY, SPIDERS AND DIRTY TRICKS
... or, how to seize the moment
by doing silly things

On the evening of Tuesday, November 14, 2000, with just under two weeks to go in the Canadian federal election campaign, the clouds parted, an angelic chorus sang and a gift descended from heaven.

The gift took the form of a CBC television documentary, by veteran journalist Paul Hunter. Titled "The Fundamental Day," the documentary ran for only a few minutes, and it did not break any new ground (not, at least, for any of the bone-tired Liberal war room operatives who were watching it). But by the time he was done, Hunter had transformed the first Canadian national election campaign of the new millennium.

"Fundamental Day" told the story of Stockwell Day, the telegenic former treasurer from Alberta, who, through a combination of luck, perseverance and circumstance, had come to be the leader of Her Majesty's Loyal Opposition in the fall of 2000. Because he was functionally bilingual, and because he had an arguably good record as Alberta's minister of finance, Day was an early favourite to lead the Canadian Reform Alliance, the fledgling political protest party that grew out of the ashes of Reform. In a leadership vote held in a grimy Toronto hotel in early July 2000, Day had even soundly trounced the founder and leader of the Reform Party, Preston Manning.

Throughout the summer of 2000, the new leader of the Canadian Alliance received a lot of glowing press reviews, most often in the pages of the *National Post*, and also in the Southam News chain, principally owned by media baron Conrad Black until late 2000. Black made no secret of his detestation of Liberal Party leader Jean Chrétien; in one *Times of London* article in November 1999, in fact, Black had boasted that by the time he got through with Canada's prime minister, there would not be enough left "to squeeze through an eye dropper." So, in editorial after editorial, in news item after news item, Black's employees depicted Day in the most flattering light; conversely, Black's minions repeatedly characterized Chrétien as a criminal, or a simpleton, or both. By the time fall rolled around, the Liberal Party's popularity had shrunk, somewhat, while Day's Reform Alliance party was experiencing a modest growth in support.

Stockwell Day, however, had a past, and it was not one that would be helpful to his political fortunes in a pluralistic, urban democracy. I had first started paying attention to the former evangelical pastor and auctioneer in late 1998, when I stumbled across three letters sent by Day's father, a former Social Credit supporter named Stockwell Day Senior, to the Western Canada Concept (WCC). The WCC was the political vehicle of Douglas Christie, the British Columbia man who, according to the Law Society of Upper Canada, has "made common cause" with Canadian Holocaust deniers such as James Keegstra and Ernst Zundel. The WCC itself opposes abortion, bilingualism and immigration, which it states "can result in Western Canada becoming just as crowded and degenerate as the third world."

In his missives to the WCC's official organ, the *Western Separatist Papers*, Stock Senior unburdened himself of a few opinions. Such as that gays were "sodomites." And that Canada should only admit immigrants who "look like us." And that our immigration offices resembled "the Harlem Globetrotters" basketball team. And that Mr. Christie was his "captain." So Stockwell Day's father had written some inappropriate letters—so what? Stock Junior could hardly be saddled with the apparent sins of his father. A few more minutes on the Internet, however, revealed that Stock Junior had also spoken with great candour about all manner of social subjects, and all while a member of the Alberta Legislature or Cabinet.

A sampling of these Stockwell Day Junior statements was most revealing. On abortion, Day had strong views; in a story in the *Edmonton Journal* in June 1995, for example, Day had said: "Women who become pregnant through rape or incest should not qualify for government-funded abortions unless their pregnancy is life-threatening." In a March 2000 story in the same newspaper, Day likened Canadians who favour reproductive choice to child abusers. He declared: "The thinking is, if you can cut a child to pieces or burn them alive with salt solution while they're still in the womb, what's wrong with knocking them around a little when they're outside the womb?"

The would-be Alliance leader also did not hesitate to express himself in an intemperate fashion about other subjects. Those Canadians who chose to live common law, he indicated in an April 2000 speech during the Alliance leadership race, are contributing to "escalating social problems." Single parents and their children, meanwhile, Day told the Alberta legislature in May 1991 "[are] significantly associated with rates of both violent crime and burglary." The children found in single-parent families, he added in a news item in the *Calgary Herald* in June 1992, "are statistically more susceptible to social problems, emotional problems, behavioural problems... That can lead, in some cases, to juvenile crime.

It can also lead to drug and substance abuse. That's the statistical reality." Adherents of non-Christian faiths, Day told *Alberta Report* in March 1984, "will not be in Christ's presence for an eternity. You can call that Hell." Even author John Steinbeck was not immune from Day's sense of moral outrage. In March 1994, the *Calgary Herald* reported that Day wished to ban *Of Mice and Men* because it contained "profane" language. Said Day: "When you're talking about school children, you have to respect the fact that most Canadians profess to be of the Christian faith and they're sending their kids to school... They don't need to be exposed to the name of Jesus Christ being taken in a blasphemous sense."

Gays and lesbians, however, occupied a special place in Day's social construct. Homosexuality, he declared in the *Edmonton Journal* in August 1997, is "a lifestyle choice that doesn't deserve this kind of attention." A fellow Alberta politician, who had brought a group of gay leaders into the legislature in July 1986, had committed an "offence to the Lord," Day told the *Calgary Herald*. To *Alberta Report* in February 1992, the equally homophobic far-right magazine that has trumpeted Day from his earliest incarnation as a politician, he stated that "homosexuality is a mental disorder that can be cured through counselling." And in the pages of a July 1986 edition of the *Herald*, Day insinuated that AIDS was divine punishment for homosexual behaviour: "I believe that everybody has the freedom to make their own choices on how they're going to live... My personal belief in scripture leads me to believe there are negative consequences incurred when we engage in activities the Bible warns us of our engaging in."

All of these statements by Stockwell Day were known, to a greater or lesser extent, in Alberta political circles. After Day declared his candidacy for the Reform Alliance leadership in March 2000, it became imperative for his advisers to spare no effort in keeping such statements away from the Canadian voting public. In this, they were greatly assisted by the *National Post* and Southam News chain. Even in news stories, the *Post* sought to depict Day, and Liberal efforts to criticize him, in terms that were most helpful to the Reform Alliance.

That was why Paul Hunter's documentary about Day's fundamentalist religious views was so important. For months, Liberals had been attempting to draw the media's attention to evidence of Day's apparent extremism. For months, the media, particularly those many segments of it owned by Conrad Black, had declined to pay virtually any attention. Or, as in the case of the *Post*'s editorialists and reporting staff, it had sought to depict the Liberals as the real extremists.

The documentary started with a discussion of Day's involvement with a private Bible school in Bentley, Alberta, in the 1980s. The school, which was found by a December 1984 Alberta government inquiry to possess a curriculum that "violated principles of tolerance and understanding [towards] Jews, blacks and Indians," employed Day as a pastor for more than five years. Hunter's story described how Day was indifferent towards the Conservative government's criticism of the Bentley Christian centre. "God's law is clear," Day shrugged. "Standards of education are not set by government but by God, his Bible, the home and the school."

The CBC report went on to document Day's efforts to prevent a museum in his riding from receiving a small grant for a study of gay and lesbian history; recognizing the historical contributions of gay and lesbians to Alberta's history was "a mistake," he declared. The documentary then described Day's attempts, as a cabinet minister, to prevent gays and lesbians from receiving legal protections against discrimination. A clip of Day recorded him stating: "I think people need the right to say no to, for instance, to sex education programs that would include homosexual material. We'll look at fences there. I think there should be fences around adoptions. We'll look at fences there."

After recalling some of Day's hardline views on abortion, Hunter's report turned to a final issue: creationism.

For many months, Liberals had been hearing rumours that Stockwell Day was an enthusiastic adherent of creationism. There had been no reporting about any of this, however, and Day resisted saying much about his faith in public. Creationism itself, as a religious philosophy, contains many conflicting elements. Some creationists believe that the earth is flat, and is covered by some sort of dome or firmament. Others are geocentrists who insist that, while not flat, the earth is the centre of the solar system. Young earth creationists, of which Day may be one, claim a literal interpretation of the Bible as a basis for their beliefs, and believe that the planet is 6,000 to 10,000 years old, that all life was created in six days, and that death and decay came as a result of Adam and Eve's Fall. There are other creationist derivatives, including Old Earth creationism, cap creationism, day-age creationism, "intelligent design" creationism, and so on.

In Hunter's documentary, Day's particular variant of creationism is vividly described for the viewer by Red Deer College's Pliny Hayes. In 1997, Hayes recounted, Day had attended a discussion about evolution during the college's Christian Awareness Week. Curious, Hayes and some of his students wanted to see what Day had to say. Recalls Hayes: "... he prefaced his comments with a smile and a question: 'Are any of my friends from the press present?' When no one responded, he then went on to say a number of things. One, that the earth is 6,000 years old. That Adam and Eve are real people. That humans co-existed with dinosaurs. That there's as much [evidence] for ... creationism as there is for evolution. And that he's upset that creationism can't be taught in public schools."

Seconds after Hunter's report disappeared from the television screen in my small Ottawa hotel room, I called Francie Ducros and Cyrus Reporter, two of the Liberal staffers I was working with on the party's election campaign communications team. Ducros was the prime minister's director of communications, and oversaw all of the campaign's communications; Reporter was chief of staff to Health Minister Allan Rock, and another formidable media spinner. For much of our ten-minute discussion, Reporter and I simply laughed. "Can you believe this?" Reporter asked me. "Can you believe it?"

"Oh, yes," I said. "It's what we've been waiting for."

Stockwell Day was a creationist. This, in and of itself, was politically irrelevant. Like every other Canadian, Day has a constitutional right to believe in whatever he desires. Like any aspiring politician, Day's religious views were immaterial to his fitness for public office.

That, at least, was the theory. If a politician rigorously maintained a distinction between his or her religion, and his or her legislative agenda, no one could legitimately have cause for complaint. Modern legislative decision-making in Canada and the United States has embraced the notion that a wall properly exists between Church and State. But what about politicians who consistently attempt to infect the public agenda with their religious views? What about them?

In a telling, and underreported, speech before a group of educators in April 2000, while still a candidate for the Alliance leadership, Stockwell Day made it clear that he was not one who believed a politician could, or perhaps even should, keep Church and State separate. "[It is not] possible to demand that the convictions I express on Sunday should have nothing to do with the way I live my life the other six days of the week," he said. Day was telling the truth. Throughout his political career, as a backbencher and as a powerful member of Alberta's cabinet, Day had consistently attempted to impose his personal morality, and his religious faith, on others. On gays and lesbians. On pro-choice women. On common law partners. Stockwell Day did not ever hesitate to use the law to advance his religious convictions, even with respect to John Steinbeck novels.

Now, with only a few days left in a hotly contested election campaign, a major Canadian media organization had confirmed that fact in a detailed and dramatic fashion. I believed that, whether they were creationists or not, Canadian voters had no desire to elect a prime minister who would attempt to stick his religion in their faces. Day, however, had already tried to do so in Alberta. How could (or should) Canadians be told that Day might do the same thing to the country?

James Carville, who knows a thing or two about doing battle with the sort of far-right political establishment that periodically offers up the likes of Stockwell Day, muses about this. Before Day's election as leader of Reform Alliance, I spoke to the Democrats' top political consultant. Told about Day's views on abortion, Carville suggests that Liberals resist the temptation to say nothing. If one's political opponent has dropped a sticky moral issue into the middle of an election campaign, one is entitled to discuss the issue, says Carville. "I think you have got to [be] pretty nonpolitical... and, you know, kind of say: 'Sometimes in politics, people sometimes have to discuss unpleasant things, and you know we have some very real differences between us. And, unpleasant as it may be, the most unpleasant alternative would be for you not to know what they are.' You know?" He pauses. "[Day] states that he doesn't favour abortion, even in the case of rape and incest. So you should state that it is a long-held policy of our government that Canadian women are smart enough, and they should be able to make these choices themselves."

What about a case where criticizing a political opponent's views—his willingness to mix his religious views with his politics—is necessary?

Carville laughs. "The first rule is to make a joke about yourself," he says. "The second rule is that there is nothing wrong, since time immemorial, about going after someone in a nice funny way, you know? Nothing wrong with that at all."

That is what I did. With the full knowledge, and, in some cases, full participation, of much of the national Liberal campaign's senior staff, I decided to use a little humour to make my point. And my point was twofold: one, Stockwell Day's religion plays a significant role in his politics; and, two, Canadians are entitled to know about that, and consider its political implications for themselves.

Early the next morning, I ensured that every Liberal candidate was sent a videotaped copy of Paul Hunter's documentary by courier, along with a transcript. The war room's lead writer, Ken Polk, a long-time Chrétien aide, then produced a couple of tough "talking points" documents to highlight what the CBC had revealed. Karl Littler, a senior adviser to Finance Minister Paul Martin, supplied me with some of the material I intended to use. And one of the campaign's press officers, Sophie Galarneau, refined a line I planned to use the next day on *Canada AM*.

Throughout the election, I had been drafted by the Liberal Party to appear on various television and radio political panels. Because I was no longer an employee of the prime minister, or anyone else in government, for that matter, I was able to say things that many others could not. As a result, I had been called all manner of canine derivatives: I was "an attack dog," said the *Globe and Mail*; I was a "Liberal pit bull," declared a columnist with the Sun Media chain. Meanwhile, Day's party had also called me names, his caucus members grumbling about how nasty I was. For example, John Reynolds, a Reform Alliance member of Parliament darkly pronounced on me in the *Toronto Star*: "He's the master of dirty tricks... I would put nothing past him." The criticisms, generally, were all part of the game. My rule of thumb is that, whenever a politician or a politico is called a "statesman" by an opponent, it is time to worry. When the other side is calling that same person all sorts of names, it is safe to assume that he or she is probably being effective.

Canada AM's political panel was regarded as one of the most-watched in the country. I had been appearing on the panel before and during the election, usually facing off with Stockwell Day's grumpy chief of staff, Rod Love (who liked to boast to reporters that he had never lost an election). The night before my November 16 *Canada AM* appearance, I quietly spoke with Jonathan Murphy, director of the Liberal caucus research bureau. Murphy assigned a young staffer, Matthew Graham, to scour Ottawa and find what I was looking for. Late that night, Graham showed up at my door with the prize in a Wal-Mart bag. I wrote him a cheque, and he left.

Early the next morning, I met with Ken Polk and John Milloy at the Liberal Party's war room on the eighth floor of a bland Ottawa business tower. Milloy, an Oxford graduate, was the head of the Liberal war room. The three of us discussed lines and the day's stories, and then I hurriedly walked over to the CTV offices, carrying a Labatt Blue gym bag.

In the studio, I sat beside the only other pundit present, the Alliance's Tim Powers, and placed the gym bag beside my chair. A technician clipped a tiny microphone to my lapel and looped an earpiece over my shoulder so that I could hear what was being said outside the Ottawa studio. Powers, a fair-minded lobbyist and former Tory from Atlantic Canada, had joined the Alliance some months before the election. Despite the fact that we disagreed about most everything, he was bright and affable, and we had become friendly. Unlike Rod Love, Powers displayed a sense of humour.

The host of the political segment was Valerie Pringle. In the Toronto studio with her were representatives of the NDP and the Tories; a Bloc Québécois talking head was being beamed in from Quebec City.

Typically, when a network broadcasts one of these pundit segments, anywhere between five to eight minutes is given to the participants to duke it out. If that does not sound like a lot of time, it isn't. The minutes fly past like an express train. Normally, the host throws out a question about some issue in that day's headlines, or about something that happened earlier that week. On the *Canada AM* panels, whenever the Conservative, NDP or Bloc participant said something critical—most often about the Liberal government, but also about the Reform

BARNEY, SPIDERS AND DIRTY TRICKS

Alliance—I ignored them. There is no point, in these debates, wasting precious seconds on opponents who represent no real electoral threat.

In the case of Powers and I, however, the rule was Leave No Charge Unanswered. He was my principal opposition, and vice versa. While an estimated two million Canadians looked on, we would go at each other hammer and tongs, exploiting whatever weakness the other side had, highlighting whatever achievement we needed to highlight. The best approach was to be tough, but not be a bully or a sulk. If humour could be used, that was good, too. Sometimes, if the conversation got too heated, the pundits would end up speaking loudly and at the same time. For the most part, however, Pringle and her co-host, Dan Matheson, kept us from doing that.

On the morning in question, the panel batted around the usual stuff: polls, policies, prognostications. Time was slipping by, fast. When it appeared that I might lose my opportunity, I interrupted Powers. "Yeah, yeah, yeah, whatever," I said. "Valerie, you say you want to talk about the past week. Let's do that. In the past day or so, we have learned that Stockwell Day apparently believes that the world is 6,000 years old, Adam and Eve were real people and—my personal favourite—humans walked the earth with dinosaurs."

Powers looked at me as I reached down to open my gym bag. I continued: "Valerie, I just want to remind Mr. Day that *The Flintstones* was not a documentary." I then quickly extracted a large, stuffed, purple Barney from my bag. I held Barney up to the camera while Powers collapsed in laughter and so did all the rest. "And this is the only dinosaur that recently co-existed with humans."

Of all the things I have done in politics, over many, many years, probably nothing has had the impact of those few seconds on *Canada AM*—waving around a Barney dinosaur and suggesting that *The Flintstones*, in the now-immortal words of Karl Littler and Sophie Galarneau, "was not a documentary." In election campaigns, something does not happen if it does not happen on television. To that, I have added another axiom: television is about pictures, not words. Barney the dinosaur, purchased for $75 the night before, had helped me to create a visual about Stockwell Day; using a little bit of humour, we had tapped into a public suspicion that Day was prepared to impose his religious views on everyone else and, possibly, that he was a kook. In a lengthy piece published the day after Jean Chrétien was re-elected with a massive majority, columnist Paul Wells, in the *National Post*, no less, had this to say about the Barney stunt: "The transformation of Mr. Day, from Stock to Laughingstock, was complete." The stunt was discussed in the pages of the *Economist*, the *New York Times* and *Time* magazine, and got a tip of the hat in the June 2001 issue of the U.S. political magazine *Campaigns and Elections,* which declared that my Barney moment "drove home the point" that Stockwell Day was an extremist who couldn't be trusted.

Powers and I left the studio together; he was still laughing. We shook hands and parted ways. Back at Liberal headquarters, I was greeted by a dozen staff people who wanted to see Barney. One of them suggested we auction the doll off at a party fundraiser. After I settled in at my desk, I received a call to inform me that the prime minister had been asked about my Barney stunt by reporters. The PM had shrugged it off, saying I had "the right" to do what I did. While campaigning in British Columbia, Stockwell Day, for his part, remarked—effectively, I thought—that "the real dinosaurs" were located in the Liberal Party caucus. He repeated, however, his conviction that creationist theory should be taught alongside evolutionary theory in Canadian schools, then stalked off.

The infamous Barney, meanwhile, can now be found somewhere in my basement, where my sons, ages one and three, refuse to surrender it.

Was Barney a dirty trick? Plenty of people thought so. Conservative columnists called me a "smear doctor" and even a "hatemonger." One

BARNEY, SPIDERS AND DIRTY TRICKS

race-baiting Ottawa-area radio host, Lowell Green, devoted an entire program to the subject, calling me "a sewer rat" and "diabolical." He suggested that listeners pray for the redemption of my soul. The *Sun* chain's Earl MacRae actually equated me with Joseph Goebbels.

But Barney had the desired effect. It kept Paul Hunter's documentary in the news and in the opinion pages for a few more days; it kept Day on the defensive about his hidden moral agenda; and it unleashed, as one CTV reporter told me, "ten million water-cooler conversations about Stockwell Day's craziness, and whether he wanted to bash down the wall between Church and State." Which, of course, had been the objective.

Really dirty tricks have been a feature of election campaigns for a long, long time. Following the Watergate scandal in the United States in the early 1970s—where a synonym for dirty tricks, ratfucking, was publicized by one of the indicted players in that drama—so-called dirty tricks were highly unpopular. Spying, invasion of privacy and so on became verboten, and for a time campaigns took on a distinctly Pollyannaish aspect. It was inevitable that the pendulum would swing back, and it did. Towards the end of the 1970s, stunts, dirty tricks, and skulduggery were back with a vengeance. (Because the very term "dirty tricks" prompts fear and loathing in even the most jaded political consultant, I am forced in this chapter to dwell upon examples that principally concern only me.)

Dirty tricks are as old as politics itself, it seems. As far back as 54 B.C., for example, letters written by Cicero to his colleague Atticus, amply testify to the longevity of such electoral nastiness. The political system of Rome was then characterized by *consules flagrant infamia*, Cicero wrote; meaning, "the consuls are ablaze with scandal." Cicero tells his friend that a closed-door session concerning the misconduct of several politicians was stirring up *magnus timor candidatorum*, or "great fear among the candidates." The problem apparently related to the revelation that a certain candidate had been bought, but did not stay bought. According to Cicero, one Gaius Memmius stood in the Senate to read an agreement that he and a fellow candidate had made with certain Roman consuls to pay them a great deal of money for suborning witnesses, should they be elected. The agreement detailed sums to be paid, and who was involved in the conspiracy. History goes on to record that Memmius was successful in his objective: he effectively destroyed the political careers of those he named, but, tellingly, did irreparable damage to his own career, as well.

The types of "dirty tricks" available to political hacks are limited only by the imagination, and, sometimes, by the law. Cell phones are monitored by companies that later sell tapes and transcripts to the media or political partisans. Private detectives are hired to poke through a candidate's garbage—called Dumpster diving—hoping to unearth some scandal. Telephone conversations are regularly recorded to trap or embarrass an opponent. Sometimes, campaigns are even infiltrated by moles from the other side. In the summer of 1984, I was a young Liberal, assigned to assist Senator Phillippe Gigantes in trying to elect some Grits under the very troubled leadership of John Turner. As the Liberal effort lurched from one disaster to another, the so-called strategists who supposedly ran the campaign were growing increasingly, and visibly, desperate. One memorable day, Gigantes met with one of these people (I will not name him because he left politics thereafter, and never came back). Following the meeting, Gigantes sat down with me, shaking his head. I asked him what was wrong.

The person with whom he'd just met, he said, "wants to pay for someone to act as a mole on the Tory press plane so that we can get some dirt, and find out what the reporters are writing," said Gigantes. "What an asshole."

"What did you say to him?"

Gigantes laughed. "I told him to save his money. I told him that, if there is any dirt to be had on a campaign plane, he can buy an account of it in the newspaper the very next day. And for just 25 cents!"

Dirty tricks do not work, principally because they are dirty tricks. Other political consultants feel similarly. U.S. political commentator Larry Sabato argues in his best-selling book, *Dirty Little Secrets*, that "such tactics frequently go too far, becoming acts that either constitute or lead to significant impairment in the conduct of public affairs—[which is] our definition of corruption." As would have been the case in the never-realized Liberal "mole" plot, the dividends paid by such tactics are far outweighed by the damage that inevitably results when one is "found out." Polling data shows, not surprisingly, the voting public and the media look on such trickery as highly inappropriate, and those who engage in such tricks are seen as worse than those they seek to expose: a February 1999 U.S. Gallup poll, for example, showed that fully three-quarters of those surveyed considered ethical political behaviour to be "very important."

In the 1962 Canadian federal election campaign, to cite another example, flamboyant Liberal cabinet minister Judy LaMarsh followed Conservative leader John Diefenbaker across Canada as part of what she called a "Truth Squad," providing what she called "constructive criticism" of the Dief and his policies. The Truth Squad effort dramatically backfired on LaMarsh and the Liberals, however, because Diefenbaker was able to persuade voters that LaMarsh was using gutter tactics to win popular support. LaMarsh was widely castigated for the effort—she was even forced to publicly concede that she was "accident prone"—and Diefenbaker was re-elected, albeit with a minority government.

Donald Segretti, the Watergate player who served time in prison for his excesses and is widely credited with inventing the term "ratfucking," brought dirty tricking to a historically low level. Some of the tricks favoured by Segretti, and catalogued in Bob Woodward and Carl Bernstein's *All the President's Men*, included planting moles, forging embarrassing letters, stealing documents and disrupting Democratic events by calling in cancellations to hotels.

Dirty tricks are often confused with political stunts and gimmicks, but they should not be. A dirty trick, by its very name, speaks to its essential illegitimacy, whereas a good stunt or gimmick can be a funny or trenchant way to make a political point. A stunt is not a dirty trick. It is worth remembering, however, that an effective stunt will often be called "dirty" by political adversaries who are targeted or by partisan media commentators. Stunts are frequently used to poke fun at the opposition, or to somehow humanize a candidate—to make them appear more fun or more sympathetic. Candidates are attracted to such stunts, principally because they are cheap. A good stunt can attract a lot of media coverage at no cost. As one wag put it, they earn votes with irreverence, and there is nothing dirty about that. They can backfire, of course: Stockwell Day's decision to arrive at his first press conference as Opposition leader atop a Sea-Doo and wearing a wetsuit prompted a lot of derisive laughter. For Day, the chorus of criticism was serious enough to force him to good-naturedly poke fun at himself for having attempted the stunt in the first place.

In the unsuccessful 1996 provincial British Columbia Liberal campaign, which I helped to run, we used one political stunt to great advantage. One sunny afternoon in May of that year, in a cluttered office space in Richmond, brewing executive James Villeneuve and I were speaking in a conference call with Gordon Campbell, leader of the provincial political party. Villeneuve, a superior political communicator who would later chair the successful 2000 campaign of Toronto mayor Mel Lastman, had flown out West to assist the B.C. Liberals in the race. We were preparing Campbell for his appearance on a radio drive-in show the next morning. The B.C. election race was well underway, and our stalwart group was struggling, mightily, to unseat the well-organized and well-funded New Democrats of Glen Clark. Our opponents were well ahead of us in the polls. At one point, I suggested that radio drive-in shows were not the ideal place to ruminate aloud about complex policy matters. Villeneuve recalled Bill Clinton's fabled saxophone recital on the Arsenio Hall show in 1992. Laughingly, we asked the B.C. Liberal leader whether he played an instrument.

"Well, yes," he said. "I play guitar, sometimes. But I'm not very good."

Villeneuve and I pounced like the hungry jackals we so resemble. Could he think of a song or two to strum on the radio program? "Sure," said Campbell. He called back a few hours later. Not only had Campbell located a song to play, he had written one. It was a funny and catchy little ditty, sung in a respectable alto, and all about the three-dozen or so tax increases Glen Clark's NDP had foisted upon the weary voters of B.C. He called it "Taxman Glen."

The song was a huge hit; people loved to see a politician who did not take himself so seriously that he could not have fun. Everywhere Campbell went in the province, people requested that he sing "Taxman Glen." In a matter of days, the B.C. Liberals started to inch back up in the polls. And on election night, Campbell and his party actually acquired 41 per cent of the popular vote, fully three points ahead of Clark's NDP, but, thanks to the vagaries of riding boundary laws that seemed to favour the incumbent, the NDP eked out a few more seats.

Sending dead flowers to a losing campaign, or ordering a lot of C.O.D. pizzas to be delivered to one's opponent, are examples of the sort of puerile behaviour that some consultants and political veterans can succumb to. But pranks are best when they are funny, not malicious. Democratic campaign operative Joe Trippi recalls one wonderful example of this in *Dirty Little Secrets*. Trippi had been part of the team overseeing the 1984 presidential campaign of Walter F. Mondale. Recalls Trippi: "I was running Pennsylvania for Mondale in the 1984 primary against Gary Hart. We had this huge Mondale for President dinner, with four or five thousand people there. Then, after dessert, I see out of the corner of my eye that all the waiters are bringing out plates of fortune cookies, and it hits me about ten minutes later that I never ordered any cookies. To my shock and horror, Mondale gets up to give his speech, grabs a cookie, opens it, and reads, as they all did, 'Hart Wins Pennsylvania.' Mondale got this horrid, pale look on his face..."

There are three things that distinguish political stunts that work from those that do not. The first essential ingredient in any effective political stunt, dirty or otherwise, is information. At the epicentre of the stunt has to be some kernel of truth that a campaign wishes to communicate to voters. It can be about one's own candidate or one's opponent. But it has to be true.

Opposition research, or oppo, has mushroomed into a significant political cottage industry because of this need for information that is as truthful as it is relevant. As noted in the previous chapter, the best oppo information is that which is found on the public record: bills sponsored by a political opponent, voting records, public statements, spending, tax filings, criminal records, bankruptcy notices and the like. While some politicos do not hesitate to dig for information that is not part of the public record, it is almost always a bad idea. In the case of Stockwell Day's unique perspective on the co-existence of humans and dinosaurs, for instance, I and others toiling on the Liberal Party's campaign were aware of Day's views many months before they became public. We did not attempt to publicize any of what we knew, however, because the media hadn't yet reported on the issue. If we had done so, we would have risked the charge that we were probing a man's personal life, no matter how true the allegations might have been.

In the United States, some political consultants have built careers upon ferreting out information that is not readily found on the public record. The title of one book that has sold well in American political circles, by veteran journalist Louis J. Rose, says it all: *How To Investigate Your Friends and Enemies*. In his slender volume, Rose describes how to glean information by scrutinizing real estate documents, learning the identities of the owners of numbered companies, investigating business deals and using freedom of information legislation. Another U.S.-based group, the Centre for Public Integrity, publishes a book titled *Citizen Muckraking*. It details how to access information on the public record, as well as how to legally tape a telephone conversation (get the parties' consent), intercept a cellular phone communication (illegal in most jurisdictions) or place hidden video cameras (again, almost never, because of the risk of a civil or criminal charge of trespass).

I believe that political consultants should not seek out—or use—information not readily found on the public record, for a stunt or any other purpose. Scandals, embarrassments and improprieties are best served up by reporters, not consultants working in backrooms. Leaking the public record scandalous stuff to reporters, so that they can decide what to do with it, is an integral part of the political game. Sometimes it is done for revenge, sometimes to make the leader feel like a big player, sometimes to float a "trial balloon"—to determine whether a proposal would enjoy some support. Often, leaks are done to damage the other side. If it was obtained from the public record—and if it is timely and accurate—it not only *can* be leaked, it *should* be.

The second essential ingredient in any good political stunt is relevance. It is not enough that one's allegation is true, it also has to be compelling to the voting public. In today's media environment, where consumers of news are bombarded with an endless stream of imagery and information, the competition for a position on the elusive "public agenda" is fierce. Press releases and press conferences are largely the vestiges of another political era; for the most part, they are ignored by reporters. As commentators like Shanto Iyengar and Bill Fox have written, television has revolutionized the way in which politics is reported by the media. It is, in fact, the way in which most voters obtain information about the choices they will make on voting day. Television, writes Iyengar, an expert on negative campaigning, is "news that matters." If a campaign, whether national or local, hopes to get its message out, it needs to get on television. Therefore, the campaign needs a strategy that understands television, and is capable of capturing television's attention. That is why stunts have become more and more commonplace in political campaigns: television loves visuals, and policy discussions are rarely visual.

Chickens and Pinocchio are two hackneyed visual stunts that have been frequently deployed to capture the attention of television cameras. For example, as I had done with Conservative Prime Minister Kim Campbell in 1993, to mock her refusal to debate a multibillion-dollar purchase of combat helicopters, many others have made use of the partisan in a chicken-suit gag. Ohio Republicans, for example, have sent a six-foot-tall singing chicken to an upscale Democratic event in Cleveland, to present a candidate with a Liberal of the Year Award. And in 1996, B.C. Liberal campaign manager Greg Lyle developed a devastating spot depicting NDP Premier Glen Clark with a nose that grew, like Pinocchio, every time the narrator recounted another one of his falsehoods. The Pinocchio stunt has been used many times before, however, such as in the celebrated 1989 New Jersey gubernatorial race by Democratic Congressman Jim Florio, as well as in the 1999 Israeli prime ministerial contest, where visitors to Ehud Barak's Web site could watch as Benjamin Netanyahu's nose grew.

The third and final ingredient in a good political stunt is difficult to define, but is best likened to effectiveness. Not only must there be a true story at the centre of the stunt, and not only must it be relevant to the voter: it must also be effective. But what is an effective political stunt? An example of what is *not* effective, perhaps, may provide one answer.

In July 2000, the Reform Alliance, apparently weary of my public criticisms of both the party and its leader, Stockwell Day, developed a section of its official Web site called "Spinning Warren's Web." The section even featured a small graphic of my head, superimposed on the body of a six-legged spider on its web. In the first instalment in the running stunt, the Reform Alliance declared: "The Chrétien Liberals, fearing the surging popularity of Stockwell Day and the Canadian Alliance, have hired 1997 Liberal loser-turned-lobbyist Warren Kinsella as their professional purveyor of paranoia . . . Warren can find vast right-wing conspiracies at work in any gathering of two or three people to the political right of Joe Clark, and is not one to let facts get in the way of truth." For a short period during the summer of 2000, then, whenever I commented on a policy position taken by Day or his party, the Reform Alliance would issue a new "Spinning Warren's Web" release.

When contacted about the Web site by Robert Fife, a political writer for the *National Post*, I shrugged it off. In the resulting story, Fife wrote:

> Mr. Kinsella, who has a reputation as a no-holds-barred political infighter who helped run the Liberal war room in the 1993 election, took the attack on his credibility with grace and a touch of humour. 'I just think it's hilarious. It's a great kick, and it's kind of a compliment,' he said. 'I guess the boys in the Alliance have kind of forgotten who the real adversary is and it ain't Warren Kinsella. It's Jean Chrétien.' An Alliance official said the decision to set up a rapid-response team was made yesterday to counter the Liberals' plans to 'resort to fear and drive-by smear.' 'When these accusations come, we are going to knock them out of the park, fast and furious. We are going to chip away at the credibility of Warren,' the official said.

That may have been the plan, but it didn't seem to work out that way. The stunt was not very effective, most journalists conceded, because it had a venomous tone, and because it reflected a poor strategy—going after someone whose name was not going to be appearing on a ballot. The only places where "Spinning Warren's Web" was receiving glowing reviews, in fact, were on the Internet portals of the neo-Nazi Freedom-Site and British Holocaust denier and racist David Irving.

Interestingly, in May 2001, a Guelph, Ontario, anti-racist activist named Matthew Lauder revealed that he had infiltrated a number of far-right groups over a period of two years. In a story he wrote and posted on the Internet, he alleged that the Alliance had shared information about me with the likes of Paul Fromm and Marc Lemire. Fromm is a former schoolteacher who lost his job due to his involvement with neo-Nazi groups. Lemire is the "Web master" of the largest Canadian Internet hate site, the Freedom-Site. In his exposé, Lauder writes:

> ... Fromm mentioned that there was "much communication" between him and the Alliance regarding the building of a "file" to put Warren Kinsella, a Liberal Party advisor and author, into disrepute. According to Fromm, the Canadian Alliance wanted revenge for an article criticizing the party. Fromm suggested that they were actively gathering information for the Canadian Alliance to "ruin Kinsella's reputation."
>
> During the summer of 2000, the Canadian Alliance published an article on its Web site criticizing Kinsella.... Likewise, Lemire posted a number of articles that attacked Kinsella and urged interested readers to contact the Canadian Alliance Party.
>
> However, involvement by Fromm and Lemire in the Canadian Alliance did not stop at the alleged advisory level; they were, in fact, full

voting members of the party. But the honeymoon with the Alliance came to a quick end in the early fall of 2000. Fearing a scandal, the National Council of the Canadian Alliance quickly terminated Fromm's membership..."

The *National Post* investigated Lauder's revelations in June 2001. Lemire told reporter Jonathon Gatehouse: "As for if we were approached by people in the Canadian Alliance to give them information on Kinsella . . . Well, that's between us and them." One of the Alliance's veteran MPs—rural Alberta's Leon Benoit—told Gatehouse that he had met with Fromm twice on Parliament Hill to discuss immigration. Even more surprising was that Benoit said he saw nothing wrong with meeting with a man long associated with white supremacist and neo-Nazi groups. As for the Alliance, no public comment was made on whether its officials had exchanged information with Fromm and Lemire about me.

Notwithstanding the Alliance's lack of success with the web stunt, Day apparently authorized another version of "Spinning Warren's Web" that quickly threw the Alliance leader and his party into damage control mode. In the release, Day insinuated, possibly because I had been so critical of his apparent homophobia, that I was "obsessed" with homosexual sex. On the same day the release appeared on the Internet, a number of lawyers contacted me to counsel that I sue for defamation; some even offered their services. I decided to give the Reform Alliance an opportunity to withdraw the statement. Repeated phone calls to Day's chief of staff, Rod Love, were never returned; the former chief, Rick Anderson, sympathized but said he could offer no solution. As a last resort, I contacted the Reform Alliance leader's amiable director of communications, Jim Armour, who, after a five-minute conversation in which I suggested that the "obsessed with homosexual sex" line was over the top, agreed to quickly remove it, which he did.

Sensing that I might be able to turn "Spinning Warren's Web" into an advantage, I asked the *Ottawa Citizen* whether I could contribute an opinion column on the stunt. The newspaper's editors quickly agreed. This is some of what the *Citizen* printed, under the headline "Diary of a Grit Arachnid":

> My transformation into a spider was rather sudden. There I was one day, walking along on two legs and (mostly) minding my own business, and—all of a sudden—whammo! CCRAP leader Stockwell Day transformed me into an arachnid.
>
> I am not making this up. It is there for all the world to observe. Check out CCRAP's nifty web site, at www.canadianalliance.ca, and you will easily locate an entire section devoted to Yours Truly, Spiderman.... There is even a little graphic of my smiling head, superimposed upon a six-legged spider, scooting across a web. (Yes, six legs.)...
>
> While all of this spider stuff delighted my four-year-old, who rather liked the idea that Daddy's head can now be found on an insect's body, I must confess that I was puzzled. Had Mr. Day's much-touted 'freedom train' perhaps gone off the rails? Had he lost his proverbial caboose? Was his beloved 'agenda of respect' now something else entirely?
>
> ... The one who I appear to irritate the most [with my public criticisms of Reform Alliance policies], however, seems to be Mr. Day. That, I

fear, is the reason that he is spending your tax dollars to obtain transcripts of every word that I utter, or write. It is also why, I surmise, he calls me a 'loser,' 'character assassin,' 'sleazy,' 'scare-monger,' 'chief drive-by smear artist' and (my personal favourite) 'creepy.' . . .

Personally (as you have no doubt surmised), I am rather enjoying all of this attention. My book about organized racism, *Web of Hate*, is coming out in a third edition in the Spring of 2001, so this incessant web talk is good for sales. My daughter thinks it is swell that her father is a spider. And, in partisan terms, I am also pleased to note that Mr. Day believes that I am his principal opponent, and not Jean Chrétien—the most popular Prime Minister ever.

But, as a proud Grit arachnid, I remain bewildered about one thing: would you vote for a dummy who doesn't even know that spiders have eight legs, not *six*?"

After that, "Spinning Warren's Web" quickly fell into disuse, then disappeared. Stockwell Day and the Reform Alliance, it appears, had finally remembered that their principal opponent was a popular Liberal prime minister, not one of his more enthusiastic supporters.

Weeks later, in his Washington office, James Carville listens to an account of the Reform Alliance's attempt at political stunt-making. When he hears that the stunt targeted a political consultant, and not an actual *politician*, he laughs aloud. "Shee-it," he says. "I think all of that is kind of borderline silly. That's having a campaign about a campaign. You have to have a campaign about issues, about hopes and dreams and fears and that kind of stuff. Right? That's what it's all about. When you forget that, you lose!"

Again: Dirty tricks don't work because, well, they're *dirty*. Political stunts, if delivered with a dollop of humour and a sense of timing, can be highly effective in an election campaign. But the message that lies at the centre of the stunt has to be relevant to voters; it has to make them *think*. If the message is meaningless, or too obscure, voters will regard the stunt-makers as a bunch of political people acting like jackasses.

Which, of course, is a thought that occurs to voters quite a lot.

CHAPTER SIX

THE NEW COWBOYS
... or, how to use a phone (or a modem)
to reach out and beat someone

As one might expect of a former chairman of the Republican National Committee (RNC), and perhaps even a lawyer from Yazoo City in Mississippi, Haley Barbour is the very picture of calm. It is the 2000 Republican National Convention in Philadelphia, and it is summer, and it is hot. Standing in a noisy corridor at the Loews Philadelphia Hotel, shifting from one foot to the other, pausing to shake hands with those walking by, Barbour does not look as though he is easily fazed. He is, after all, the man who in 1994 single-handedly rebuilt the G.O.P. in Congress. And he is also the man who ensured that the party narrowly recaptured the White House with George W. Bush in the fall of 2000, by being better organized on the ground, in places like Florida.

Barbour grins, or shares a quick joke, with some of the conservative partisans who pause to exchange a few words with the man who, possibly more than any other alive, knows how to get their fellow Republicans elected. He is of average height, and of slightly more-than-average weight. He has thick, greying hair and a Mississippi accent that is as smooth and sweet as syrup. He is funny—quipping that Bill Clinton could sell "Fords to Chevrolet dealers." He is partisan, too—noting that Clinton is also the "factually challenged" president. Haley Barbour is a diehard, never-give-up Republican. He always has been.

Between handshakes and small talk, Barbour returns his attention to his Canadian acquaintance and is unfailingly polite in answering questions, even though the questions concern negative campaigning and how to make use of some of the new technology to go neg in a manner that is effective. Barbour is clearly familiar with all of the methodologies mentioned by his inquisitor—the Internet as a communications tool, push polling, frugging—but he is wary. As long as he is on the record, he will only say that negative campaigning does indeed work, and that technology helps to ensure that it works. But the chief practitioners of negativity, he says with a straight face, are the Democrats of Al Gore, and not the Republicans of George W. Bush. "There's no doubt," Barbour says. "Negative campaigns and negative ads work. But they don't always work. There is a risk involved. And Gore, particularly, is subject to that risk because he has such high negatives going in."

All around Barbour there is an awful lot of things going on. The convention that will see the election of George Bush and Dick Cheney to the position of G.O.P. standard-bearers is a cyclone of activity and sights and sounds. An estimated 45,000 people are in attendance at the convention, with just under 5,000 of those being actual delegates and alternates. Outnumbering them are 10,000 or so volunteers, and 15,000 accredited media people, as well as thousands of observers and retailers. Over at the convention centre, the Republicans have put on something they have called "PoliticalFest." Those who are so inclined can get their picture taken stepping out of the door of an Air Force One set, or sitting behind the desk of a fake Oval Office, complete with vases filled with flowers and important-looking papers placed here and there. Beneath red, white and blue banners, Ronald Reagan's shiny black armoured limousine has been put on display, as well as one of Pat Nixon's gowns. There is a pair of Teddy Roosevelt's shoes, and a seat liberated from the Ford Theatre, where John Wilkes Booth assassinated Abraham Lincoln. In the streets between the hotel, the convention centre and the Comcast-Spectacor's First Union Centre, where the actual voting and speechifying are taking place, there are a lot of protestors, but they are generally behaving themselves. The delegates are overwhelmingly white and clean-cut.

Haley Barbour, born in 1948 in the sweaty Mississippi Delta, surveys what he sees, but does not let on whether he thinks it is good or not. He believes George W. Bush will win, but he is cautious. He believes Republicans will re-take Congress, but he is cautious about that, too. He is generally well known for this refusal to engage in an overabundance of G.O.P. jingoism. On the contrary: when the party makes mistakes—and it has made plenty in the past decade or so—Barbour will not hesitate to be critical. Around the time Bill Clinton clobbered Bob Dole in the 1992 presidential race, and around the same time he became chairman of the RNC, Barbour warned Republicans of the dangers associated with policies that many Americans considered to be extremist. Like Dole, Barbour is a "big tent" Republican—meaning, a Republican who tries to broaden the G.O.P. base beyond wealthy, white heterosexual males. "We need our heads examined if we let abortion be the threshold issue of Republicanism," he says. In his maiden speech as G.O.P. chair, he bluntly assessed what he saw at his party's 1992 convention in Houston: "We came across as shrill, strident and hard-edged."

In person, Barbour is funny and charming. He listens carefully to every question that is posed to him, nodding slowly. When he is asked about push polling, however, the nodding stops. "You know," he drawls, his eyes diplomatically searching the ceiling of the Loews Hotel, "when I first came along, push polling actually meant something. It was when you took a poll and you'd have pushy questions in it. The purpose of the push poll wasn't to see what someone's position was on an issue. It was to try and poison the environment. And, um . . ." He trails off.

As a Republican bigwig, there is good reason for Haley Barbour to be hesitant about push polling. In early 2000, with the outcome of the nomination for the Republican presidential candidate still far from certain, Barbour's party was seriously bruised by the issue. In February of that year, John McCain accused George W. Bush of push polling in South Carolina; that is, getting his supporters to dial up Republicans and ask them a series of loaded questions calculated to destroy McCain's reputation.

The Bush campaign did not deny that it was asking voters what it called "tough questions" about John McCain. But it strenuously denied that the questions were part of a push poll. To buttress the point, the Bush people released the script of the survey about John McCain. The release did not assist Bush's cause. One question asked respondents how they felt about McCain's "plan" to "increase taxes on charitable contributions to churches, colleges and charities by $20 billion." Another queried whether Americans approved of McCain's "legislation that proposed the largest tax increase in United States history." The survey went on to question whether McCain deserved support, since his "campaign finance proposals would give labour unions and the media a bigger influence on the outcome of elections."

The American Association for Public Opinion Research (AAPOR) defines a push poll as something very much like what George W. Bush's campaign authorized in South Carolina. Says AAPOR in its code of ethics:

> A push poll is a telemarketing technique in which telephone calls are used to canvass potential voters, feeding them false or misleading 'information'

> about a candidate under the pretense of taking a poll to see how this 'information' affects voter preferences. In fact, the intent is not to measure public opinion, but to manipulate it—to 'push' voters away from one candidate and toward the opposing candidate. Such polls defame selected candidates by spreading false or misleading information about them. The intent is to disseminate campaign propaganda under the guise of a legitimate public opinion poll.

The issue, in the South Carolina controversy, was about whether the critical information passed along was in any way misleading or inaccurate. At its depths, the South Carolina contretemps saw McCain claiming that a 14-year-old boy had been reduced to tears by one of the Bush push pollsters, who had called the war hero "a cheat, a liar and a fraud." Perhaps even Haley Barbour, in a candid moment, would have been forced to acknowledge that the "facts" underpinning the Bush campaign poll were not entirely above reproach.

For example, McCain's relevant legislative record as a senator was as follows: he had attempted to oblige tobacco companies to pay some $500 billion of smoking-related medical costs. He had worked to remove loopholes and deductions from the United States tax code. He had made an effort to ban unregulated contributions to political parties, including his own. In the hands of the Bush campaign's spinners, and its alleged push-pollsters, those legislative measures became "the largest tax increase in United States history," an increase "on taxes on charitable contributions to churches," and a way to "give labour unions and the media a bigger influence on the outcome of elections." Were the Bush campaign's characterizations of McCain unfair, or inaccurate? The best judge, in this case, is the best political columnist in the United States—

William Saletan of the online magazine *Slate*, who dismissed the Bush poll as a "sham." Wrote Saletan: "[The Bush poll's] purpose is not just to measure public opinion but to alter it, by figuring out how to deliver a message full of negative, distorted information that will push voters away from McCain... Is push-polling worse than 'real' polling? Yes, because it's more dishonest."

While dishonest, push polls are not nearly as rare as they should be. It seems that whenever an election is hotly contested—and, more frequently, whenever political consultants temporarily take leave of their senses—push polling occurs. In March 1999, for example, a pollster closely associated with the Canadian Reform Alliance (as well as the Progressive Conservatives of Ontario premier Mike Harris) was forced to apologize to the Jewish community when he developed a push poll containing some offensive questions. Tory pollster John Mykytyshyn apologized "unreservedly" to Jews in the Toronto-area riding of Thornhill for actually asking residents if a candidate's involvement with the Canadian Jewish Congress would affect their voting decision. Another question devised by Mykytyshyn asked if voters would be influenced by the knowledge that a candidate "was the son of Holocaust survivors." (The Liberal candidate in the riding, coincidentally enough, was the son of a Holocaust survivor, and was the brother of the president of the Canadian Jewish Congress.) In a letter to the congress, Mykytyshyn claimed that the push poll developed by his Canadian Voter Contact firm had "a valid research objective underpinning [it, but] there is absolutely no excuse for the insensitivity of questions that caused concern in your community." Mykytyshyn was fired from the provincial Tory campaign team after the controversy became public. (A year later, he was fired from the Canadian Alliance executive for calling Atlantic Canadians "lazy.")

A push poll is really not a poll at all. It is a political communication technique, or, sometimes, a telemarketing technique, disguised as a poll.

Unlike legitimate public opinion surveys, push polls are not developed to collect information; they are, instead, designed to disseminate information (or rumours, or even lies) unhelpful to an opponent. Because push pollsters must reach a large number of voters to be effective—usually thousands, as opposed to hundreds contacted for a standard survey of public opinion—push polls are very brief. Although he did not say so in his interview in Philadelphia, Haley Barbour and his fellow Republicans might have known that George W. Bush's alleged South Carolina push poll was, at a minimum, 20 minutes in length. Even with a campaign as well financed as Bush's, spending that much time with thousands of potential voters is neither cost-effective nor smart. If the South Carolina effort was in fact a push poll, it was a poorly designed one. Suspicious voters can spot push polls not only by their abbreviated length; if a polling firm does not clearly identify itself at the outset, the chances are good that a push poll is about to follow.

Almost all political polling, to be fair, contains information that is critical of an opponent. The information considered negative is presented to potential voters, or to potential consumers of a product, to determine what kinds of messages or facts will affect a voting or buying decision. Russell D. Renka, a Missouri political scientist and expert on polling techniques, emphasizes this point: "Be warned—it is perfectly legitimate for good polls to address the most touchy or delicate subject. In fact, those are often the things most worthwhile to know and understand." Most often, exploring touchy subjects with polling is the means by which a campaign will decide how (or if) it should launch an attack on some aspect of an opponent's record.

In 1994, Haley Barbour lived up to his reputation as a smart political operator, and developed one of the first systems to "inoculate" against push polling. Barbour recalled that in 1982, 1986 and in later years, the Democrats and their allies in the labour movement had, in his view, made use of push polling, with great effectiveness, to frighten senior citizens about what Republican candidates would do to Social Security. By 1990, the Republican National Committee had developed an early warning system in certain states to alert G.O.P. operatives about Democrat efforts to fear-monger on the issue. By 1994, Larry Sabato reports in *Dirty Little Secrets*, Barbour concluded: "What the Hell, we know they're going to do it, they've shown their hand, so let's go on out there and take remedial action before they go after us." At a cost of $800,000 Barbour developed his inoculation plan. More than 25,000 seniors would be called in fifty key swing districts in the Midwest of the United States, and read the following message: "Republicans are for the Balanced Budget Amendment, and you are going to get called and told that Republicans will cut Social Security to balance the budget. But Republicans won't touch Social Security. So when you get called, I hope you will tell whoever calls that you know it's not true." The inoculation worked, and the Republicans captured Congress.

Push polls are not the only unethical weapons in a campaign's arsenal. While few politicos wish to discuss the practice, polling agencies exist, on both sides of the border, that will produce results that reflect not the political reality but what their client wants. Following the 1984 federal Liberal leadership campaign, for example, many supporters of candidate Jean Chrétien believed their man was sandbagged by polling done by agencies that had "torqued" the results—manipulated the numbers to make Chrétien look bad and make John Turner look good. The danger inherent in such practices is obvious; notwithstanding the attempt to fool Grit delegates and the media, John Turner went down to one of the worst election results in the history of the Liberal Party in September 1984. False polling numbers may be persuasive to delegates at political conventions, but they are far less meaningful to voters.

Frugging is another polling method whose absence could probably improve democracy. Frugging—or, Fundraising Under the Guise of Polling—are telephone calls, or letters, made to solicit funds, but not information. Frugging, like push polling, pretends to be some sort of a survey. It is a technique that some political parties use, but also more than a few advocacy groups and charities. In the United States, the Marketing Research Association has led the charge against frugging. In one of its bulletins on the practice, the association states: "The use of a poll to conduct fundraising has raised the distrust of the public to a point where they refuse to cooperate with researchers trying to obtain the opinions of any number of issues, including political campaigns, and governments." In Canada, the anti-frugging battle is led by the National Society of Fundraising Executives (NSFRE), which strongly condemned the practice late in 2000.

The Canadian Civil Liberties Association is one of many advocacy groups that recently engaged in what the NSFRE considered to be frugging. In a six-page "survey" on civil liberties, mailed out with a six-day time limit to reply, and signed by respected author June Callwood, one question asks: "Do you agree or disagree with the following statement: 'Citizens need a strong, respected organization like the Canadian Civil Liberties Association to protect our freedom of expression, privacy and other vital rights and freedoms'?" Those who agreed were then asked to endorse this statement: "Yes, I believe the Canadian Civil Liberties Association is Canada's most prestigious, principled and effective voice for the protection of my civil liberties." Respondents were thereafter offered an opportunity to contribute an amount ranging from $35 to $1,000 to "protect and enhance my threatened rights and freedoms." When Alan Borovoy, the principled group's general counsel, was questioned by the NSFRE about his group's apparent use of frugging, he replied that the objective had merely been to recruit new members. The NSFRE suggested a legitimate poll might be a better course, but Borovoy replied that his organization "couldn't afford" one.

Sugging and mugging, meanwhile, are practices related to frugging, but are less relevant to political campaigns. Sugging campaigns are devised to sell a product or service to someone, while mugging communications are devised to use "polling" tactics to market something.

Despite the occasional lapses, which include push polling, frugging, sugging and mugging, the majority of public opinion polling in North America, political or otherwise, is conducted ethically. The reasons for this vary, but most political consultants seem to agree that questionable practices are simply wrong. In *Campaign Warriors*, an academic study of the business of political consulting by James Thurber and Candice Nelson, the authors present an exhaustive survey of the views of American campaign operatives. In 200 in-depth telephone interviews with senior political consultants, Thurber and Nelson found that more than 71 per cent of consultants regard push polls as unethical. More Republicans than Democrats considered push polling to be acceptable, but one function of these kinds of "polls"—scaring voters, or suppressing voter turnout for one's opponent—is seen as acceptable by more Democrats than Republicans. Thurber and Nelson conclude: "This evidence is a strike against the conventional wisdom that political consultants only care about winning, and will try to win at all costs." Push polling, and frugging, and all of its derivatives, are clearly dangerous to those who make use of them. But what of legitimate polling? Is real polling—a multibillion-dollar business globally—something with which voters should be concerned?

There is no doubt that good polling and good pollsters are beloved by political consultants, because both are inevitably needed to assist any political campaign in securing victory. For nearly 200 years, politicians and their campaign teams have flat out adored solid public opinion research. The first known published political poll showed up in the *Harrisburg Pennsylvanian* newspaper in 1824. In the survey, popular support was measured—"without discrimination of parties," the newspaper declared—and Andrew Jackson was found to be the most likely winner in his presidential race against John Quincy Adams. Jackson eventually did win, but the results were ultimately decided in a narrow vote in the House of Representatives. Following 1824, such polls were not uncommon in the United States, and were sometimes even commissioned by newspapers. (Hotels commissioned polls, too: guests registering for the night were asked to indicate their presidential choice.)

These embryonic political polls all suffered from one principal shortcoming: the pollsters made no attempt to ensure that their results reflected an accurate sample of the voters they had contacted. Put simply, the "sample" used by the pollsters did not properly reflect the total voter population: the raw polling data had not been weighted to ensure that the final result did not overrepresent the opinions of a particular demographic category or geographic region. The most notorious case of bad sampling came in 1936, when the much-read *Literary Digest* declared in a section titled "America Speaks" that Kansas governor Alfred Landon would defeat Franklin Delano Roosevelt in that year's presidential race by a factor of two to one. (He didn't.) To arrive at its erroneous result, the *Digest* had mailed out an incredible ten million ballots, and received two million replies. The publication's well-publicized error could be traced back to the fact that its mailing list was not made up of registered voters, but phone directories and automobile registrations. In the midst of the Great Depression, it had occurred to no one at the *Digest* that the vast majority of those Americans found on such lists would be well-to-do Republicans, and not a more representative sample of voters. The *Digest* folded the next year.

A better approach to polling, and sampling, came shortly before the *Literary Digest* would destroy its reputation. In 1932, one Mrs. Ola Babcock Miller achieved the distinction of being the first political candidate to employ a scientific, and properly sampled, public opinion poll. Miller, a former newspaper publisher in Iowa, where no Democrat had been elected to high state office since the Civil War, was placed on the party's ticket, but given little hope of success. Miller had a secret weapon, however: her son-in-law, George Gallup, who had just finished his Ph.D. in psychology. Using what he taught himself about proper poll sampling techniques, Gallup determined that his mother-in-law would win. She did, becoming Iowa's secretary of state.

The work of Gallup, and the likes of Elmo Roper, Louis Harris and so on, helped to ensure that public opinion research would become a vital part of the modern political process, or a part, at least, of every well-funded North American political campaign that was to follow in the latter two-thirds of the twentieth century. As any seasoned politico should know, the so-called "horse race" figures that emerge from public opinion polling (e.g., "Who will you vote for on election day?") are interesting but not crucial. What a campaign needs to win, and what good polling hopefully provides, is information on which a political team can base its decisions. These typically focus upon three areas: the candidate, the public and specific topics or issues. For example, a political poll early in a campaign will ask voters whether they have heard about a candidate, and the candidate's opponent. If the answer is yes in both instances, the poll will then try to find out whether the impressions of those candidates are positive or negative, and why.

At the next level, respondents will be probed on more than their impressions about the field of candidates. They will be asked for their views about particular issues, as well. Statements will typically be made about a certain issue—for example, "Nuclear proliferation is a dangerous trend"—and then potential voters will be asked to indicate whether they strongly agree, agree, disagree or strongly disagree. Another important series of questions concern the voters themselves—their age, gender, occupation, income level, place of residence, political affiliation and so on. This helps to determine if a certain issue is important to a certain group of voters, and whether the candidate has a reasonable prospect of attracting those voters by speaking up about that issue.

More than perhaps anyone else in Canada, Greg Lyle understands that the success of a political campaign depends upon good public opinion research and using that research to communicate well to voters, because, at the end of the day, political campaigns are really just about one thing: communicating.

Lyle is considered, in both Conservative and Liberal circles, to be a bona fide strategic genius. More than most, Lyle knows the importance of using public opinion polling to make the right decisions at the right time. He has been a campaign manager for the British Columbia Liberals, a chief of staff to Manitoba's Conservative premier, Gary Filmon, and even, briefly, an adviser to novelist Jeffrey Archer's ill-fated campaign to become London's first mayor.

Sitting in his large office in downtown Toronto, snowflakes drifting past his window, Greg Lyle leans back in his chair and gives an enigmatic smile. He is in his late thirties, bearded, with glasses and a genial manner. It is easy to become intimidated by his obvious intelligence; campaigners from one end of Canada to another recount stories about the formidable amount of political knowledge tucked away in his head. At the moment, he is a partner in Navigator, a fledgling firm led by a small group of Conservative political professionals, who consult with both governments and the private sector. One of his key areas of expertise is knowing how to ascertain, and analyze, what people think. "A weak analysis of [political polling] focuses on what people say," says Lyle. "A strong analysis focuses on *why* they are thinking about voting in a particular way."

There are basically four steps to developing a good political poll. The first is to determine the appropriate sample, that is, avoiding the *Literary Digest* faux pas. How does one identify a very small fraction of a much larger group in such a way that the fraction accurately reflects the composition of the whole? For the most part, random sampling is the answer. If a poll is, as is most often the case, being conducted on the telephone, some kind of random digit dialing computer program will be used. The size of the actual sample is largely determined by how large a margin of error is acceptable, because the smaller the sample, the larger will be the margin for error in the projected results. How much the campaign can afford to spend also helps to determine the sample size; the bigger the sample, the bigger the cost.

The second step is the preparation of a questionnaire. In a push poll, for example, the scrupulously neutral approach usually employed in the development of a good questionnaire is abandoned. While a series of loaded questions may produce results that make a candidate feel good, they do not offer up results that truly reflect public opinion. That is why a campaign must retain a pollster with experience in developing a series of questions that do not dictate a certain result. Says Lyle: "The biggest danger is missing out on something—missing a variable. That is why a good questionnaire is imperative."

The third step in the development of a public opinion poll is to collect the data, that is, to reach out to the voters. This part of the process almost always involves the telephone. Newspaper, magazine, direct mail and Internet surveys tend to elicit results from only the most committed voters, and are therefore highly suspect. While there are some weaknesses associated with the telephone—for example, it is often difficult for a pollster to develop a rapport with a respondent, and the ubiquity of answering machines and unlisted numbers makes it very difficult to actually reach people—it remains the best available technology for collecting public opinion data. Lyle raises another potential danger: "So long as a campaign is using a professional research firm, you won't get many problems. But you get problems when a campaign tries to save money, and uses volunteers. Studies show that biased interviewers will give verbal cues to respondents, and, because people like to get along, they will respond to those cues and suppress vital information."

The fourth and final step is probably the most complex of all: interpreting the numbers. Says he: "In any comprehensive analysis, what we are really interested in is not *what* our campaign support is, but *why*. How do we increase it? How do we avoid losing support? What should we be doing, and what shouldn't we be doing?" He pauses. "Too many campaigns chase their tails: they just react to what is in the paper that day. A good campaign, on the other hand, plans where they are going. And a good plan helps campaigns choose the arguments they are going to push, to get the support that they need."

There are a number of different types of polls. The first has no official name, but is sometimes called the "pre-decision poll." For those who can afford it (and many cannot—a good one may run to more than $20,000), it is a device that helps aspiring politicians to determine whether or not to throw their hat into the proverbial ring. It tests name recognition and an opponent's areas of vulnerability, and it also provides a summary of issues important to the voters, and which way the voters are leaning in their voting intentions. Lyle considers this poll to be one of the most crucial: "The first step is to decide what you have to decide. This kind of poll tells you which is the best campaign to run, if you are going to run."

Another important type of poll is the benchmark—the one poll that a campaign must do if it is to do any polling at all. The benchmark, in the simplest terms, helps campaigns make later decisions about advertising, fundraising, policy platforms and communications strategies.

A third type of survey, called tracking polls, allow campaigns to measure daily fluctuations in public opinion, and to decide whether a decision made earlier had been a good one.

A fourth type of poll, focus groups, is not really a poll at all. Focus groups bring together small groups of people, usually no more than twenty, to discuss a predetermined set of questions, led by a moderator and observed by a cameraperson behind one-way glass. Focus groups take several hours to do properly, and, unlike polls, are not quantitative but qualitative. That means they are used to probe deeper on opinions of the public, but don't necessarily get a statistically accurate sampling of selfsame public opinion.

In a winning political campaign, good polling, and good focus groups, are crucial. In late 1999, Greg Lyle and other Canadian political consultants were invited to help prepare Jeffrey Archer for a run at London's mayoralty. In a confidential series of memos Lyle prepared for Archer, he described the "five major tasks" facing the British Conservative stalwart: strategy development, policy assessment, communications testing, targeting and tracking. In each case, Lyle underscored the need for a solid research base. In one memorandum, Lyle wrote:

> Effective polling doesn't just satisfy our curiosity about the political environment, it provides the campaign with the information needed to ensure the campaign's key decisions are informed decisions... What arguments work best to build support for Archer? What arguments work best to take support away from any opponents? What contrasts work best in comparing Archer to his opponents to build the ballot question? Who are our target voters?

Archer abruptly withdrew from the mayoralty race in the fall of 1999, when it was discovered that he had persuaded a friend to provide him with a false alibi in a defamation case many years earlier. The case related to a newspaper's claims that Archer had spent a night with a prostitute; the alibi witness assisted Archer in his successful lawsuit against the newspaper and the prostitute, and in obtaining a judgment for millions of pounds.

Tracking polls, questionnaires and sample sizes, as well as confidential memoranda to Jeffrey Archer aside, what possible relevance do public opinion polls have to those who are not political consultants? Do they matter to real people?

For many years, debates have raged amongst pollsters, politicos and media types about whether polls are actual communication vehicles; that is, does the reporting of a poll result have some kind of impact on voting decisions? It would seem most governments believe this is the case. In many Western democracies, for example, the reporting of polls is often restricted during electoral writ periods, presumably because election bureaucrats fear their impact. And, during most election campaigns, parties regularly leak polls to the media in order to give the impression of momentum or to counter a suspicion that a campaign is in trouble. Pollsters, meanwhile, generally maintain the public position that there is no evidence to show that publicity about surveys has an additional effect on public opinion. Privately, however, they will admit the reverse. They know that voters read polls, and that polls influence voters' thinking, particularly near the end of a campaign.

Jean Chrétien, for one, believes that the simple reporting of poll numbers by the media can be an effective communication tool. And he should know: he has more than 30 years of experience in national politics, and is the most popular prime minister in the history of polling. In his autobiography, *Straight from the Heart*, Chrétien rejects notions that polls are benign. He writes: "While it is still debatable whether [polls] reflect instability or cause it, no one can doubt that they have changed the electoral process. Every time they fluctuate, great careers and important policies go up and down with them. The media distribute them as news items, yet their effect is incredible."

Greg Lyle scoffs at the suggestion that political polls are mere "snapshots" of public opinion, or that surveys do not influence voting decisions. "Chrétien is right," says Lyle, who has done battle with Chrétien's Liberal Party more than once. "Polls make a difference, in three ways. One, if your candidate is getting a very low poll result, it becomes very hard to be taken seriously. Polls are a key way for telling someone whether a party is a viable choice on election day. Two, polls create momentum—and momentum can spell life or death. Anybody who has ever worked on a campaign knows that. Thirdly and finally, polls create an effect on the media, and how they report about you. They frame the dialogue."

And framing the dialogue, of course, is what winning political campaigns are all about.

The biggest political story of the nineties arrived, in the early morning hours of Sunday, January 18, 1998. It did not appear on the front pages of the *Washington Post*, or the *New York Times*, or the *Globe and Mail*. No: it first appeared on the Internet. The story was written on a battered old 486 computer in a dingy apartment in a part of Hollywood not often visited by tourists. Here is what it said:

> NEWSWEEK KILLS STORY ON WHITE HOUSE INTERN
> BLOCKBUSTER REPORT: 23-YEAR OLD, FORMER WHITE
> HOUSE INTERN, SEX RELATIONSHIP WITH PRESIDENT
> **World Exclusive** **Must Credit the DRUDGE
> REPORT**
>
> At the last minute, at 6 p.m. on Saturday evening, newsweek magazine killed a story that was destined to shake official Washington to its foundation: A White House intern carried on a sexual affair with the President of the United States!
>
> The drudge report has learned that reporter Michael Isikoff developed the story of his career, only to have it spiked by top newsweek suits

hours before publication. A young woman, 23, sexually involved with the love of her life, the President of the United States, since she was a 21-year-old intern at the White House. She was a frequent visitor to a small study just off the Oval Office where she claims to have indulged the president's sexual preference. Reports of the relationship spread in White House quarters and she was moved to a job at the Pentagon, where she worked until last week.

The young intern wrote long love letters to President Clinton, which she delivered through a delivery service. She was a frequent visitor at the White House after midnight, where she checked in the wave logs as visiting a secretary named Betty Curry, 57. The drudge report has learned that tapes of intimate phone conversations exist. The relationship between the president and the young woman became strained when the president believed that the young woman was bragging about the affair to others. NEWSWEEK and Isikoff were planning to name the woman. Word of the story's impeding release caused blind chaos in media circles; time magazine spent Saturday scrambling for its own version of the story, the drudge report has learned...

Not so long afterwards, Lucianne Goldberg lets loose with a throaty laugh, thickened by too much coffee and too many years of Marlboro Lights (smoked using an 18-carat Dunhill holder from Harrods, no less). She has just been asked whether there is any chance that the

Internet posting by her "very good friend" Matt Drudge on January 18, 1998—about a president of the United States having a tawdry affair with a naive young White House intern, and the history that it helped to create—will ever be repeated again anytime soon. "That was a huge, huge story," she says, ensconced in her West Side Manhattan office, where her eponymous Web site registers hundreds of thousands of hits every week. "I don't think there'll be anything like it for a long, long time."

Does that mean that people in politics have learned their lesson? That they will be wary, now that the Internet is available to punish them for earthly indiscretions? Goldberg finds that one particularly funny. She howls with laughter. "Listen, sweetheart, people in politics are never going to change," says the woman who, along with Monica Lewinsky, very nearly toppled a president. "They're still having affairs, they're still stealing money. But it's the speed of the thing. It's a fact: with the Internet, we can get it on a Web site and out to a million people in three seconds. And Matt can get it out to more people than that!"

Lucianne Goldberg, a.k.a. Lucianne Steinberger, a.k.a. Lucy Cummings, is like that. Brash, tough, outspoken, she is not one for nuance, or equivocation. She speaks entirely in pithy quotes, all the time. Making use of a mix of Matt Drudge, the Internet, and a sordid political scandal, Goldberg took on a very popular (and powerful) president. That president narrowly escaped impeachment in the U.S. Senate, imperilled his marriage and most probably helped to defeat his Democratic Party successor, Al Gore. But Lucianne Goldberg is still standing, and still smiling—even prospering.

Before the Internet, and before what became known as Zippergate, Goldberg had previously achieved distinction for authoring a few novels of the steamy variety, such as *Madame Cleo's Girls*, which was about a trio of top-rung prostitutes ("Chick stuff," she calls it). She also ghost-authored a few books for others. But what Goldberg knew most of all was her way around the scandal circuit. Born in 1935 in Boston, raised near Washington, she was the daughter of a government physicist. When she got old enough to write, she offered what she likes to call "the dish" in a gossip column for a local paper. She even worked on the presidential campaigns of John F. Kennedy and Lyndon Baines Johnson, and alleges that LBJ tweaked her nipples in a White House elevator.

And then, somewhere along the way, she became a Republican. Tall, buxom and quick-witted, Goldberg became an actual bona fide spy on behalf of Richard Nixon's dark 1972 campaign for president. Goldberg was the Nixon campaign's mole on the campaign plane of Democratic candidate George McGovern. Working under the guise of a reporter for something called the Women's News Service, Goldberg filed dozens of reports on supposed McGovern staff shenanigans to her infamous boss, Washington lawyer Murray Chotiner. She was paid $1,000 a week for her spy work, plus $12,000 for expenses; her code name was "Chapman's Friend," and even Richard Nixon can be heard using that appellation in the White House tapes. Thirty of her salacious reports, dictated to a secretary at Chotiner's firm, can now be found at the U.S. national archives. Later, she described herself as "a human tape recorder" for Richard Nixon's campaign, capturing every detail she could, for maximum political damage.

Many years later, using some new technology and a new set of facts, she did it all over again. This time, her target was Bill Clinton, and her chosen technology was the World Wide Web.

Goldberg had known Linda Tripp, a non-political staffer at the White House, since the summer of 1996. They met because Tripp had been the last person to see White House counsel Vincent Foster alive. Foster, a close friend of the Clintons, had died by his own hand, but right-wing conspiracy theorists insisted it was a homicide. At first, Goldberg wanted Tripp to act as a source for a book about Foster's death; as the two got to know each other, Goldberg thought Tripp might be able to do a White House exposé herself. A single mother living in

Maryland, Tripp had worked under the George Bush and Bill Clinton administrations in a variety of positions, and knew many of the relevant political players. But Goldberg eventually concluded that Tripp could not write, and Tripp was afraid that she would lose her job. They agreed to put the project on the back burner.

A year went by. In the fall of 1997, Tripp told Goldberg an extraordinary story: a reporter from *Newsweek*, Michael Isikoff, following up on tips from his own sources, one of them Goldberg herself, had contacted Tripp to question her about a young woman Tripp knew. The young woman was having sexual liaisons in the Oval Office with the president of the United States (then under a number of investigations by conservative Independent Counsel Kenneth Starr). Tripp wanted Goldberg's advice about what to do.

Certain of two things—one, that Linda Tripp would eventually be called to testify about her Pentagon friend Monica Lewinsky and, two, that no one would believe her testimony—Goldberg decided to push Tripp to tape her telephone conversations with Lewinsky. Otherwise, she said, the Clinton "machine" would destroy Tripp and her family. Tripp apparently accepted Goldberg's advice; she started to secretly tape Lewinsky's recollections about her affair with the president of the United States.

Goldberg arranged for Isikoff and Tripp to meet again. The *Newsweek* reporter sat stone-faced as the two women told him that they possessed tapes of Lewinsky's recollections. In the days that followed, lawyers representing Kenneth Starr targeted Goldberg, Tripp and Lewinsky, seeking confirmation of the affair with Clinton. Tripp, for one, was terrified; so too Lewinsky. Goldberg started calling around for lawyers willing to represent her friend Linda.

As Isikoff was preparing to go to print with his story about the affair—and Kenneth Starr's investigators were scrambling to beat Isikoff with evidence they could possibly use in a prosecution of Bill Clinton for something, anything—Lucianne Goldberg received a call from Matt Drudge. A former paperboy and 7-Eleven shelf stocker, Drudge was in his thirties, and running a Web site out of his basement apartment in Hollywood. His father had bought the computer for him at Radio Shack. Drudge had no university education and no background in journalism. But he had lots of friends like Lucianne Goldberg, people who delighted in feeding him gossip. Along with a few links to newspapers and columnists, he posted tidbits on his Web site, which he called the Drudge Report.

Goldberg has claimed that Drudge had the entire story when he called her at home, around midnight on January 17, 1998. Goldberg says Drudge was seeking confirmation about the Lewinsky story; according to her, she had never spoken to him before. Why Goldberg would so quickly confirm the story to a total stranger named Matt Drudge, a story worth a lot of money in the tabloid press, is difficult to understand. But she insists that she did so because the pair "shared" a hatred of Bill Clinton. She later told the *Washington Post*: "I wasn't going to lie to [Drudge] . . . I mean the man had all the information. He'd already written it when he called me. He read me parts of it. It would have been kind of dumb of me to say, 'Huh?'"

Matt Drudge mused about the story for a few hours, and then he posted it on his Web site. The rest, as they say, is history. The story bearing Monica Lewinsky's name would not have happened at all, says Goldberg, were it not for the wonders of the Internet. "I'll tell you why," she says, lighting another cigarette. "Because it would have gone mainstream and we could not have controlled it. Isikoff had 60 per cent of the story. He would have run with it, and the White House and the liberal establishment would have found a way to spin it and it eventually would have died. They would have been able to go with Monica is a bimbo, Monica is a stalker. They were all set to do that, in fact, and they started doing it . . . They would have been able to co-opt a mainstream newspaper. But they couldn't, if it was squeezed out through the Internet. And that is what happened."

When Drudge's story "squeezed out," as Goldberg puts it, there could be no denying the facts: the Internet had become an integral part of one of the biggest political stories anyone had ever seen. His posting rapidly showed up in countless e-mails, discussion groups and chat rooms. Mainstream media organizations felt that they could not ignore the story. In time—and not a lot of time—more than two million people a day were clicking onto Matt Drudge's Web site to learn the latest about the scandal that gripped the United States for the entirety of 1998. Bill Clinton barely escaped with his political hide, while Drudge got a big book deal and television show. Goldberg got a syndicated radio program and lots of infamy. As a political communications tool, all agreed: the Internet had certainly arrived.

In political campaigns around the globe, the Internet is now used to fundraise, to do opposition research and to communicate with voters and candidates. In the mid-1990s, national campaigns in the United States, Canada and Europe made some use of Web sites. For the most part, however, the sites were novelties, and not many political consultants took the new technology seriously. In early 1998, however, a former professional wrestler named Jesse Ventura decided to enter the gubernatorial race in Minnesota for Ross Perot's Reform Party. A more improbable, and unlikely, candidate one could not find. One of the first things Ventura did was to register a Web site, at www.jesseventura.org, for less than $200.

Phil Madsen, Ventura's Web master, recalls what happened next: "From the first day, our Web site purpose was clear; to produce volunteers, money and votes in support of Jesse Ventura . . . We set out to build and service a base of on-line supporters from which the volunteers, money and votes would come. Early on, Jesse decided the Web site would be operated like a cul-de-sac and not a crossroads. The site would not be a place for people to arrive at and then exit via links we provided. Once people entered our site, we wanted them to stay and look around. No links to external Web sites were provided. Early in the campaign, users would enter the site and view five to seven pages per visit. As election day approached, and as we added more pages to the site, users viewed nine to eleven pages per visit. We had about 2 million hits on the site from February through November, with about 75 per cent coming in the three weeks before and after the election." The Web site did what it was supposed to do, but far beyond Ventura and Madsen's expectations. Ventura's astonishing win, the *New York Times* noted, was "a victory that some attribute to effective use of the Internet as a tool for mobilizing volunteers and voters." Soon, every campaign, large or small, wanted a presence on the World Wide Web.

Most political consultants agree that a Web site needs to be more than visually appealing. It must also reflect the strategy adopted by the overall campaign that has commissioned it. Among the factors that consultants believe are key to good Web sites is rapid response, that is, ensuring that the information found on it is updated within minutes or hours, not days. Also important is the Web site's ability to attract volunteers; for example, Florida governor Jeb Bush picked up more than 1,000 campaign workers in 1998 through on-line recruitment. Another useful dimension is a political Web site's ability to communicate, rapidly and effectively, with the media and supporters. In the November 2000 federal election campaign, for example, all of the major Canadian political parties used their Web sites to contact candidates or to amplify messages in the news media.

But one of the biggest advantages the Internet now offers candidates, far and above anything else, is money. In the first week or so following the 2000 New Hampshire primary, John McCain raised an incredible

$2.6 million on the Internet. In all, McCain, whose campaign consulted with Jesse Ventura's Web master before it got started, raised more than $4.1 million from 40,000 individual donors, not big corporations and lobby groups. While he was still a hot political commodity, McCain's Web site was attracting money to the tune of about $100,000 a day. At that point, more than ten million Americans had visited the McCain Web site. McCain's campaign loved Web fundraising, and not simply because they were raising an astonishing amount of money. The donated dollars, McCain told the media on his tour at the time, were "clean." Almost half came from the wallets and purses of individual citizens who had never before contributed to a campaign; they were not lobbyists. And the fact that donations were paid by credit card was also tremendously helpful; that ensured that monies were immediately available for use by the campaign.

Pierre Bourque, a former Ottawa-area municipal politician, was one of the first in Canada to harness the Internet's political power, and he did so long before Jesse Ventura or John McCain. In 1994, Bourque started writing a column about the Internet in a small-circulation weekly called the *Hill Times*, which has a dedicated following in Parliament Hill's corridors of power. Says Bourque: "Folks would ask me where they could find certain things on-line and they would often suggest sites to me too, and relate experiences to me too. So, one day I decided to compile my favourite bookmarks onto one handy Web site . . . Something went right, because not only did people start coming back to it, and they told their friends and acquaintances about it. [And] all of my user growth has occurred by word of mouth rather than by advertising." Called Bourque's Newswatch, the Web site went on-line in January 1998, the same month Matt Drudge broke the Monica Lewinsky story. The Web site is now visited by tens of thousands of Canadian politicians, consultants and bureaucrats daily. Visually, it resembles the Drudge Report, to which it is sometimes compared. But unlike Drudge, Bourque is no mere purveyor of cybergossip. The *Online Journalism Review*, no less, has called him one of the "top fifty international players in the new media." (Although, it should be noted, Lucianne Goldberg, on her own Web site, describes Bourque as "the Canadian Drudge, Pierre Bourque. If our Canadian posters don't know about this lively page yet, they should click it. It's majorly cool.")

Many of the politicians who regularly visit his Web site, Bourque suggests, do not fully appreciate the Net's tremendous value, particularly in the gathering and dissemination of political information, nasty or otherwise. "Our current crop of elected politicians are, to a large extent, way behind the times in terms of understanding how potent the Internet is now, indeed how powerful it is fast becoming," he says. "They simply don't yet have the day-to-day hands-on experience to gauge its value. But that's a generational thing, which will change as new blood flows into the political class." Conversely, Bourque says he is encouraged by the number of political consultants who now take the Web seriously. These consultants, he says, know that in a twenty-four-hour news cycle, it is imperative to have a Web presence that is quick, newsy and interesting.

A good political Web site needs to be more than a pamphlet handed out door-to-door; it needs to be functional, a tool for both collecting and disseminating information needed to win. The site's home page should be clean and uncluttered. Inside, it is a good idea to offer a list of party officials, and possibly even a riding map, so that potential supporters know who to contact. A list of elected officials is also needed, for obvious reasons. Calendars of events are extremely useful, as is an e-mail hyperlink to campaign headquarters. In one section, a full list of press releases, backgrounders and speeches are vital, and possibly even links to other sites. (Linking is sometimes risky, however: one Liberal cabinet minister in Vancouver found, to her horror, that her site connected constituents to on-line pornography.)

"Elected officials, political parties and backroomers alike have barely scratched the surface of how the Net can heighten relationships with political fundraisers, party membership and Canadians, in general," says Bourque. "In other words, the Internet is an incredibly sophisticated tool and I believe political groups can gain terrific advantage for their agendas with appropriate manipulation of this medium."

Manipulation of voters, many consultants believe, is an unwanted consequence of the Internet's huge growth as a political communications medium. Because Web sites can be established by anybody possessing a modem, a computer and a grudge, the possibilities for on-line maleficence are virtually limitless. In 1996, for example, a mischievous college student established a Bob Dole for President Web page that, at first glance, looked like a genuine site for the Republican presidential candidate. The Web offering was actually designed to defame Dole and harm his campaign. In Canada's last federal election, dozens of political Web sites popped up on the Web designed to attack particular candidates. While the Liberal leader received his fair share of criticism, such as at the caustic www.dumpchretien.com, Stockwell Day was the target of many more on-line roastings. One offensive site depicted Day as Italian fascist leader Benito Mussolini, and unfairly likened his party to Nazism. Other anti-Day prank sights, however, were simply funny: one featured a number of professional animated cartoons of Day, and took good-natured shots at his policies.

The most infamous political Web site of all was designed by the Halifax firm that produces the hit CBC television show *This Hour Has 22 Minutes*. On the site, it was noted that Day and his party favoured the use of national referenda to make legislative changes. The pranksters at *22 Minutes* had therefore come up with a novel referendum question: "We demand that the government of Canada force Stockwell Day to change his first name to Doris." Said the Web page: "If you support Stockwell Day's effort to allow citizen-initiated referenda in Canada, be the first on your block to have a referendum of your own! If you want a national referendum on the very important issue below, please join the online petition. *22 Minutes* and Stockwell Day—Putting democracy back in the hands of the people!" By clicking on a button, surfers were given the opportunity to vote for the Doris Day name change; at its peak, Canadians were indicating their support every three seconds. Approximately one million votes ended up being cast in favour of the change from Stockwell Day to Doris Day. The Web stunt attracted media attention around the world; the premier U.S.-based "serious" political Web site, www.politicsonline.com, highlighted the Day petition in its year-end wrap-up, calling it "wildly successful" and a "neat idea."

Unfortunately, some unofficial Web politics are not nearly as comedic as the *This Hour Has 22 Minutes* petition. According to Phil Noble, the international political consultant who founded www.politicsonline.com, the average Internet user generally tends to be a committed voter, mostly under the age of thirty-five, well educated and with a libertarian and/or conservative bent. This has particularly been the case in Internet chat rooms, bulletin boards and discussion sites. Contributors to these parts of the Web reveal themselves to be often on the fringes of the right wing, expressing opinions in language that can be fairly regarded as vicious and certainly libellous. Lars Nelson of the *New York Daily News* had the most memorable description of the Internet in this regard: it is "a vanity press for the demented."

Other Web troublemakers delight in another approach, called cybersquatting—buying up Internet domain names before legitimate campaigns can do so. In the fall of 2000, one such character bought the domain names of Liberal Party candidates, and demanded a large sum to release them. He was figuratively told to jump in the lake. Pierre Bourque, who runs a well-populated discussion room on his Web site, is familiar with the trend. Says Bourque: "[The essence of the] Web is a gigantic repository of information from official and unofficial sources.

It is a conduit for thought, both enlightened and mischievous, earnest and disingenuous. In many cases, the truth in that vast pool of information lies in the eyes of the beholder. From a political point of view, that allows for the rise of deception, red herrings and disinformation, all powerful tools in that arena where reality can often be defined as a matter of opinion." And political disinformation, Bourque admits, has become a significant problem of late.

For instance, political e-mail dirty tricks—and experts like Bourque agree that e-mail "remains the killer Internet application"—have sprouted like weeds in recent years. In Jesse Ventura's home state of Minnesota, the year 2000 Senate race witnessed a nasty mudslinging match between the state's Republican senator and his Democratic-Farmer-Labour candidate opponent. A series of unpleasant e-mails, written by a person called "Katie Stevens"—but coming from none other than the G.O.P. senator's lead opposition research operative—labelled the Democrat "two faced," among other things too defamatory to reprint. Unbeknownst to the G.O.P. consultants, virtually everything on the Internet is tracked and logged, and the offending e-mails were quickly traced back to the Republican team. As a result, an actual criminal investigation was launched under Minnesota's Fair Campaign Practices Act.

Not all e-mails associated with politics are illicit. During the most recent U.S. presidential race, both leading candidates sent out daily e-mail messages that featured access to snappy-looking pop-up windows, streaming video clips of candidates and mountains of useful information. Millions received the missives and, presumably, were assisted in decisions they made on Election Day. But, as with any technology, there are ample opportunities for abuse.

The Internet-based campaign against the MAI—the Multilateral Agreement on Investment—which was aimed at further liberalizing

THE NEW COWBOYS

trade on a global scale, was, in the view of those who favoured the agreement, an excellent example of such abuse. To those opposed to globalization, it was the MAI itself that represented an abuse. On one point, both sides agree: the international Internet campaign against the MAI was an astounding success.

The anti-MAI drama goes back to 1995, when trade ministers from most of the world's leading industrial economies had been working to hammer out a new worldwide agreement on rules for foreign investment. The ministers expected they would be able to conclude an agreement by the end of 1998. They were wrong.

In political seismological terms, there have been three major Internet events. One was the leak of the Clinton-Lewinsky affair to Matt Drudge by Lucianne Goldberg. The second was the incredible fundraising successes of John McCain. And the third was the derailment of 1999's Seattle MAI talks, by a few thousand activists who knew how to mobilize people using the Internet. Seattle was memorable for its fierce street battles, and for televised clips of astonished-looking trade ministers being prevented from getting out of their hotel rooms, much less meeting.

For many months before the protestors converged on Seattle, anti-globalization forces had been using homemade Web sites and mass e-mailing lists to generate a tremendous amount of support for their cause. The Internet was used to do everything from circulate anti-MAI polemics, to arrange for bed-and-board for those planning to protest in Seattle. Just one Web site, www.indymedia.org's "Battle of Seattle," received nearly two million hits during the ill-fated trade conference. By Seattle's conclusion, trade ministers flew home with no agreement, and with a keener appreciation for the huge potential political power of the Internet. The anti-MAI groups claimed victory.

One of the few politicians who has continued to track the anti-globalization effort on the World Wide Web is a former premier of

Quebec, Pierre Marc Johnson. Now a lawyer in Montreal, Johnson's impressive curriculum vitae suggests that his views are worth heeding; along with his political successes, Johnson is a medical doctor, a lawyer and a professor at McGill University. He has been a vice chair of the Prime Minister's National Round Table on the Environment and the Economy, and he has been an adviser to the Secretary-General of the United Nations Conference on Environment and Development. And, at the moment, he believes that the Internet can transform small advocacy groups into political giants. Seattle proved that, he says.

During a discussion in Toronto, Johnson says: "The Internet allows mobilization; it is as simple as that, particularly for persons whose main mode of work is communicating and networking. It is now possible to do it instantly, efficiently and almost at no cost." The men and women he knows well—the ones who were working towards concluding an MAI agreement—were simply flummoxed by the Internet-based lobby, says Johnson. "It was this unbelievable uproar," he recalls. "They got these e-mails. They got messages from constituents, against the MAI. It was powerful—it was incredibly powerful."

The failure of Seattle as well as the failure of the MAT the year before, he writes, were huge political events, and not simply because trade representatives failed in their drive to develop international trade liberalization rules and freer investment provisions:

> The MAI Seattle debacle was partially caused by the surprise effect of the attack. In Seattle, the use of the Net allowed mobilization of many thousands in the streets. This in turn gave good shots for the 6:00 o'clock TV news. [The Internet's] use also allowed for coalitions, common drafting of positions and press communiqués. The best communicators, from the radical end of the

spectrum, appropriated for themselves the voices of discontent with the WTO negotiations. The power they unleashed gave the impression of a coherent, cohesive and generalized opposition . . . the use of the Net is an instrument of broad mobilization, as long as there is an object to mobilize about.

In Seattle, there was.

Johnson is hesitant to be too critical of the political class, of which he was formerly a very well known member. He gently emphasizes that, even now, "we are all trying to catch up on this stuff." But the fact remains, he says, that politicians, and the people who work for them, are woefully underequipped to deal with the negative implications of Internet activism. "Governments," he says, "are starting to get nervous. They did all of these negotiations [before Seattle] . . . and then they ended up being surprised as hell by what happened there."

The moral in all of this, to the likes of Lucianne Goldberg, is simple. The rules of the game have changed. Given the final word, Goldberg says: "Every political party has their Web site, sure. But political operatives have figured out that the Web, now, is where they can leak stuff. They know it can get stuff out fast. You don't have to go through the bureaucracy at the *Washington Post* or *Time* magazine or the *New York Times* anymore." She laughs her deep, husky laugh.

"We consider ourselves the new cowboys, you know. We don't have to do anything [political activists] used to have to do. As long as it's checked out, we just let it fly. We don't have to ask anyone's permission, ever again."

CHAPTER SEVEN

INK-STAINED WRETCHES AND WRETCHESSES
... or, why all political journalists must die

Political journalists—and I write this as someone who has *been* one, and as someone who has even taught *unsuspecting youngsters* how to be one—are regarded by politicians as duplicitous, lazy, amoral confidence artists. They are seen as cynical, soulless sophists, to a one. If Jesus Christ himself was one of their confidential sources, they would burn him in a New York minute, just to get the scoop on his resurrection.

When political consultants, regardless of party affiliation, age, race, gender or place of origin, are asked about reporters, their eyes will start to look for the nearest exit. When pressed, they will mumble something about how they have plenty of friends who are political journalists, or that there are some reporters who they trust, or that they understand that the media are "professionals" and have a job to do. But put away the tape recorder, get a few beers into them, and the truth will eventually tumble out. Political consultants, and, usually, the politicians they represent, hate political journalists. Hate 'em.

In the past couple of decades or so, relationships between politicos and hacks—never easy to begin with—have deteriorated rather dramatically. Statistics do not lie, generally, and the statistics tell the story. In their 2000 Brookings Institution study called *Campaign Warriors: Political Consultants in Elections*, American University professors James Thurber and Candice Nelson reveal the results of a survey that was, in part, about consultants and reporters. Thurber and Nelson conducted 200 in-depth interviews in 1997 and 1998 with the principals in a number of major U.S. political consulting firms, and found that political activists are "full of negativity" about the news media.

Nearly 70 per cent of political consultants, for example, rated the job that journalists do as "poor" or no better than "fair." It did not matter what party the consultants were affiliated with, the vast majority regarded reporters as stinkers. Only 1.5 per cent described journalists as "excellent." (This works out to be approximately 3 of the 200 consultants interviewed, in case you are wondering.)

The older the consultant, the worse his or her views of the fourth estate. Wrote Thurber and Nelson: "Political consultants who have been around longer develop more concrete attitudes toward the media. The experiences or run-ins [sic] they have had over the years may have reinforced their beliefs about journalists." Reporters and editors in search of a silver lining in this statistical storm cloud may point to one statistic: Thurber and Nelson found that "only 30 per cent" of the consultants polled had actually worked for a media organization. *Ipso facto*, most political flaks cannot be expected to understand the doings of political hacks. But not so fast. Employing tortuous sentence structure, the pair of academics note: "Not only were the consultants who had worked in the media not more likely to rate political journalists more favourably, they actually gave more *negative* [their emphasis] ratings. Seventy-five per cent of those consultants who had worked for the news media, compared to 65 per cent of all other consultants, rated today's political journalists as fair or poor." Of all of the consultants consulted, 50 per cent said journalists were, in fact, getting worse.

Concluded Thurber and Nelson: "Considering the evidence ... the results are striking. Political consultants dislike the media... [They] do not like political journalists." Political consultants must, however, accept one immutable law of nature. They are bound together with media people in perpetuity, metaphorical groom and bride in a diabolic marriage without end. One cannot properly exist without the other. Political consultants need reporters to tell nice stories about the candidates they wish to elect, and, naturally enough, unpleasant stories about their electoral opponents. Political reporters, meanwhile, need consultants to provide them with the stories that sell newspapers and boost ratings.

To endure this relationship—and, if possible, prosper in it—different political consultants have developed different methodologies for dealing with political journalists. As a public service, here are mine:

[
KINSELLA'S TWELVE HANDY TIPS FOR SURVIVING
ENCOUNTERS WITH UNETHICAL, UNSCRUPULOUS,
UNPRINCIPLED POLITICAL JOURNALISTS
]

TIP ONE: THE PRESS IS THE ENEMY

President Richard M. Nixon once declared that the press is the enemy and, on this single occasion, he was right. For any political consultant hoping to remain one, it is essential that he or she recall that reporters are different from the rest of us. Their stock-in-trade is misfortune, conflict and an unkillable distrust of political success. As U.S. television host and former political staffer Chris Matthews puts it in his best-selling book *Hardball*: "Their mission is to produce a good story, and in their business it's generally the bad news that makes the best headlines. Failure, misery, disaster—that's what makes the bells go off in a journalist's nervous system: the kind of story where somebody gets hurt." Don't be the one who gets hurt.

TIP TWO: LEAVE NO CHARGE UNANSWERED

James Carville's rule applies to the words of both political journalists and political opponents, and it has become particularly crucial since the advent of a twenty-four-hour, seven-day-a-week news cycle. Any critical statement offered up by a reporter or the other side, no matter how imbecilic or nonsensical it may seem at first blush, must be taken seriously, and pronto. If the charge appears to be getting ready to blast off into the political stratosphere, then, fight back. Says Carville: "Make sure you go on the offensive right away. Rush the passer. Blitz. Send in the linebackers, send in the cornerbacks. Send the punter in from the sidelines." There are a lot of sports analogies going on there, but Carville's point is a truism. Hit back or lose. In politics, it is fatal to simply shrug off a criticism that may initially seem minuscule or ridiculous, or to wait too long to reply. Barry Goldwater thought Tony Schwartz's "Daisy" spot was ridiculous, too, until it was too late.

TIP THREE: NOTHING IS OFF THE RECORD

If a political staffer says something to a journalist that is "off the record," they are generally right to assume that the journalist will not print or broadcast their identity somewhere. The staffer is wrong to assume that the journalist will not tell a few dozen friends the identity of his or her source later that night at Hooters. If you decide to go ahead and blab, remember to clarify the rules out loud. Speaking to a reporter

INK-STAINED WRETCHES AND WRETCHESSES

on "background" means no use of the source's name, but quotes and vague descriptions of titles are acceptable; "deep background" means no information that can even remotely suggest the identity of the source. ("Sources said" stories are the product of deep backgrounding.) Finally, the most misunderstood rule—"off the record"—means just that: nothing said by a source can be used. Period. But, before you step forward to play the role of someone's Deep Throat, it is worth remembering that, sooner or later, you will be outed. Despite all evidence to the contrary, political parties are filled with smart people, and some of them are very good at figuring out the name of a particular reporter's "anonymous source." And remember this, too: if a reporter thinks the story you leaked to them is better than any story you will give to them in the future, they will not hesitate to burn you. So proceed with caution.

TIP FOUR: POLITICS IS WAR

That's what journalists think, anyway. Notwithstanding the reality—and the reality is that voters say they are fed up to the teeth with stories about politicians' endless squabbling—political reporters cannot resist battlefield rhetoric. To them, mortality itself is at stake. Take, for example, some of the verbiage that flew around at the time of the 1992 New Hampshire primary. From CNN on February 13: "[Paul] Tsongas knew when he took the lead, they'd be *gunning for him*. Tom Harkin was the first to *open fire*... The stream of *salvos* into the Tsongas camp may only be *light artillery* compared to what's ahead." From NBC the next day: "[Clinton's] opponents are like sharks with *blood in the water*..." From *Newsweek* on February 10: "[Clinton] will slowly *bleed to death, die of a thousand cuts* in the Summer and Fall..." You get the picture. Every smart political consultant knows that defeats are never as final, or their causes as definitive, as reporters think. But, if one's campaign ever hopes to get coverage, describing differences in apocalyptic terminology is never a bad idea. So come out with guns a-blazing, as it were. The media will lap it up.

TIP FIVE: KEEP IT SIMPLE, STUPID

The KISS rule existed long before Carville tacked a version of it ("It's the economy, stupid") on the wall of Bill Clinton's War Room in Little Rock. There are two reasons why consultants need to always ensure their communications are really, really, really simple. First, an overwhelming majority of voters are rushing kids to hockey games, ballet classes, or trying to get to work on time. They do not have enough hours in the day (or night) to sleep, let alone research party platforms. Voters want to know what they want to know fast, and in simplistic terms (which is another reason negative political ads work with them: they are simple and contain a single digestible fact). Second, political reporters are divisible into two categories: they are either lazy or busy. Either way, reporters do not have the time or the inclination to analyze and synthesize reams of policy documents. Keeping one's message simple does not imply that voters or reporters lack the grey matter to understand; it merely acknowledges that they lack the *time*.

TIP SIX: GET IT RIGHT THE FIRST TIME

Political reporters, as evil as they may seem to consultants, are not an entirely bad lot. The majority can and will forgive a candidate's unwitting minor errors, as long as the flubs aren't happening every other minute. But God help the politician who makes an error of fact that is, well, funny. Reporters love to laugh at politicians, and so do voters. So press accounts of Dan Quayle's June 1992 visit to an elementary school in Trenton, New Jersey, should be required reading for anyone seeking public office. Sitting next to twelve-year-old William Figueroa to help him with his studies—while a horde of television cameras recorded the exchange—the U.S. vice-president made a horrifying and historic error of fact. Young William had gone to the board to spell the word "potato," which he did, correctly. Young Dan instructed William to add the letter "e" to the end of the word. Published accounts note that the assembled press in the classroom grew very, very quiet, somewhat like hunters do just before they are about to shoot some lumbering beast in the woods. The next day, William Figueroa threw more dirt on Quayle's figurative coffin at a press conference, when the grade-schooler soberly pointed out that the vice-president seemed like a nice guy, but he "needed to study more." Indeed.

TIP SEVEN: SWORDS ARE FOR FALLING ON

During the last federal election campaign, Stockwell Day (who, it should be noted, bears more than a passing resemblance to Dan Quayle) decided to use Niagara Falls as a backdrop to a campaign announcement. Standing at the falls' edge, Day attempted to draw an analogy between the flow of Lake Erie from "north to south" and the "brain drain" from Canada to the United States. A reporter from the area pointed out to Day that, in fact, the relevant body of water drained from "south to north." Missing a golden opportunity to poke fun at himself, and thereby seem as human as the rest of us, Day darkly warned that he would "check the record, and if someone has wrongly informed me about the flow of this particular water, I'll be having a pretty interesting discussion with them." Not only did Day succeed in making himself *look* like a dummy, he also came across *sounding* like a dummy who couldn't take responsibility for his own mistakes. The lesson, here, is that candidates should, if the circumstances warrant, 'fess up, laugh at themselves, then move on. Periodically falling on one's sword is excellent politics.

TIP EIGHT: THE ORCHESTRA PIT

Many years back, Roger Ailes started out as a prop boy on the *Mike Douglas Show*. By age 28, he was executive producer. One day, Richard Nixon appeared on the show, and was highly impressed with Ailes (who, as Joe McGinnis recalls in his seminal book *The Selling of the President*, bluntly told Nixon that "television isn't a gimmick"). Ailes went on to work for a string of Republican leaders, from Nixon to Reagan to Bush, racking up victory after victory. But Ailes contributed one line to history that amply testifies to his genius. "It's my orchestra pit theory of politics," said Ailes. "If you have two guys on stage, and one says, 'I have a solution to the Middle East problem,' and the other guy falls in the orchestra pit, who do you think is going to be on the evening news?"

Statistics bear out Ailes's pithy observation. From 1960 to 1992, Thomas E. Patterson diligently tracked every story written in *Time* or *Newsweek* about major party candidates for his book *Out of Order*. In every U.S. election before 1980, "good news" dominated bad. After that, the situation reversed. In the 1960s, about 75 per cent of political coverage had been "good news;" in the 1990s, 40 per cent. When given a choice, political reporters will always write negative stuff; it is their heroin. Candidates (and voters) who request that journalists publish or broadcast "good news for a change" are wasting their breath, and sound nauseatingly Pollyannaish, as well. Give the nattering nabobs of negativity, as William Safire called them, the fix they want. Get tough. Go neg. Hit back, hard. Kick ass. It's the only way to get a reporter's attention.

TIP NINE: SPIN IS B.S.

. . . and not in the way that political reporters think: which is that so-called "spin" is false. Spin is merely a word that describes attempts to put a favourable gloss on something. It is akin to editorializing about one's own candidate, or the opposition's candidate. Putting a favourable gloss on a falsity is, well, lying. And if you lie, you will get caught. Count on it. Spin is overrated and overdone because so many political reporters are so suspicious of it—they sense that they are being manipulated by a backroom sleaze who has a bigger salary and a bigger car.

Unless you are invited to spin, don't. Even if you're invited to, proceed with caution. Reporters are in the facts business; give them the facts they need to do their job. When they call, they already possess a "thesis" about the story they want to write; apart from murder, the only thing that prevents them from publishing or broadcasting that thesis is *facts*. Fancy talk simply won't work—or, as one politician once put it to me, "You can't shine shit."

Former Clinton adviser Dick Morris also dismisses spin, albeit from a slightly different perspective, calling it a "mutually reinforcing conceit." Says he: "Consultants and press secretaries overly pride themselves on their ability to manipulate press coverage, which they really can't. The media revels in the assumption that its slant and bias are so important that they are worthy of the skills of great manipulators, which they really aren't." There are simply too many daily newspapers, and too many television stations, for any single spin campaign to make much of a difference. As above: just the facts, ma'am.

TIP TEN: TV IS PICTURES

Study after study show that the vast majority of voters get their political information from TV. (TV reporters, meanwhile, get their agenda and research from newspaper coverage, but not much else.) In political terms, the existential reality is this: if something did not happen on television, it did not happen at all. Step one: get your candidate on TV. Step two: on television, emotion counts more than facts—or, as B.C. Liberal leader Gordon Campbell once told me ruefully: "It's 10 per cent what you say, 20 per cent how you say it, and 70 per cent how you look." Television news executives will try to deny this, but in the depths of their souls they know it is true.

Political news coverage on TV is all about melodrama. Former NBC News chief Reuven Frank, no less, confirmed as much in a memo which he circulated to his staff: "Every news story should . . . display the attributes of fiction or drama. It should have structure and conflict, problem and denouement, rising action and falling action, a middle and end. These are not only the essentials of drama; they are the essentials of [TV news] narrative." Too much emotion in the "cool" medium that is television is inadvisable, as Marshall McLuhan lectured the world in 1960, after the "cool" John F. Kennedy beat the "hot" Richard M. Nixon in a televised presidential debate.

TIP ELEVEN: SOUND BITES EARN EARNED MEDIA

"Earned" media is what political consultants call advertising they don't have to pay for—principally, helpful news stories. They love earned media because it is cheaper than other forms of political advertising, and because it is regarded as more neutral, and therefore more credible, by potential voters. Writes political scientist William Kerbel: "Media coverage has become a campaign resource as important as money, for money will come only to candidates perceived to be viable—which is to say, perceived to be viable by the press." To capture earned media, therefore, political consultants need to remember that folks in the news business love stuff that is dynamic. This means that newshounds don't like to write about substantive issues; instead, they like to cover events that have some connection to a substantive theme. Most of the time, they think that politics is a game, so they churn out stories about how a particular campaign is a horse race, or a battle, and so on. (Heaven forbid that they should actually suggest that it is a clash of ideas.)

INK-STAINED WRETCHES AND WRETCHESSES

The brass ring—in this horse race, or battle, or whatever it is—is the sound bite. Political consultants are perpetually dreaming up creative ways to get a sound bite (i.e. a pithy quote) on the news, because sound bites attract the interest of voters. Back in the late 1960s, the average U.S. network political sound bite was 42.3 seconds. By the end of the century, it had shrunk to 9.8 seconds. This, to me, is not necessarily a bad thing; after all, if you can't say it in a few seconds, it probably can't be said. Dick Morris, who is smarter than the average bear, agrees: "A good campaign strategy may take months to formulate, but it should take no more than a few words to express." Good sound bites get earned media. Earned media gets money, credibility and votes. *Ipso facto*, get a sound bite now.

TIP TWELVE: THE MEDIA IS A SPECIAL INTEREST GROUP

One of the nastiest viruses that journalists are exposed to in journalism school is that the public "has a right to know." Personally, I can't say if the public always has a right to know. (For example, I still cling to the belief that Bill Clinton's fling with a White House intern was between Clinton, his God and his wife.) But I do know one thing: the public mostly does not give a rat's ass about what the media care about. To them, the media is just another special interest group. Therefore, reports about individual speeches by candidates, policy platforms, "scandals," or what the media lovingly call "defining moments" in televised debates are usually irrelevant to voters. Plenty of studies show that voters tend to look for information that corroborates what they already believe or suspect; most often, they are not looking for a clever political spot to change their mind.

In a 500-channel universe, no single media outlet commands unswerving loyalty anymore: voters are very selective, and they see media reports as just one of a number of sources of information they use to make ballot decisions. To wit, voters care about issues, not blowjobs in the White House. Says William Kerbel: "Left to their own devices, citizens . . . tend not to ask the sort of horserace, strategy or personality questions that obsess political reporters."

But reporters cannot help themselves. They are creatures obsessed.

In Washington, D.C., route 495 is called the Beltway. On a map, the Beltway runs more or less in a circle around the U.S. capital, and captures places where political hacks and flaks abound—Alexandria, Arlington, and so on. When something happens in Official Washington that excites reporters and politicos, it is said to be "inside the Beltway." In Canada, some of my friends and I have used a similar phrase. If a development has folks on Parliament Hill atwitter, but the ordinary voter doesn't give two hoots about it, it is a "North of the Queensway" story.

For 36 days in the fall of 2000, I was imprisoned in a small, grimy and poorly ventilated space, helping out on the Liberal Party's national campaign. In all of that time, I can count on one hand the number of times a reporter called up to discuss bona fide policy issues. It did not particularly matter, it seemed, that more than 60 per cent of Canadians who were polled during the election were saying that they considered health care to be their biggest concern. It did not matter that a sizable number also wanted to discuss taxation. No: what interested reporters were trivialities like what NDP leader Alexa McDonough was wearing that day, or what leader Stockwell Day listened to on his CD player, or what was going on inside the Liberal Party's "war room."

If Canadians heard a lot about the Liberal, Tory, Alliance and NDP "war rooms" over the course of the writ period, they can be forgiven for wondering why. Reporters were transfixed by the subject of war rooms. Utterly and completely transfixed. I am not exaggerating when I say that every day a reporter or a producer of a program would dial up to request a tour of the Liberal Party's "war room." We would always say no because we naively believed elections should be about actual issues, and not about a bunch of young people and computers crammed into a smelly room, churning out press releases and whatnot. But they kept on calling. (One CTV television crew even filmed the outside of the Liberal Party's headquarters, ostensibly hoping to spot something war-roomish through the mirrored windows.)

Occasionally, I would get irritated with a reporter making such a request, and ask them whether "real Canadians" really gave a sweet damn about these so-called war rooms. Late in the campaign, an equally irritated CBC television producer said the subject was "important." I asked him why, given what the polls said about what Canadian themselves considered important, things like the future of health care, and taxation, and social programs. His answer was simply to repeat that war rooms were "important."

That is codswallop. Everywhere Jean Chrétien went in the campaign, he spoke about the issues that count to Canadians. But the news coverage did not reflect that nearly enough. When no reporters were looking, I spoke to a few senior members of the Alliance, Tory and NDP parties to confirm that they all feel similarly. Far too many journalists, they told me, find writing about political process a lot easier than actually writing about policy. Jaime Watt, the Ontario Progressive Conservative strategist who produced the devastatingly effective ads that helped elect Mike Harris, puts it this way: "Reporters love talking about process, because they are constant outsiders. They love anything that lets them be players, that lets them be in on the process. I think readers don't care about [political process], but reporters are obsessed."

Because most Canadian reporters and journalists were aggravated by the notion that the Liberal Party would likely be re-elected with an unprecedented third majority, they needed to figure out some way to explain why the Liberal Party would be re-elected with an unprecedented third majority. So, late in the campaign, segments of the media abandoned their interest in war rooms and took up a new theme: the 2000 federal election was too full of negativity and not enough policy. From one editorial page to the next, all of the political parties were sternly admonished for being "too negative." The media, meanwhile, suggested with a straight face that it was not in the least bit complicit in any of this.

I am one of those partisans who believes that elections are about choices, and that political parties are permitted, if not required, to sometimes be critical about the choices offered by a political opponent. But I would also argue that, if the news media has essentially absolved itself of the role of writing intelligently about policy, then it is inevitable that coverage of an election will be less than relevant to real people, the ones who live south of the Queensway.

Journalists, however, remain a force of nature. Try as you might, you cannot (and should not) ignore them. One fine day back in 1992, I was manning my desk in the Office of the Leader of the Official Opposition, when I got a phone call from someone claiming to be near the thirteenth floor of a downtown Ottawa office tower, a block away. The Royal Canadian Mounted Police had just raided an office, the caller said, and the office belonged to a lobbying firm called Government Consultants International (GCI).

GCI, I knew, was one of the most powerful lobbying operations in the country. Among other things, it was the place of employment of Patrick MacAdam, a university friend of Brian Mulroney, who had served as Mulroney's caucus liaison. He was a canny operator, a man widely regarded as one of the most influential unelected Tories in Canada. And the RCMP, allegedly, had raided his office as well as his home.

I discussed the tip with one of the press people in Chrétien's office. We agreed that it was worth checking out, although certainly not by any of us. It was suggested that I speak with Bob Fife, Ottawa bureau chief for the Sun newspapers. Fife was reputed to be a good investigator, with lots of contacts around town. I called Fife, identified myself and asked that we speak off the record. Fife quickly agreed, so I told him as much as I knew about the alleged RCMP raid, and wished him luck. I hung up and forgot about the matter.

At first, Fife told me much, much later, when Fife called him, MacAdam denied that the RCMP had visited his home or former place of business. But the raids had, in fact, taken place. In March and October 1994, MacAdam was charged with five different counts relating to some undeclared taxes. MacAdam called the whole matter "a bookkeeping error," but in June 1997, an Ontario provincial court judge ruled otherwise. Judge Patrick White fined MacAdam $164,610 for tax evasion, adding that he would have sent the former lobbyist to jail if it were not for some health and financial problems. The 62-year-old Tory bigwig was placed on probation for a year and ordered to perform 150 hours of community service. The fine was equivalent to the amount of tax MacAdam had evaded. MacAdam paid his debt to society; time went by, and MacAdam reinvented himself as a freelance writer.

Another fine day, another call: I was told that MacAdam, writing a first-person piece for the *Ottawa Sun* tabloid, had identified me as Fife's source. He seemed to be irritated that people would be interested in police raids at the homes and offices of prominent political people. I immediately rang up MacAdam's editor, Mark Bonokowski (who would later leave the journalism business to unsuccessfully run for a nomination as a Reform Alliance candidate in an Ottawa-area riding). I told him that I did not understand how MacAdam had published what he did. Bonokowski imperiously announced that MacAdam was correct, and that was that.

Shortly afterwards, Bob Fife (who would later become Ottawa bureau chief of the *National Post*) called me at the Vancouver firm where I was working. As I took notes, Fife admitted that he had told MacAdam the identity of his confidential source—namely, me—and he was sorry. He said he had never done anything like that before. "I'm sorry, I'm sorry," he said. I asked him why he had broken his word. He couldn't really explain. I hung up.

That experience taught me that there is no such thing as off the record. It taught me that I should never forget that some political journalists *will* burn a confidential source if they feel they must. And it taught me that reporters on Parliament or Capitol Hill, while they like to dish out pious pronouncements about politicians, and lots of tough judgments, are sometimes guilty of lapses of their own.

[KINSELLA'S REPORT CARDS ON POLITICAL JOURNALISTS]

Every so often, political journalists like to put together "report cards" about active politicians. They will provide a short critique of the politician's record, then assign a letter grade, just like back in high school. Politicians and political staffers profess to be uninterested in these puerile exercises, but that is a fib. I have seen bad grades send experienced politicians into deep funks lasting for weeks. Good grades, meanwhile, get boasted about.

As a public service—and not because I am a sado-masochist who wants his book to receive lots of lousy reviews from political journalists, who are notoriously thin-skinned—I've decided it's high time we turned the tables. I have worked in politics, in different capacities, for many years. I have a degree in journalism, and I have taught the subject at the bachelor's and master's level. I have also worked as a journalist, in different parts of the country. So I figure I am as qualified as anybody to offer a report card on a few journalists. It is my fervent and sincere hope that my report card will give voters a helpful guide to who is worth reading, or listening to, and who isn't.

First, a few reference points. In my opinion, a great political journalist is someone who does it differently: someone like I. F. Stone, who pored through mountains of documents to ferret out good stories. Or John Wesley Dafoe of the *Winnipeg Free Press*, who turned down offers of knighthood and Senate seats to pursue his craft. Or the *Washington Post*'s Bob Woodward and Carl Bernstein, who refused to follow the capital's journalistic pack and brought down a corrupt president. Those are the great political journalists—the ones who pay attention to detail, the ones who remain scrupulously fair, the ones who refuse to do what everyone else does. Those are the ones who deserve an A for their work. And they are a rare breed, indeed.

Being a B-level political reporter is no mark of shame, however. A political reporter or columnist who receives a B isn't an Izzy Stone or a Bob Woodward, because they may occasionally succumb to pack journalism, or partisanship, or a bit of intellectual laziness. But their work is still above average. The C-level political journalists, meanwhile, are the ones who are boring or seem to be afraid to write a story that their colleagues aren't writing; they are the ones who may sometimes appear to be sloppy, or lazy, or both. D-level reporters and columnists—and, naturally enough, those who receive a failing grade—should consider another line of work.

If nothing else, I (and my co-conspirators, who include a few senior elected people who are not courageous enough to be named) have enjoyed this little exercise. I fully expect journalistic retribution, but that's okay. In this book, one of my arguments has been that political journalists need a kick in the ass. If one or two of them don't kick back —or if they don't get a colleague to do so on their behalf—I'll eat my favourite baseball cap (the one inscribed WE POOL'EM, YOU RULE'EM).

In alphabetical order, then, here is a report card on some members of the Canadian political journalist ruling class:

JIM BROWN: A veteran reporter with the Canadian Press (CP), Brown is highly influential, given that his stories run in more newspapers than any other reporter's in Ottawa. CP reporters can generally be counted upon to be fairer than most of their colleagues, and Brown is one of the fairest of the fair. Not flashy, mind you, but political consultants and staffers distrust flashy reporters. Flashy is for Liberace's wardrobe, not political coverage. **Grade: B+.**

JOAN BRYDEN: Bryden has one of the media's best networks within the Liberal government, which is good news for her employers at Southam News, because most of that agency's writers don't. Liberals like Bryden, because they don't feel she's out to get them. Unlike that of a lot of Hill hacks, Bryden's political analysis is usually pretty good. Seems sane, too, which makes her completely unique amongst her colleagues. **Grade A-.**

DALTON CAMP: Erudite, politically experienced, and drives the proto-Reformers batty, which, for that reason alone, makes his columns in the *Toronto Star* and *Hill Times* worthwhile reading. Camp's a lifelong Tory, but despite that, he has become, inexplicably somehow, a favourite of senior Liberal cabinet ministers. **Grade: A-.**

COLUMNISTS AND EDITORIALISTS AT THE NATIONAL POST: Nice folks, some of them: Natasha Hassan, Jon Kay and John Williamson stand out as clear, thoughtful writers. But the editorials the rest of their colleagues write on Canadian politics are plumb crazy. Some members of this group think poor people, along with the sick, are a bunch of whiners. And they measure quality of life entirely in marginal tax rates, which explains why for the first two years of their existence, they acted like the press office for the Reform Alliance. **Average grade: D.**

RICHARD CLEROUX: A former *Globe and Mail* writer, author of a best-selling book about espionage, Cleroux is now a regular Internet political columnist with the Sun media chain. He is also an ubiquitous presence on assorted pundit panels. An inveterate gossip and a bit of a leftie, Cleroux provides a nice antidote to the sort of corporate back-slapping coverage found too often in other places. Pays too much attention to the ravings of nutbars on the Internet, however. **Grade: B.**

ANDREW COYNE: Andrew is an unashamed right-wing polemicist, like everyone else at the *Post*, but no red-necked mouth-breather is he. *Au contraire*: Coyne has long been regarded by lots of folks, even members of the Liberal cabinet, as thoughtful and fair, and he's a federalist, to boot. He was seized for a time with the Shawinigate Stockholm Syndrome that afflicted others at the *Post*, but generally is capable of cogent (if ultra-conservative) argument. **Grade: B.**

MIKE DUFFY: Duff, as his many friends call him, is a native of Prince Edward Island who has developed a formidable knowledge of Ottawa politics from his many years at the CBC and, now, CTV. He's not out to destroy anyone's life or career, which is always a refreshing change. Duffy's underrated and underutilized by his employers, and he shouldn't be. **Grade: B+.**

BOB FIFE: The bureau chief for the *National Post* doesn't get an F simply because he committed the heinous sin of burning a source (i.e., me). At least he called me to confess and apologize, for which he deserves some credit. He has also long been regarded as a reporter who will eviscerate anyone from any political party, which means he knows how to be fair. But since Fife assumed a post at the *Post*, some things have changed. In just one "news story" about a mission early in 2000 by Prime Minister Jean Chrétien to the Middle East, Fife wrote that the trip was "ill-fated" and "disastrous" and that the prime minister, himself, was "past his prime," "ignorant," "embarrassing," "flying by the seat of his pants," "insulting" and "ill-informed." For good measure, Fife sniffed that the prime minister had "tarnished Canada's reputation." Oh, really? A few million Canadian voters seemed to think otherwise, when the next election rolled around. **Grade: F.**

DOUGLAS FISHER: The so-called dean of the press corps, Fisher (as he continually reminds his readership) is a former member of Parliament with the CCF, the forerunner of the New Democratic Party. He should have stuck with that. Some of his columns exhibit obvious distaste for any programs designed to help aboriginals living in near–Third World conditions (said columns being unpleasant and wrong, but certainly not boring). Apart from those, Fisher has for many years been typing quite a few coma-inducing thumbsuckers for the Sun chain about things voters don't care about, such as obscure parliamentary events from five decades ago. Each one gives a whole new rationale for forced mandatory retirement. Snooze city. **Grade: C.**

ALLAN FOTHERINGHAM: Zowee, Dr. Foth, are you still around? We all thought you were dead! **Grade: F.**

DIANE FRANCIS: In person, she's as sweet as pie. But I had one telling run-in with Francis's typewriter, when she quoted a prominent white supremacist in one of the unpleasant anti-immigration screeds she hammers out for the *Post*. (She's an immigrant herself, for what it's worth.) When I and many others pointed out to her why it's a mistake to bestow media credibility on a neo-Nazi, Francis reacted with fury. In one e-mail she sent to me, awash with her characteristic modesty, she wrote: "I am interested in fixing our immigration/refugee situation and the message, not the messenger is important here." After pointing out that a single letter to the editor had been printed to protest the use of a racist as her "messenger," Francis added: "That's the end of it so don't bother me any more." Fine by me. **Grade: F.**

FRANK MAGAZINE: It's hard to say who really writes for *Frank*. It's easier to say who supplies it with material: anyone with an axe to grind, which is precisely everyone on Parliament Hill (me included). The most notorious name associated with the satirical rag is Michael Bate. A musician and former Canadian Press reporter, Bate has been at the helm of *Frank* for about a decade. In that time, he and his anonymous team have deflated the egos of a lot of pompous types in Ottawa, which can't be anything but good. But along the way, he has launched jihads against some people in the corridors of power by attacking their children. His magazine's "contest" about raping the daughter of Brian Mulroney, and its vicious ongoing commentary about one of Chrétien's sons, have been way beyond the pale—and Bate privately admits it. His hypocrisy doesn't end there: everyone whose children attend his wife's Ottawa-area Montessori school are off limits. Early in the magazine's existence, Bate and his colleagues actually assisted in the publication of a white supremacist group's newsletter. Later on, when the newsletter's publishing contract ended, Bate used his magazine to ridicule his former far-right clients. The magazine lost me as a reader in 1995 when they published my home address, thereby making it easier for assorted violent neo-Nazis (the ones I had written about in *Web of Hate*) to find me and my wife. The Ottawa Crown attorney's office said Bate's magazine deserved to be charged with a criminal offence for that one. Me, I'll just grade it. **Grade: F.**

GRAHAM FRASER: Earnest, thoughtful, thorough, competent, and the author of far too many column inches—at both the *Globe and Mail* and now the *Toronto Star*—about constitutional amendments, which few Canadians care about, and fewer still like. In-depth constitutional coverage: more boring than a leisurely drive through Saskatchewan. Graham, get a new gig. **Grade: B-.**

EDDIE GREENSPON: Brainy, friendly, decent and unofficial press secretary to the cabinet ministers he likes (most of the time, he likes just one), Greenspon is a best-selling author and has been the *Globe*'s Ottawa bureau chief. If he was told by *Globe* management to stop filing columns filled to the rim with anonymous sources, he would experience the worst case of writer's block since J. D. Salinger. "Stenographer to certain senior Liberal strategists" should be engraved on his business card. **Grade: B-.**

CHANTAL HÉBERT: The *Toronto Star* columnist, who previously worked in the French media, dislikes Jean Chrétien. Lots of French reporters hate him, but I somehow expect more from Hébert—she's clearly smart. **Grade: C.**

CLARE HOY: A pugilistic and proud right winger, Hoy is wonderful: he doesn't give a shit what anyone else thinks, which makes him one of the most honest political columnists around (it has also gotten him fired, at least once). Writes for the *Hill Times,* where he has bashed me but good. I disagree with him most of the time, but he will take on anyone, which makes him unique among the toadying types who are his colleagues. **Grade: B+.**

RAFE MAIR: Even though he is far removed from the insularity of Ottawa—he works way out on the Left Coast, shouting into microphones at CKNW radio in Vancouver—Mair, a former politician, is feared and loathed far and wide (mostly by Liberals, but not exclusively). In demographic terms, talk radio has always been decidedly right wing, and on that score, Mair does not disappoint. What makes him unique, and therefore valuable, is his willingness to challenge some of the orthodoxies of Canada's conservative cabals. **Grade: B+.**

DON MARTIN: The *Calgary Herald* national affairs columnist (and former colleague of mine) is funny and fair. Writing for a rabid pro-Alliance rag like the *Herald* can't be easy, which is why Martin deserves a good mark. **Grade: A-.**

LAWRENCE MARTIN: Author of one volume of a supposed two-volume biography of Jean Chrétien, Martin is a columnist for Southam News. He penned one whopper during the 2000 federal election, suggesting that, if the Grits won, they'd owe most of the victory to the author of this book, thereby demonstrating, conclusively, that he is utterly bonkers. He's thorough, and he loves detail, which is to his everlasting credit. Tallest free-standing newspaper columnist in Canada. **Grade: B.**

ANDREW MCINTOSH: An investigative journalist for the *National Post*, in an earlier incarnation he was one of Stevie Cameron's researchers on her anti-Mulroney book, *On the Take*. He clearly relishes flinging mud at prime ministers. As pretty much everyone in Canada knows by now, McIntosh was determined to transform Chrétien's hometown of Shawinigan, Quebec, into something synonymous with the Watergate apartment complex. For months, McIntosh has been a veritable journalistic St.George, charging out to slay the twin-headed dragon of prime ministerial perfidy and misdeeds. In just one noteworthy dispatch, McIntosh informed us that the prime minister sold off his shares in a golf course "in a bid to quell months of controversy"—in the absence of comment from the prime minister, McIntosh can apparently read Chrétien's mind. The prime minister has been "rebuked" by "conflict-of-interest scholars" for all of this, he goes on to report, although we are not told who, precisely, did the rebuking, or the *Post*'s criteria for conflict-of-interest scholarship. He won a National Newspaper Award for his coverage but whatever McIntosh reports, the Canadian public does not seem to give a damn. **Grade: D.**

JASON MOSCOVITZ: Well-connected, well-regarded, well-spoken. A long-time CBC political reporter, Moscovitz is smart and decent. Why he remains a political reporter, therefore, is an impenetrable mystery. **Grade: B+.**

NATIONAL POST: My Liberal friends—and many folks at the *Post* itself—will be utterly horrified to learn that I (and quite a few other Grits, secretly) love this newspaper. Love it. To me, it has a quality that too many other broadsheets do not—namely, a clear, consistent personality. Sure, it can be mean, and it can be politically contradictory. Sure, its "personality" is that of a youthful, miserly, misogynistic, self-absorbed neo-con. But those things make it even *more* interesting, to me. I don't have to agree with its assorted positions on public policy issues—and I don't, believe me—to recognize good writing and passion when I see it. Where the *Post* has lately gone off the rails, however, is with its crazy fixation on "Shawinigate," and is willingness to use its news pages to promote the Canadian Alliance in a way that is as flimsy as it is transparent. That said, other papers could learn from the *Post*, which consistently looks great and which consistently projects a single (if flawed) political vision. **Grade: A-.**

DON NEWMAN: Senior political editor for CBC news in Ottawa, Newman is well-liked, well-informed, and his "Politics" program on Newsworld is followed religiously by every political hack in Ottawa.

That is because, at one time or another, they have all been on it. Put bluntly, this simply means he is watched by a few hundred people who breathe the same air, eat the same food, golf at the same golf courses—and are utterly disconnected from the day-to-day reality of life for millions of real people. Not Newman's fault, but he remains an unindicted co-conspirator. Ottawa paying attention to Ottawa: yecch. **Grade: A-.**

CRAIG OLIVER: Oliver has been around Ottawa since Jesus was a little feller, but his longevity has not interfered with his enthusiasm for a good old-fashioned political dust-'em-up. When he tells some of his engaging stories, he actually makes politics sound interesting again, which is no easy thing. While he was personal friends with the likes of Pierre Trudeau, Oliver is always even-handed. He's been struggling with an eye problem for a while, but you would never know it from his onscreen commentaries and analysis. **Grade: A.**

VAUGHN PALMER: The best political columnist in Canada only writes about B.C. politics. That's good news for his many readers at the *Vancover Sun*, but bad news for the rest of the country. Trenchant, dogged, smart, gifted: this guy's got it all. **Grade: A+.**

SASA PETRICIC: Little-known CBC reporter, but that may change. A former cartoonist with the Carleton University student newspaper in the '80s, Petricic has come a long way. He is likeable, friendly and fair. His stories, moreover, often probe subjects other political reporters discount, but which they shouldn't—things like the Internet, or advocacy advertising. On Parliament Hill, any reporter who is truly fair will always have lots of fans, in every party. **Grade: B+.**

JEFFREY SIMPSON: Nice fellow, if a tad professorial. I used to think he was a lawyer, because he thinks like one, but I do not mean this as an insult (I'm one myself, after all). Most-read column he does for the *Globe* is the one in which, every year, he admits his mistakes. Too bad few of his colleagues follow his example, because they make plenty. **Grade: B.**

JIM TRAVERS: Travers used to be managing editor at the *Toronto Star*, then later became one of their Ottawa columnists. A lot of doubts were expressed about whether he would make the transition to lesser mortal status, but Travers has gone on to be a columnist who does not follow the pack. He is usually one of the first to challenge the Parliamentary Press Gallery's conventional wisdom, and that is a good thing in the Town That Independent Thinking Forgot. Most columnists wouldn't know how to conduct research if their lives depended on it, but Travers's opinions are usually based upon a solid foundation of fact. **Grade: B+.**

BILL WALKER: The *Toronto Star*'s former bureau chief—now in Washington—still looks like he is about 14 years old, but his reporting is always solid and trustworthy. **Grade: B.**

PAUL WELLS: Most days, politicos think Wells is one of the better political columnists in Ottawa, because he can be prolific and witty and perceptive. Freshness is good, in fruit, vegetables and political journalism. Wells can be fresh. In the past, Wells has called me a "big mouth" and "a spotlight-hogging Toronto lawyer"—which is true if not particularly nice. Recently I learned to be extra careful with Wells, after he took some stuff I'd given him, refashioned it into stainless steel, and deposited it between my shoulder blades in a column clearly designed to bring me down a peg or two. **Grade: B.**

GREG WESTON: How an award-winning journalist and author like Weston could end up at the *Sun* in Ottawa, after a prolonged absence of years, in which he chased riches in the movie business, puzzles many, me included. His stuff is very fair, very thorough and very detailed, none of which is a hallmark of *Sun*-style journalism. It'll be interesting to see how long he lasts there. My bet: not very. **Grade: A-.**

HUGH WINSOR: Apart from his penchant for writing too much and too often about the minutiae of federal broadcast regulatory agencies, Winsor is unique for his ability to dig up the dirt on both the political and bureaucratic classes. Many of his colleagues are good at the former, but not the latter. He's not afraid to tilt at windmills admired by the rest of the pack, too, which never hurts. **Grade: B+.**

Don't get me wrong. I do not mean to suggest that the Parliamentary Press Gallery is full of venal miscreants. Some of them, as noted, possess redeeming features. One or two of them are even somewhat likeable. But I, along with a lot of other political consultants, some of whom are former reporters themselves, have become decidedly wary of political journalists. As the research of political scientists James Thurber and Candice Nelson suggests, the more political consultants see and hear of political journalists, the less they like.

Some of this is due to sour grapes, of course. Politicos are frustrated by the fact that this rebellious, ill-mannered, ink-stained pack of jackals has, in a very real sense, more power and influence than they do. They are also irritated by their near-total inability to keep the media pack under control. But what political consultants think, at the end of the day, is irrelevant. What matters is what the voters think, and, overwhelmingly, they hold journalists in as much contempt as they reserve for politicos and lawyers. (I've been all three—journalist, lawyer and politico—so I know all about this contempt stuff, believe me.)

The priorities and prognostications of political journalists have no bearing on the day-to-day challenges facing most voters. Randy

McCauley, Jean Chrétien's witty former press secretary, puts it succinctly: "Parliament Hill, or Capitol Hill, are a few square kilometres surrounded by reality." Intellectually, smart reporters seem to know this. In practical terms, they don't ever do anything about it, and they continue to write about politics in the same old way they always did.

And that, perhaps more than anything else, is why so many of them deserve less-than-stellar grades.

CONCLUSION

CAMPAIGNS MATTER
... or, Kinsella's tips on how to survive the next election

Do campaigns matter? The consensus amongst political consultants, at least, is that they do.

In recent years, those latter two words—campaigns matter—have become a sort of awkward rallying cry for those who devote their time and judgment to political contests. There has been a well-read book bearing that title. There have been more than a dozen international political science conferences put together to answer that question, most of them concluding, with greater or lesser degrees of enthusiasm, that the answer is yes. And most everyone concerned, from respected academics, to the consultants who consign themselves to the nasty and brutish (but not always short) world of electoral politics, have repeated the phrase in plenty of books and interviews. Even political reporters have insisted that yes, indeed, campaigns matter. (If they were to do otherwise, of course, they would be admitting to the irrelevance of their chosen career.)

But do campaigns *really* matter as much as the political commentariat asserts? Or are campaigns utterly irrelevant to the lives of real people—those who sneer or head to the kitchen for a glass of milk when a political spot is broadcast? The truth, I think, may lie somewhere between those two poles, but more closely to the former than the latter. If campaigns are designed to inform voters about the choices available to them in democratic contests, if they highlight differences, and if they motivate voters to express themselves on the basis of those differences, then campaigns do what they are supposed to do. Political campaigns may not be the prettiest of dialectical exercises, as even the likes of James Carville or Haley Barbour would be inclined to admit, but they seem to meet the two basic requirements: information and motivation. Campaigners try to inform voters, and, once informed, voters are, hopefully, persuaded to move their way or, at least, to move away from the alternatives.

Not surprisingly, I am one of those who believes that campaigns matter despite, or, perhaps, because of, much-documented declining rates of voter participation in elections. That said, I have to concede that the "campaigns matter" claim has a hollow, defensive ring. It is as if political consultants, and their clients, continue to worry that the reverse is true. It is as if—and this is even worse—they had something to do with the circumstances that led to the disinterest, disaffection and disenfranchisement that now besets too many election campaigns.

So the doubts stubbornly persist here and there, and especially recently: do campaigns matter?

The question isn't entirely irrelevant, especially coming, as it does, at the conclusion of a book about the grittier side of political campaign tactics. In recent years, a small but influential number of university professors have asserted that, well, campaigns *don't* really matter at all.

People make up their minds about voting choices based upon things over which political consultants have no control, they say. For example, some of them have developed mathematical models to track changes in personal income, gross domestic product and so on, and then predicted campaign winners based upon economic results. Not policy, and certainly not hardball campaign strategy.

One of the better-known members of the "campaigns don't matter" school is the much-quoted James E. Campbell, at the State University of New York at Buffalo. Campbell asserts that, as far as he and like-minded thinkers are concerned, the economy is the answer to every question. Data assembled by Campbell shows the following: since World War Two, in eight out of the ten presidential elections where the United States has enjoyed annual GDP of at least 2.5 per cent, the incumbent has won. The two exceptions, he allows, were Democrat Hubert H. Humphrey in 1968, whose candidacy was battered by the ongoing Vietnam War, and the Republicans' Gerald R. Ford in 1976, who was the target of anger for the sins of Watergate and the pardon of Richard Nixon. Until recently, Campbell was attracting a lot of academic converts, and he was causing much consternation among political consultants. Until recently.

The definitive rebuttal to Campbell is this: Florida. Florida, Florida, Florida.

In 2000, the Democrats held the White House, and the GDP was closing in on a whopping 6 per cent. Despite that, and, most significantly, because of some pretty good tactical campaigning on the ground, George W. Bush's team defeated the incumbent party's candidate, Al Gore, and thereby captured all of Florida's electoral college votes. Gore was considered smarter and more mature than his rival. But the 2000 presidential campaign *wasn't* all about the economy, stupid (to mangle Carville's line). It was principally about who campaigned better. Bush did, Gore didn't. *Ipso facto*, campaigns matter.

I started this book by accepting as a truism that campaigns should matter to voters. Perhaps I shouldn't have done so. Perhaps I should have spent more time arguing for the proposition that modern electoral politics are legitimate, and that the way we make democratic choices is affected by campaigns.

I didn't, and I won't. This book's starting point—its starting point long before the weeks-long nail-biter in Florida—is that campaigns count. They matter. It is not even a debatable point anymore. The *methodologies* of campaigns—tough advertising, opposition research, quick response, the Internet, polling, earned media, stunts and so on—are therefore all exceedingly important, as well.

Professor Campbell's statistics are interesting. But there is only one statistic that matters to me in the election campaigns in which I participate. It came to me one morning a few years ago, while I was driving to a campaign office somewhere out West. I was listening to CBC Radio, as usual. (Which reminds me: a good Liberal friend, Scott Sheppard, once remarked to me that "CBC Radio, *Globe and Mail* Liberals" are always out of touch with voters—not "AM Radio, *Toronto Sun* Liberals," like him. He was right.) As I listened to CBC, the radio host mentioned that, about two decades ago, only about one out of every five households were two-income. By the nineties, the commentator noted, nearly four out of every five households were two-income.

It would be an overstatement to say that I very nearly drove my car off the road, but not by much. In every campaign I have been involved with since, I have cornered fellow partisans to lecture them about that statistic. Most of the time, they feign interest, and go back to whatever they were doing before.

They shouldn't. In June 2001, I and some other political consultants gathered in Washington to share trade secrets—and to chat with people like Mark Mellman. Bulky, bearded and brilliant, Mellman has been a pollster to Bill Clinton and Al Gore. And he, too, subscribes to the notion that voters have a lot of things on their minds, but politics isn't one of them. "The voters we are talking to," he says, "are not very interested in what we have to say.... It's therefore very important in campaigns to say things over and over again."

Why aren't voters interested? Because, as that two-income statistic suggests, voters are busy. Very busy. During an average day during an average campaign, voters spend far more time contemplating the availability of parking spaces than they do the minutiae of a party's policy platform. "Most of the time, voters don't even have a notional idea of what a candidate stands for," says Mellman. "That's why so many of them vote because of a candidate's image." The lives of voters are preoccupied with too many real-life challenges—getting the kids to school on time, getting the bills paid on time, getting enough time to sleep. For politicians, and the political hacks who try to get them elected, this represents the biggest challenge of all, not Professor Campbell's theories. Given the difficulties of ordinary existence, how do campaigns attract, and hold, the attention of ordinary people?

I hope this book has been about the answers to that question. It has been about using every trick in the book—every dirty trick, my detractors will tell you—to grab the attention of busy voters. It has been about how to make voters indicate a preference for your candidate.

At the end of all of this, however, it occurred to me that voters, being as busy as CBC Radio tells us that they are, need a little bit more. They need, I think, some tips on how to make their way through an election campaign without losing their marbles, or their temper, or both. With all of the crafty campaign techniques now bombarding voters, they need help to separate the good from the bad, the meaningful from the meaningless.

[KINSELLA'S SEVEN-POINT VOTER'S GUIDE TO KICKING ASS]

RULE ONE: *Just because someone tells you something is "negative campaigning" doesn't mean it is.* "Negative ads" and "negative campaigns" have been defined in so many different ways, no one is quite sure what "negative" means any more. What too many people seem to accept, however, is that "negative" politics is bad for democracy. That is what the late Kenneth Burke, the noted expert on rhetorical theory, calls letting language do our thinking for us. One of the better studies in this area is by the Annenberg Campaign Mapping Project (ACMP). ACMP divided campaign discourse into three types: *advocacy*, which are arguments in favour of a politician's position; *contrast*, which are arguments contrasting two or more political choices; and, *attack*, which are arguments critical of an opponent or the opponent's position on something. Only the last type can be fairly seen as "negative," but all three are often lumped together as just that. It is worth remembering that the Annenberg study found that attack ads actually contain a far greater percentage of "policy words" and more issue content than contrast or advocacy ads. And a 1998 national U.S. poll, also by Annenberg, concluded that voters regard contrast ads as "responsible" and "useful." So what's "negative" about any of that? Nothing. Reporters like to call tough campaign messages "negative" because they prefer to report on conflict not agreement. Political opponents like to call the other side's ads "negative" because they know voters believe they don't like negative ads, and hope to win support by condemning the opposition's use of them. Don't believe the hype. Most of the time, when you hear a politician is being "negative," it's not true. They're merely being political.

RULE TWO: *So-called "negative" campaigning isn't becoming more widespread.* Every campaign I have worked on, one wag once remarked, has always been called the most negative campaign yet. I wish I had thought of that line myself, because seldom have truer words been spoken; after every campaign, journalists churn out pious thumb-sucker editorials about how awful and nasty and unpleasant the latest election had been (more than once, I've been handed much of the blame for rendering them more negative). But the academics who know this area best, such as the University of Pennsylvania's Katherine Hall Jamieson, have produced study after study to show that so-called "negativity" in political campaigns has become less frequent over the years, not more. Because the press loves to focus on the inflammatory stuff during elections, you will see and read more about it. But that doesn't mean it is happening more frequently. According to Jamieson, "attack" campaigning has actually remained steady since 1960. Claims that the widespread use of "negative" stuff is to blame for shrinking numbers of people casting ballots are also suspect. "Contrast" ads, which Jamieson tracked in the 1996 Clinton-Dole presidential race, actually "increased both turnout and vote share." So there.

RULE THREE: *Don't get sucked in by reporting about strategy and tactics; policy is what counts most, and you know it.* Reporters love—and I mean *love*—writing about strategy and tactics. If they have a choice between writing a piece about a policy issue (which requires actual research) and political backroom shenanigans (which doesn't), they will opt for the shenanigans, ten times out of ten. First off, it lends itself more readily to the battlefield/sports analogy language political journalists so adore. Second, it suggests that they have privileged access to the smoke-filled backrooms. Third, it allows them to write or broadcast pretty much whatever the hell they want, without having to worry about things like objectivity or even fairness (it also allows reporters to interview other reporters, which is navel-gazing in its purest form, and which they also dearly love). Finally, it can't be disproved. By that, I mean strategy and tactics are pretty woolly concepts. I've been involved in campaigns where I read in a newspaper that our strategy was "X," and I knew it was "Y." I couldn't call in to the paper's editors to deny it, because that would mean letting our opponents (who read the papers, too) know by implication that our secret strategy was, if not "Y," then most likely "X."

A 1996 Media Studies Centre/Roper Centre poll found that fully 50 per cent of voters felt that way too much attention was being paid to who was "ahead" in races, and not enough to the issues. If the media ever heeded the polls and focus groups they commission for themselves, they'd stop writing about political process immediately, and they'd start writing about policy, because that's what their customers want. But they won't, trust me. They love the superficial stuff. It makes them feel like insiders.

RULE FOUR: *Don't be suspicious when you hear that political campaigns are researching the public record of the other side—be grateful.* Politicians, and aspiring politicians, have records, and by that I don't mean criminal records (although some of them have those, too). I mean a public record that tells voters something about how they can be expected to conduct themselves in office: things like their stands on different policies, or if they have a fondness for junkets and expense accounts, or their willingness to put partisanship ahead of principle, or whether they are a dummy or not. Not things like extramarital affairs, or divorces, or past use of marijuana: nothing like that. Just the things that matter—the things that are found on the public record. Whenever the media learn that opposition research teams are taking a look at these things that matter, they will call it "dirty tricks." Every time. But letting voters know about a politician's public record isn't dirty tricks—it's a public service. If the media aren't inclined to do it (see rule three, above), then it is incumbent upon political parties to step up to the plate.

There are clear limits to what is acceptable in oppo, and the public knows what they are. A 1998 survey by the Sorensen Institute for Political

Leadership at the University of Virginia found that its respondents considered to be "very or somewhat fair" criticizing one's opponent for "talking one way and voting another" (80.7 per cent); "his or her voting record" (75.8 per cent); "his or her business practices" (71 per cent); "taking money from special interest groups" (70.7 per cent). Political consultants are also aware of the limits to political discourse. In January 1994, for example, the American Association of Political Consultants passed a code of ethics bylaw, calling upon members not to make appeals based upon racism, gender and so on; to refrain from false and misleading attacks on an opponent and the opponent's family; and to document carefully each and every criticism they voice about an opponent. Oppo, when it restricts itself to the public record of a candidate, is always right and proper. If you still doubt that, cast your mind back to 1972: do you think a crook like Richard Nixon would have been re-elected had the Democrats been doing some smart oppo on the activities of his aptly named Committee to Re-Elect the President (CREEP)? Not on your life.

RULE FIVE: *Be a smart consumer of campaign polling—and don't let pollsters do your thinking for you.* There's a good reason why governments of every conceivable stripe have banned polling in the days immediately preceding election day. It's because they know that the publication of poll results influences voters. It's just common sense: if you read a poll that your chosen candidate is about to be pulverized, what's the point of bothering to help out on election day? Similarly, if you have doubts about a candidate, but you observe that most of your fellow citizens don't, there's a good chance you will be less reluctant.

After George Bush Senior beat Bob Dole in the 1988 New Hampshire primary, he called all of this political psychology stuff "the Big Mo"—as in, momentum; he had it, Dole didn't. Polls provide testimony as to whether a candidate or a political party have momentum.

And, where goes momentum, so goes voter awareness, donations and press coverage. (Political reporters are particularly enthusiastic about polling, because (a) their bosses regularly pay big bucks to commission polls, and (b) polls buttress reporters' false conviction that a campaign is a horse race.) If you don't like the sound of any of this "Big Mo" mumbo-jumbo (and you shouldn't), then *be independent*: pay attention to policy differences, not polling numbers.

RULE SIX: *Not every reporter is evil, but remember that the things that matter to them shouldn't matter to a normal person like you.* I've given a pretty hard time to political journalists in this book because, well, they deserve it. I have now spent enough years in campaign backrooms to know that most reporters are just as ethically impaired as the ethically impaired politicians. The important point to remember about them is Roger Aisle's Orchestra Pit theory: reporters are interested in writing about things that go wrong, not what goes right. These days, voters want to know about both. To ensure you are getting a balanced picture, try to find some time to read a candidate's literature. Take a look at a policy platform—most of them are on-line these days. Take in a debate or two. Call up the candidate, or the candidate's campaign, and ask for a prompt answer to a question that matters to you. Better yet, volunteer on a campaign: in that way, you're not merely getting answers to your questions, you are helping to shape the answers.

RULE SEVEN: *You matter.* The Battle of Florida, which eventually saw George W. Bush win the presidency with only a few hundred votes over Al Gore, should prove, even to the most committed cynic, that every vote counts. Bush won the presidency despite the punditocracy's predictions that Gore would clobber him. That happened for two reasons: one, Bush fought back hard against every allegation thrown at him; two, he did GOTV better than Gore—what political consultants call Get

Out The Vote. As someone who has run campaigns, and as someone who has even been foolish enough to run for office himself, take my word for it: you, the voter, have power. Use it or lose it.

Here ends the lesson.

I pretty much knew I had to write this book in March 2000, when I was attending the Liberal Party of Canada's biennial convention in Ottawa, and a kid insulted me. Sort of.

I was standing in a crowded hallway at the Ottawa Congress Centre, chatting with some reporters and some fellow Grits, when a tall young man approached. He introduced himself and said he was from British Columbia. He then reached back into the crowd and pulled forward another young man who, he explained, was his brother.

"This is the guy I was telling you about," he said, speaking to his brother. "This is the Prince of Darkness." The brother then reached across, struck mute, and shook the hand of the Prince of Darkness.

This is a true story. I am not making this up. This youngish B.C. Liberal called me the Prince of Darkness in a tone that suggested that he did not necessarily regard it as a bad thing. On the contrary: both he and his brother (who proceeded to just stare at me as I did my best to make small talk) seemed to think that it was in fact rather, well, good.

I had to laugh. If you have made it this far in this book, you will not disagree when I say that people who are involved in politics are a little odd. I mean, who else but someone involved in politics could be called the Prince of Darkness, by a total stranger, and think it was funny? Who else but someone involved in politics could *call* a total stranger the Prince of Darkness, and mean it as a compliment? Barney dolls, oppo, kids in chicken suits, push polling, Pinocchio ads, leaks on the Internet, going neg: it's a weird business, indeed.

Just after the young men walked away, I got a tap on the shoulder.

Standing before me were two of Prime Minister Jean Chrétien's senior aides, Bruce Hartley and Charlie Angelakos. They looked harried and sounded out of breath. Someone wanted to speak with me, Hartley said. Someone important.

I won't disclose who I spoke to, or what we spoke about; after all, even we oddball political folks have to have some secrets. Suffice to say, at the end of our conversation, this person—who has forgotten more about politics than this Prince of Darkness will ever know—had this to say: "It's politics. You get hit, you hit back hard. Right?"

Right.

ACKNOWLEDGEMENTS

Allan Fotheringham—or maybe it was someone else, but it doesn't really matter—once noted that political people read books differently from others. Whereas everybody else reads books from front to back, political folks do it the other way around. That's because they always check the index (or the acknowledgements page) to see if they, or anyone they know, is in the book. Only then do they buy it.

Consequently, I intend to thank everyone who was interviewed for this book, or anyone who has ever offered me their political insights in the past. That way, I not only get to offer them my sincere thanks, but I potentially get them to buy the damn thing, too. (Some folks named below, undoubtedly, may not want to be thanked, but they only have themselves to blame. They shouldn't have talked to me.) So here goes, starting from the left, where I got my political start.

ACKNOWLEDGEMENTS

In the Far West, I learned from the likes of Gary Collins, Gord Campbell, Clark Roberts, Greg Lyle, Stew Braddick, Ted Olnyk, Luigi Perna, John Eisenstat, Irv Epstein, Raymond Chan, Paul Fyssas, Ross Fitzpatrick, May Brown, John Kenney (RIP), Don Williams, George Taylor, Royce Frith, Steve Kukucha, Bill Brooks, Patrick Wong, Celso Boscariol, Dave Wizinsky, Jay Straith, David Plewes, Heather Dunsford, Herb Dhaliwal, Diana Hutchinson, Alex Pannu, Dennis Prouse, Murray Dykeman, Pam McDonald, Fraser Randall, Andre Gerolymatos, Tim Morrison, Martin MacLachlan, Svend Robinson, Mike McDonald, Dirk Ricker, Jen Reid, Stuart Pelly, Ed Barnes, Jim Sullivan, Lorne Burns, Chuck Strahl, Greg Walker, Don Millar, Renate Bublick, Mike Brooks, Adam Korbin, Prem Vinning, Kent Scarborough, Angus Reid, John Nuraney, Stan Winfield, Ted Nebbeling and Bruce Young. Special thanks go to Brad McTavish, Mark Brady and Naina Sloan. And I am immensely grateful to Toby Ward, the Canadian politico who interviewed Haley Barbour for this book, for his judgment, his loyalty and his friendship, all of which I value a great deal.

In the Nearer West, my home, I was enlightened by Nick Taylor, John Cordeau, Steve MacAdam (RIP), Colin MacDonald, Joyce Fairbairn, Sheldon Chumir (RIP), Lloyd Axworthy, Derek Raymaker, David and Izzy Asper, John Harvard, Elliott Poll, Ron Duhamel, David MacInnis, Cos Gabriele, Lee Hill, Rey Pagtakhan, Ethel Blondin-Andrew, Catherine Lappe, Dan Nearing, Jim Keelaghan and Bob Haslam. Always standing by me when I was battling Western separatists and/or kooky right-wingers, were my parents, Lorna and Doug; my brothers, Lorne and Kevin; and the two guys who have been allies the longest, Alan Macdonald and Pierre Schenk.

In Godless Central Canada, where my brood and I presently reside, there are about a million people to thank, and to whom I owe much, whether they know it or not. The list will only be partial, for which I offer *mea maxima culpa* in advance. There is James Villeneuve, Tom

ACKNOWLEDGEMENTS

Allison, Gordie Brown, Richard Patten, Rick Anderson, Eugene Bellemare, Percy Downe, Angelo Persichilli, Sheila Copps, Jane Taber, Pierre Marc Johnson, John Hayter, Benoit Chiquette, Malcolm Lester, Allan Gregg, John Hinds, Michelle Bishop, Anne and Rob Morash, Gordon Ashworth, Jim Peterson, Herb Gray, Jaime Watt, John Webster, Chris Sweeney, Emond and Heather Chiasson, David Peterson, Robert Houle, John Tory, Dennis Mills, Rob Toole, Jon and Martha Taylor, Dale Lastman, Chris Benner, John Rae, Manuel Prutschi, Mark Quinn, David Gourlay, Jeff Steiner, Marc Laframboise, Gabor Apor, Hugh Segal, John Webster, Charlie Angelakos, Chris Baker, Zoe Amos, David Zussman, Bob Murdoch, Chuck Guite, Mark Poole, Jack Warren, Bruce Drysdale, Stevie Cameron, Eric Maldoff, Beatrice Raffoul, Adrian Montgomery, Phyllis Bruce, Paul Godfrey, Gary Clement, Duncan Dee, Ian MacLeod, Dan Dunlop, Sharon Smith, Randy and Luba Pettipas, Dominic Agostino, Greg Wong, Mark Stokes, Peter Gregg, Bob Nault, Kaz Flinn, Taras Zalusky, Stan and Bernie Farber, Alice Willems, Jonathan Goldbloom, Isabel Metcalfe, Grant Kippen, Doug Wotherspoon, Greg Schmidt, Pat Neri, Monique Bondar, Francie Ducros, Mauril Belanger, Laurel Broten, Doug Melville, Greg Tsang, Tony Knill, Kevin Lee, Cal and Darrell Bricker, Jerry Yanover, Chethan Lakshman, Nathalie Gauthier, Claudette Levesque, John Chenier, Johanne Senecal, Earl Stuart, Mike Robinson, Gerald Butts, Dominic LeBlanc, Ron Drews, Jean Pelletier, Jen Nicholson, Phillip Gigantes, John Parisella, Deb Roberts, Titch Dharamsi, Tenio Evangelista, Mike Marzolini, Rob Ritter, Hugh Scott, Don Boudria, Mike Pearson, Joan Lajeunesse, Tim Barber, Alister Campbell, "Marc the Ninja," Eme Onuoha, Dan Rogers, Dan Hays, Jon Kay, Sheila Finestone, Denise Costello, Ezra Levant, Dan Rath, Bob Lay, Len Kuchar, Bill Fox, Don Guy, Hugh Blakeney, Chris Clark, George Smitherman, Scott Sheppard, Paul Pellegrini, Mary-Ellen Kenny, Jim Anderson, Jossie Higginson, Debbie Gowling, Sandra Leffler, Julienne Racicot, Maryse

ACKNOWLEDGEMENTS

Harvey, Kevin Bosch, Keith Davey, Gen LeBlanc, George Young, Phil Dewan, Christine Hampson, Diane Gemus, Bruce and Deb Davis, Stephen LeDrew, Pierre Bourque, Patrick Parisot, Dan McCarthy, Rob Steiner, Heather Bradley, Paul Genest, Mike McAdoo, Kassandra McMicking, Sergio Marchi, Jean Carle, Greg Owen, Fred Gaspar, Peter Milliken, David and Penny Collenette, Tony Genco, Tom Jakobek, John Harding, Michael Meighen, Maurizio Bevilacqua, John Duffy, John Milloy, Bruce Hartley, John Manley, Jimmy Warren, Ken Polk, Andre Ouellet, Tony Macerollo, Nick Parker, Natasha Hassan, Dan Hayward, Phil Goodwin, Pierre Tremblay, Mike Duffy, Chaviva Hosek, Joan Fraser, Sonja and Jamie Clement and countless others. Special thanks go to Graham Scott for his support and informed insight; Cyrus Reporter and Allan Rock, for their leadership and friendship; Jim Watson, for many years of support and "shameless" photo-mongering; Frank Schiller and Randy McCauley, for political smarts far beyond their collective years; and my pal Bob Richardson, who is the best political strategist and tactician I have met, anywhere.

In the Far East, I have learned much from the likes of Dominic LeBlanc, Tony Blom, Shona Kinley, Kirk Cox, Allison MacNeil, Paul Sparkes, Tim Powers, Brian Tobin, Kevin Fram, Willy Moore, Steve MacKinnon, Lawrence Macaulay, Al Graham, Meredith Naylor and Carl Gillis, to whom this book is partly dedicated. Most of all, I have had the privilege to have learned at the knee of the great Roméo LeBlanc, one of the most decent men ever to set foot on Parliament Hill.

Beyond our borders, I am grateful to James Carville, John Rowley, Betsey Wright, Haley Barbour, Rod Shealy, Phil Noble, Lynda Kaid, Tony Schwartz, Dick Morris, Lucianne Goldberg, Tobe Berkovitz, Pippa Norris, Mark Mellman, Dane Strother, Scott Howell and many others.

For those who went above and beyond the call of duty to get this book in your hands, I offer the most sincere thanks of which I am capable. Included in this small group is Grace Tsakas, my assistant, for overseeing

ACKNOWLEDGEMENTS

interview transcripts and keeping me organized. There is also Prime Minister Jean Chrétien and his wife, Aline, who have stood by me when many others would not.

Thanks, too, to my agent, Helen Heller. If this book was a good idea, you can thank Helen, who thought it up. She's the best there is. (If the book wasn't a good idea, you can blame her, too.) My publisher, meanwhile, is Anne Collins. She is precisely the kind of editor described in acknowledgements pages by her other authors: she's patient and thoughtful, and she knows how to make your stuff seem better than it actually is.

Most of all, thanks and love to Suzanne, for giving me the support I needed to get this one done, and to our little army of future cabinet ministers (and prime ministers!): Emma, Ben, Sam and Jake.

Thanks to one and all.

BIBLIOGRAPHY

Adatto, Kiku. "Sound Bite Democracy: Network Evening News Presidential Campaign Coverage, 1968 and 1988." Research Paper, Shorenstein Barone Center, John F. Kennedy School of Government, Harvard University, 1990.
Ailes, Roger. *You Are the Message: Secrets of the Master Communicators.* Homewood, IL: Dow Jones-Irwin, 1988.
Ansolabehere, Stephen, and Shanto Iyengar. *Going Negative: How Campaign Advertisements Shrink and Polarize the Electorate.* New York: The Free Press, 1995.
Ansolabehere, Stephen, Shanto Iyengar, Adam Simon, and Nicholas Valentino. "Does Attack Advertising Demobilize the Electorate?" *American Political Science Review* 88 (1994): 829–38.
Arterton, F. Christopher. "Campaign Organizations Confront the Media-Political Environment." In *Race for the Presidency*, edited by James D. Barber. New York: Prentice-Hall, 1978.

BIBLIOGRAPHY

Asher, Herbert. *Polling and the Public: What Every Citizen Should Know.* Washington, D.C.: Congressional Quarterly Press, 1988.

Atkin, Charles, and Gary Heald. "Effects of Political Advertising." *Public Opinion Quarterly* 40 (Summer 1976): 216–28.

Auletta, Ken. *Three Blind Mice: How the TV Networks Lost Their Way.* New York: Random House, 1991.

Austin, Erica, and Bruce Pinkleton. "Positive and Negative Effects of Political Disaffection on the Less Experienced Voter." *Journal of Broadcasting and Electronic Media* 39 (1995): 215–35.

Bain, George. *Gotcha: How the Media Distort the News.* Toronto: Key Porter Books, 1994.

Bartels, Larry. "Messages Received: The Political Impact of Media Exposure." *American Political Science Review* 87 (1993): 267–85.

Bayer, Michael J., and Joseph Rodota. "Computerized Opposition Research." In *Campaigns and Elections: A Reader in Modern American Politics*, edited by Larry J. Sabato. Glenview, IL: Scott, Foresman and Company, 1989.

Beall, Pat. "Buy Your Own Time." *Campaigns and Elections* (July 1991): 48.

Bennett, James. "Another Tally in '96 Race: Two Months of TV Ads." *The New York Times*, 13 November 1996, D20.

Biocca, Frank, ed. *Signs, Codes and Images of Television and Political Advertising.* Vol. 2: Hillsdale, NJ: Lawrence Erlbaum Associates, 1991.

Blaemire, Robert. "Targeting: Before You Start Trying to Persuade, Figure Out Who You're Talking To." *Campaigns and Elections* (October/November 1991).

Blumenthal, Sidney. *The Permanent Campaign: Inside the World of Elite Political Operatives.* Boston: Beacon Press, 1982.

Boorstin, Daniel J. *The Image: A Guide to Pseudo-Events in America.* New York: Athenaeum, 1961.

Boyd, Gerald. *Despite Vow to Be 'Gentler,' Bush Stays on Attack. The New York Times*, 29 October 1988, 8.

Bozinoff, Lorne, and Peter MacIntosh. "Canadians Oppose Negative Advertising." *Gallup Canada*, 17 November 1988.

Broder, David S. "Beware the 'Push-Poll.'" *The Washington Post*, 9 October 1994, C7.

Burke, Kenneth. *A Rhetoric of Motives.* New York: Prentice-Hall, 1953.

Cairns, Allan. "An Election to Be Remembered: Canada 1993." *Canadian Public Policy* 20 (1994): 219–34.

Cameron, Stevie. *On the Take: Crime, Corruption and Greed in the Mulroney Years.* Toronto: Macfarlane Walter & Ross, 1994.

Cantril, Albert H. *The Opinion Connection: Polling, Politics and the Press.* Washington, D.C.: Congressional Quarterly Press, 1991.

Cappella, Joseph N., and Kathleen Hall Jamieson. "Broadcast Adwatch Effects: A Field Experiment." *Communication Research* 21, no. 3 (1994): 342–65.

———. *Spiral of Cynicism: The Press and the Public Good.* New York: Oxford University Press, 1997.

Carey, John. "How News Media Shape Campaigns." *Journal of Communication* 26 (Spring 1976): 50–57.

Carney, Tom. *Negative Political Advertisements in the 1993 Canadian Federal Election: Exploring Their Impact by the Use of Participatory Action Research.* Windsor: Department of Communication Studies, University of Windsor, 1994.

Ceci, Stephen J., and Edward L. Khan. "Jumping on the Bandwagon with the Underdog: The Impact of Attitude Polls and Polling Behaviour." *Public Opinion Quarterly* 46 (1982): 228–42.

Chrétien, Jean. *Straight from the Heart.* Toronto: Key Porter Books, 1985.

Christ, William, Esther Thorson, and Clarke Caywood. "Do Attitudes toward Political Advertising Affect Information Processing of Televised Political Commercials?" *Journal of Broadcasting and Electronic Media* 38 (1994): 251–70.

Clarkson, Stephen. "Yesterday's Man and His Blue Grits: Backward into the Future." In *The Canadian General Election of 1993*, edited by Alan Frizzell, Jon Pammett, and Anthony Westell. Ottawa: Carleton University Press, 1994.

Coffey, P. J. "A Quantitative Measure of Bias in Reporting of Political News." *Journalism Quarterly* 52 (1975): 551–53.

Combs, James E., and Dan Nimmo. *The New Propaganda: The Dictatorship of Palaver in Contemporary Politics.* New York: Longman Publishing Group, 1993.

BIBLIOGRAPHY

Cook, Philip S., Douglas Gomery, and Lawrence W. Lichty, eds. *The Future of News: Television, Newspapers, Wire Services and News Magazines.* Baltimore, MD: Johns Hopkins University Press, 1992.

Corcoran, Paul E. *Political Language and Rhetoric.* Austin: University of Texas Press, 1979.

Crouse, Timothy. *The Boys on the Bus.* New York: Random House, 1972.

Cundy, Donald T. "Image Formation, the Low Involvement Viewer, and Televised Political Advertising." *Political Communication and Persuasion* 7 (1990): 41–49.

Cunningham, Stanley B. "Sorting Out the Ethics of Propaganda." *Communication Studies* 43 (1992): 233–45.

Curran, Tim. "'Attack' Ad May Preview '92 GOP Tactics." *Roll Call,* 4 November 1991, 35.

Davey, Keith. *The Rainmaker: A Passion for Politics.* Toronto: Stoddart, 1986.

Denton, Robert E., Jr. *The Primetime Presidency of Ronald Reagan.* New York: Praeger, 1988.

Denton, Robert E., Jr., and Gary C. Woodward. *The Political Communication in America.* Westport, CN: Praeger, 1998.

De Vries, Walter. "American Campaign Consulting: Trends and Concerns." *PS: Political Science and Politics,* March 1998, 21–25.

Devlin, L. Patrick. "An Analysis of Presidential Television Commercials: 1952–1984." In *New Perspectives on Political Advertising,* edited by Lynda Kaid, Dan Nimmo, and Keith Sanders. Carbondale: South Illinois University Press, 1986.

———. "Contrast in Presidential Campaign Commercials of 1988." *American Behavioural Scientist* 32, no. 4, (March/April 1989): 389–414.

Diamond, Edwin, and Stephen Bates. *The Spot: The Rise of Political Advertising on Television.* Cambridge, MA: MIT Press, 1984.

Dionne, E. J., Jr. *Why Americans Hate Politics.* New York: Simon & Schuster, 1991.

Erikson, Robert S. "The Influence of Newspaper Endorsements in Presidential Elections: The Case of 1964." *American Journal of Political Science* 20 (May 1976): 207–33.

Faber, Ronald J., Albert R. Tims, and Kay G. Schmitt. "Negative Political Advertising and Voting Intent: The Role of Involvement and Alternative Information Sources." *Journal of Advertising* 22 (1993): 67–76.

Fallows, James. *Breaking the News: How the Media Undermine American Democracy*. New York: Pantheon Books, 1996.

Felknor, Bruce L. *Dirty Politics*. New York: Norton, 1966.

Finkel, S., and J. Greer. "A Spot Check: Casting Doubt on the Demobilizing Effect of Attack Advertising." *American Journal of Political Science* 42 (1998): 573–95.

Fleitas, Daniel W. "Bandwagon and Underdog Effects in Minimal Information Elections." *American Political Science Review* 65 (1971): 434–38.

Fletcher, Fred. "Media, Elections and Democracy." *Canadian Journal of Communication* 19 (1994): 131–50.

Fletcher, Fred, and Robert MacDermid. "Reading the Spots: The 1997 Federal Campaign." Paper presented at the annual conference of the Canadian Political Sciences Association, Ottawa, June 1998.

Fox, William J. *Spinwars: Politics and New Media*. Toronto: Key Porter Books, 1999.

Fraser, Graham. *Playing for Keeps: The Making of the Prime Minister 1988*. Toronto: McClelland & Stewart, 1989.

Friedenberg, Robert V. *Communication Consultants in Political Campaigns: Ballot Box Warriors*. Westport, CT: Praeger, 1997.

Garramone, Gina. "Voter Responses to Negative Political Ads." *Journalism Quarterly* 61 (1984): 250–59.

———. "Effects of Negative Political Advertising: The Roles of Sponsors and Rebuttal." *Journal of Broadcasting and Electronic Media* 29 (1985): 147–59.

Goldwater, Barry. *With No Apologies*. New York: Morrow, 1979.

Graton, Michel. *So What Are the Boys Saying? An Inside Look at Brian Mulroney in Power*. Toronto: McGraw-Hill Ryerson, 1987.

Greenspon, Edward, and Jeff Sallot. "How Campbell Self-Destructed." *The Globe and Mail*, 27 October 1993, A1.

Griese, Noel L. "Rosser Reeves and the 1952 Eisenhower TV Spot Blitz." *Journal of Advertising* 4 (1975): 34–38. Hollitz, John E. "Eisenhower and the

BIBLIOGRAPHY

Admen: The Television 'Spot' Campaign of 1952." *Wisconsin Magazine of History* 66 (Autumn 1982): 25–39.

Grossman, Laurence K. *The Electric Republic: Reshaping Democracy in the Information Age.* New York: Vintage, 1995.

Hall, J. A. "When Political Campaigns Turn to Slime: Establishing a Virginia Fair Campaign Practices Committee." *Journal of Law and Politics* 7 (1990–91): 353–77.

Hansborough, Mac. "Dial N for Negative: Using Phones to Make Your Attacks Heard but Not Seen." *Campaigns and Elections* 13 (April 1992): 58–61.

Harris, John F. "Va. Republicans Say Democrats Are Slinging a Little Mud in Their Poll Questions." *The Washington Post,* 18 August 1993, D1.

Harwood, John, and Daniel Pearl. "In Waning Campaign Hours, Candidates Turn to Phone 'Push-polling' to Step Up the Attack." *Wall Street Journal,* 9 November 1994, A24.

Herbert, Christopher J. "Listen Up: A Guide for the Focus Group Observer." *Campaigns and Elections,* (July 1994): 42.

Herbst, Susan. *Numbered Voices: How Opinion Polling Has Shaped American P olitics.* Chicago: University of Chicago Press, 1993.

Hertsgaard, Mark. *On Bended Knee: The Press and the Reagan Presidency.* New York: Shocken, 1989.

Hickman, Harrison. "Public Polls and Election Participants." In *Polling and Presidential Election Coverage,* edited by Paul J. Lavrakas and Jack K. Holley. Newbury Park, Calif.: Sage, 1991.

Hill, Ronald. "An Exploration of Voter Responses to Political Advertisements." *Journal of Advertising* 18 (1989): 14–22.

Hofstadter, Richard. *The Paranoid Style in American Politics and Other Essays.* New York: Knopf, 1965.

Holbrook, T. *Do Campaigns Matter?* Thousand Oaks, CA: Sage, 1996.

Hooper, Michael. "Party and Newspaper Endorsement as Predictors of Voter Choice." *Journalism Quarterly* 46 (Summer 1969): 303–05.

Iyengar, Shanto. *Is Anyone Responsible?* Chicago: University of Chicago Press, 1991.

Iyengar, Shanto, and Donald Kinder. *News that Matters: Television and American Opinion.* Chicago: University of Chicago Press, 1991.

James, Karen, and Paul Hensel. "Negative Advertising: The Malicious Strain of Comparative Advertising." *Journal of Advertising* 20 (1991): 53–69.

Jamieson, Kathleen Hall. *Packaging the Presidency.* New York: Oxford University Press, 1984.

———. *Dirty Politics: Deception, Distraction and Democracy.* New York: Oxford University Press, 1992.

———. "Broadcast Adwatch Effects: A Field Experiment." *Communication Research* 21 (1994): 342–65.

———. *Everything You Think You Know about Politics . . . And Why You're Wrong.* New York: Basic Books, 2000.

Jamieson, Kathleen Hall, Paul Waldman, and Susan Sherr. "Eliminate the Negative? Categories of Analysis for Political Advertising." In *Crowded Airwaves: Campaign Advertising in Modern Elections*, edited by James A. Thurber, Candice Nelson, and David Dulio. Washington, D.C.: Brookings Institution Press, 2000.

Johnson-Cartee, Karen S., and Gary A. Copeland. *Negative Political Advertising: Coming of Age.* Hillsdale, NJ: Lawrence Erlbaum Associates, 1991.

———. *Inside Political Campaigns: Theory and Practice.* Westport, CT: Praeger, 1997.

Joslyn, Richard A. "Political Advertising and the Meaning of Elections." In *New Perspectives on Political Advertising*, edited by Lynda Kaid, Dan Nimmo, and K. R. Sanders. Carbondale: Southern Illinois University Press, 1986.

Kaid, Lynda Lee. "Political Advertising in the 1992 Campaign." In *The 1992 Presidential Election: A Communication Perspective*, edited by Robert Denton, Jr. Westport, CT: Praeger, 1994.

Kaid, Lynda Lee, and John Boysdon. "An Experimental Study of the Effectiveness of Negative Political Advertisements." *Communication Quarterly* 35 (1987): 193–201.

Kaid Lynda Lee, and Dorothy Davidson. "Elements of Videostyle." In *New Perspectives on Political Advertising*, edited by Lynda Kaid, Dan Nimmo, and Keith Sanders. Carbondale: Southern Illinois University Press, 1986.

Kaid, Lynda Lee, and Anne Johnston. "Negative Versus Positive Television Advertising in U.S. Presidential Campaigns, 1960–1988." *Journal of Communication* 41 (1991): 53–64.

Kaid, Lynda, et al. "Television News and Presidential Campaigns: The Legitimization of Televised Political Advertising." *Social Science Quarterly* 74 (1993): 274–85.

Kaplan, William. *Presumed Guilty: Brian Mulroney, the Airbus Affair and the Government of Canada*. Toronto: McClelland & Stewart, 1998.

Katz, Elihu, Hanna Adoni, and Pnina Parness. "Remembering the News: What the Picture Adds to Recall." *Journalism Quarterly* 54 (Summer 1977): 231–39.

Keesel, John. *Presidential Campaign Politics: Coalition Strategies and Citizen Response*. Chicago: Dorsey, 1988.

Kellner, Douglas. *Television and the Crisis of Democracy*. Boulder, CO: Westview Press, 1995.

Kent, Montague. *30-Second Politics: Political Advertising in the Eighties*. New York: Praeger, 1989.

Kolodny, Robin, and Angela Logan. "Political Consultants and the Extension of Party Goals." *PS: Political Science and Politics* 31, no. 2 (1998): 155–59.

Krasno, Jonathan, S. *Challengers, Competition, and Reelection*. New Haven, CT: Yale University Press, 1994.

Kurtz, Howard. *Spin Cycle: Inside the Clinton Propaganda Machine*. New York: The Free Press, 1998.

Ladd, Everett, and John Benson. "The Growth of News Polls in American Politics." In *Media Polls in American Politics*, edited by Thomas Mann and Gary Orren. Washington, D.C.: Brookings Institution, 1992.

Lane, Robert E., and David O. Sears. *Public Opinion*. Englewood Cliffs, NJ: Prentice-Hall, 1964.

Lang, A. "Emotion, Formal Features, and Memory for Televised Political Advertisements." In *Psychological Processes*, edited by F. Biocca. Vol. 1 of *Television and Political Advertising*. Hillsdale, NJ: Lawrence Erlbaum Associates, 1991.

Lau, R. R. "Negativity in Political Perception." *Political Behaviour* 4 (1982): 353–77.

Lee, Robert Mason. *One Hundred Monkeys: The Triumph of Popular Wisdom in Canadian Politics.* Toronto: Mcfarlane Walter & Ross, 1989.

Leonard, Thomas C. *The Power of the Press: The Birth of American Political Reporting.* New York: Oxford University Press, 1987.

Lowry, D. T., and J. A. Shidler. "The Soundbites, the Biters, and the Bitten: An Analysis of Network TV News Bias in Campaign '92." *Journalism and Mass Communication Quarterly* 97 (1995): 33–44.

Luntz, Frank. *Candidates, Consultants and Campaigns: The Style and Substance of American Electioneering.* New York: Basil Blackwell, 1988.

———. "Should a Poll Push You to Run?" *Campaigns and Elections* (March 1991).

MacInnis, Craig. "B.C. Premier's Nose out of Joint over Ad." *The Globe and Mail*, 30 April 1996, A7.

Marsh, Catherine. "Back on the Bandwagon: The Effects of Opinion Polls on Public Opinion." *British Journal of Political Science* 15 (1984): 51–74.

Martinez, Michael D., and Ted Delegal. "The Irrelevance of Negative Campaigns to Political Trust: Experimental and Survey Results." *Political Communication and Persuasion* 7 (1990): 25–40.

Mason, William M. "The Impact of Endorsements on Voting." *Sociological Methods and Research* 1 (May 1973): 463–95.

Matalin, Mary, and James Carville. *All's Fair: Love, War, and Running for President.* Random House, 1994.

Mauser, Gary. *Political Marketing: An Approach to Campaign Strategy.* New York: Praeger, 1983.

McCombs, Maxwell. "Editorial Endorsements: A Study of Influence." *Journalism Quarterly* 44 (Autumn 1967): 545–48.

McCombs, Maxwell, and Donald Shaw. "The Agenda-Setting Function of Mass Media." *Public Opinion Quarterly* 36 (1972): 176–87.

McGiniss, Joe. *The Selling of the President 1968.* New York: Trident, 1969.

McGuire, W. "The Myth of Massive Media Impact: Savagings and Salvagings." *Public Communication and Behaviour* 1 (1986): 173–257.

Mehrabian, A. "Effects of Poll Reports on Voter Preferences." *Journal of Social Psychology* 28 (1998): 2119–30.

Mellman, Mark. "Benchmark Basics and Beyond." *Campaigns and Elections* (May 1991).

Merritt, Sharyne. "Negative Political Advertising: Some Empirical Findings." *International Journal of Public Opinion Research* 13 (1984): 27–38.

Meyer, Chris, and Phil Porado. "Hit or Miss: Your Guide to Effective Media Buying." *Campaigns and Elections* (August/September 1990): 38.

Mickelson, Sig. *From Whistle Stop to Sound Bite: Four Decades of Politics and Television.* New York: Praeger, 1989.

Miller, Mark Crispin. "Political Ads: Decoding Hidden Messages." *Columbia Journalism Review* 30 (1992): 36–39.

Mittal, Banwari. "Public Assessment of TV Advertising: Faint Praise and Harsh Criticism." *Journal of Advertising Research* 34 (1994): 35–53.

Moore, David W. *The Superpollsters.* New York: Four Walls Eight Windows, 1992.

Morwitz, V. G., and C. Pluzinski. "Do Polls Reflect Opinions or Do Opinions Reflect Polls? The Impact of Political Polling on Voters' Expectation, Preferences, and Behaviour." *Journal of Consumer Research* 23 (1996): 53–67.

Mueller, Claus. *The Politics of Communication.* New York: Oxford University Press, 1973.

Neel, R. F., Jr. "Campaign Hyperbole: The Advisability of Legislating False Statements out of Politics." *Journal of Law and Politics* 2 (1985): 405–24.

Nelson, Candice J. "Inside the Beltway: Profiles of Two Political Consultants." *PS: Political Science and Politics* 31, no. 2 (1998): 162–70.

Nieves, Evelyn. "Spelling by Quayle (That's with an E)." *The New York Times,* 17 June 1992, A17.

Nimmo, Dan. *The Political Persuaders: The Techniques of Modern Election Campaigns.* Englewood Cliffs, NJ: Prentice-Hall, 1970.

Noonan, Peggy. *What I Saw at the Revolution: A Political Life in the Reagan Era.* New York: Random House, 1990.

Nordlinger, Gary. "Allocating Your Media Dollars: How and When to Use TV, Newspaper and Radio." Paper presented at the annual National Campaign Training Seminar and Trade Show, Washington, D.C., 17 June 1995.

Novazio, Robert. "An Experimental Approach to Bandwagon Research." *Political Opinion Quarterly* 41 (1977): 217–25.

Nugent, J. F. "Positively Negative." *Campaigns and Elections* 7 (1987): 47–49.

O'Sullivan, Patrick, and Seth Geiger. "Does the Watchdog Bite? Newspaper Ad Watch Articles and Political Attack Ads." *Journalism and Mass Communication Quarterly* 74 (1995): 771–85.

Patterson, Thomas, and Robert McClure. *The Unseeing Eye: The Myth of Television Power in National Elections.* New York: Putman, 1976.

Pentony, J. F. "The Effect of Negative Campaigning on Voting, Semantic Differential and Thought Listing." *Journal of Social Behaviour and Personality* 10 (1995): 631–44.

Perlmutter, David D. *The Manship School Guide to Political Communication.* Baton Rouge: Louisiana State University Press, 1999.

Perloff, Richard. *Political Communication.* Mahwah, NJ: Lawrence Earlbaum, 1998.

Perloff, Richard, and Dennis Kinsey. "Political Advertising as Seen by Consultants and Journalists." *Journal of Advertising Research* 32 (1992): 645–55.

Pfau, Michael, and Michael Burgoon. "The Efficacy of Issue and Character Attack Message Strategies in Political Campaign Communication." *Communication Reports* 2 (1989): 53–61.

Pfau, Michael, and Allan Louden. "Effectiveness of Ad-Watch Formats in Deflecting Political Attack Ads." *Communication Research* 21 (1994): 325–41.

Pfau, Michael, and Henry C. Kenski. *Attack Politics: Strategy and Defence.* Westport, CT: Praeger, 1990.

Pinkleton, Bruce. "The Effects of Negative Comparative Political Advertising on Candidate Evaluations and Advertising Evaluations: An Exploration." *Journal of Advertising* 26 (1997): 19–26.

Randolph, Sallie, G. "The Effective Press Release: Key to Free Media." In *Campaigns and Elections: A Reader in Modern American Politics*, edited by Larry J. Sabato. Glenview, IL: Scott, Foresman and Company, 1989.

Reeves, Rosser. *Reality in Advertising*. New York: Knopf, 1961.

Rhee, J. W. "How Polls Drive Campaign Coverage: The Gallup/CNN/*USA Today* Tracking Poll and *USA Today's* Coverage of the 1992 Presidential Campaign." *Political Communication* 13 (1996): 213–29.

Ridder, Rick. "Do's and Don'ts of Opposition Research." *Campaigns and Elections* 15 (August 1984): 58.

Roddy, Brian, and Gina Garramone. "Appeals and Strategies of Negative Political Advertising." *Journal of Broadcasting and Electronic Media* 32 (1988): 415–27.

Roese, W. J., and G. N. Sande. "Backlash Effects in Attack Politics." *Journal of Applied Social Psychology* 23 (1993): 632–53.

Roll, Charles W., Jr., and Albert H. Cantril. *Polls: Their Use and Misuse in Politics*. New York: Basic Books, 1972.

Romanow, Walter, Michel de Repentigny, Stanley B. Cunningham, Walter C. Soderlund, Kai Hilderbrandt. *Television Advertising in Canadian Elections: The Attack Mode, 1993*. Waterloo, Ontario: Wilfrid Laurier University Press, 1999.

Romanow, Walter, Walter Soderlund, and Richard Price. "Negative Political Advertising: An Analysis of Research in Light of Canadian Practices." In *Political Ethics: A Canadian Perspective*, edited by Jane Hiebert. Vol. 12 of *Royal Commission on Electoral Reform and Party Financing Research Studies*. Toronto: Dundurn Press, 1991.

Rosenstiel, Tom. *Strange Bedfellows*. New York: Hyperion Books, 1993.

Sabato, Larry. *The Rise of Political Consultants: New Ways of Winning Elections*. New York: Basic Books, 1981.

———. *Feeding Frenzy: How Attack Journalism Has Transformed American Politics*. New York: The Free Press, 1991.

Sabato, Larry J., and Glenn R. Simpson. *Dirty Little Secrets: The Persistence of Corruption in American Politics.* New York: The Free Press, 1991.

Safire, William. *Before the Fall.* Garden City, NY: Doubleday, 1975.

Salmon, C. T., L. N. Reid, J. Pokrywczynski, and R. W. Willett. "The Effectiveness of Advocacy Advertising Relative to News Coverage." *Communication Research* 12, no. 4 (October 1985): 546–67.

Scarrow, Howard A., with Steve Borman. "The Effects of Newspaper Endorsements on Election Outcomes: A Case Study." *Public Opinion Quarterly* 43 (Fall 1979): 388–93.

Schwartz, Tony. *The Responsive Cord.* Garden City, NY: Doubleday, 1973.

———. *Media: The Second God.* New York: Random House, 1981.

Selnow, Gary. *High-Tech Campaigns.* Westport, CT: Praeger, 1994.

Shapiro, Michael, and Robert Rieger. "Comparing Positive and Negative Political Advertising on Radio." *Journalism Quarterly* 69 (1992): 135–45.

Shea, Daniel M. *Campaign Craft: The Strategies, Tactics, and Art of Campaign Management.* Westport, CT: Praeger, 1996.

Simon, Herbert A. "Bandwagon Effects and the Possibility of Election Predictions." *Public Opinion Quarterly* 18 (1954): 245–53.

Slade White, Joe. "Lessons Learned: Through the Cutter." *Campaigns and Elections* (February 1996): 22.

Soderlund, Walter, Walter Romanow, Donald Briggs, and Ronald H. Wagenberg. *Media and Elections in Canada.* Toronto: Holt, Rinehart and Winston, 1984.

Stewart, Charles. "Voter Perception of Mudslinging in Political Communication." *Central States Speech Journal* 26 (1975): 279–86.

Stoler, Peter. *The War Against the Press.* New York: Dodd and Mead, 1986.

Straffin, Philip D. "The Bandwagon Curve." *American Journal of Political Science* 21 (1977): 695–709.

Taras, David. *The Newsmakers: The Media's Influence on Canadian Politics.* Scarborough: Nelson Canada, 1990.

Thompson, Spring. "TV Time Buying Rules: Feast and Famine." *Campaigns and Elections* (June/July 1993): 9.

Thurber, James A. "The Study of Campaign Consultants: A Subfield in Search of Theory." *PS: Political Science and Politics* 31, no. 2 (1998): 145–49.

Thurber, James A., and Candice J. Nelson. *Campaigns and Elections American Style*. Boulder, Colo.: Westview Press, 1995.

———. *Campaign Warriors: Political Consultants in Elections*. Washington, D.C.: Brookings Institution Press, 2000.

Traugott, Michael. "The Impact of Media Polls on the Public." In *Media Polls in American Politics*, edited by Thomas Mann and Gary Orren. Washington, D.C.: Bookings Institution, 1992.

Trent, Judith S., and Robert V. Friedenberg. *Political Campaign Communications: Principles and Practices*. 3d ed. Westport, CT: Praeger, 1995.

Wagenberg, Ronald, Walter Soderlund, Walter Romanow, and Donald E. Briggs. "Campaigns, Images and Polls: Mass Media Coverage of the 1984 Canadian Election." *Canadian Journal of Political Science* 21 (1988): 117–29.

Weaver, David H., and G. Cleveland Wilhoit. "Journalists—Who Are They, Really?" *Media Studies Journal* (Fall 1992): 63–79.

West, Darrell. *Air Wars: Television Advertising in Election Campaigns, 1952–1992*. 2d ed. Washington, D.C.: Congressional Quarterly Press, 1997.

White, Theodore H. *The Making of the President 1968*. New York: Atheneum, 1969.

Whitehead, Thomas. "Annals of Television: The Man from Iron City." *The New Yorker*, 27 September 1969.

Whyte, Kenneth. "The Face that Sank a Thousand Tories." *Saturday Night*, 14–18 February 1994, 58–60.

Winsor, Hugh. "How Did Tories behind Attack Ads Miss the Message?" *The Globe and Mail*, 8 December 1993, A8.

Wood, Stephen C. "Eisenhower Answers America: A Critical History." Mimeo, Department of Speech Communication, University of Rhode Island, n.d.

———. "Television's First Political Spot Ad Campaign: Eisenhower Answers America." *Presidential Studies Quarterly* (Spring 1990).

Woolstencroft, Peter. "'Doing Politics Differently': The Conservative Party and the Campaign of 1993." In *The Canadian General Election of 1993*, edited by Alan Frizzell, John Pammett, and Anthony Westell. Ottawa: Carleton University Press, 1994.

Young, Susan. "Candidates Make Push-polling Claims." *The Bangor Daily News*, 27 October 1994, A1.

Zhu, J., J. R. Milavsky, and R. Biswas. "Do Televised Debates Affect Image Perception More than Issue Knowledge?" *Human Communication Research* 20 (1994): 302–33.

ABOUT THE AUTHOR

Warren Kinsella is a lawyer, a political consultant, and a weekly columnist for the *Ottawa Citizen*. He is the author of the bestselling *Web of Hate*, on neo-Nazi and white supremacist hate groups in Canada and the U.S. He served as political aide to Jean Chrétien when Chrétien was Leader of the Opposition; he unsuccessfully ran for federal office in 1997 (a race in which he wishes he'd kicked ass); and he played key roles in two successful Chrétien campaigns. Kinsella lives in Toronto with his wife and family.